Digital Opportunities in African Businesses

International Finance Corporation Research Series

The International Finance Corporation (IFC) Research Series explores the mobilization of private sector capital in support of development and the elimination of poverty in a livable world. Publications are subject to review meetings chaired by the IFC managing director and the vice president of economics. Relevant regional or industry vice presidents and directors also participate. The peer reviewers include experts from outside the World Bank Group.

Digital Opportunities in African Businesses is the inaugural book in this series.

Digital Opportunities in African Businesses

Edited by Marcio Cruz

WORLD BANK GROUP

CONTENTS

Figures

Maps

Tables

FOREWORD

Digital technologies are a fundamental enabler for most business activities. Research shows digitalization can foster growth in productivity, jobs, exports, and incomes, as well as help reduce poverty. However, productive use of digital technologies by firms in Africa remains modest and uneven, leaving a chasm between those who are connected and those who are disconnected. As we stand on the cusp of an era in which artificial intelligence and other advanced digital technologies will become increasingly crucial, it is imperative to gauge the digital readiness of African businesses and to examine how they can fully participate in this technological transition.

This book presents new data and analysis aimed at helping African businesses make fuller use of digital technologies. It presents a wealth of new evidence, illuminating the disparities in digital use by firms and the opportunities arising from the current state of digitalization across African businesses. The book provides granular detail on digitalization in Africa, delving into adoption of digital technologies, their productive use, and the intensity of such use by various types of businesses. It also identifies potential market opportunities for profitable investments in digital infrastructure, digital platforms, and novel applications adapted to local contexts. Recent research across the World Bank Group has delivered important policy lessons for developing countries when building their digital infrastructure and economies. Building on those past efforts, and in collaboration with academics, industry experts, and International Finance Corporation (IFC) practitioners, this research breaks new ground in understanding the opportunities and barriers that African firms face when adopting and productively using digital technologies. It will also inform further dialogue between the private and public sectors in this crucial area.

Reaping digital opportunities in African businesses can help foster inclusive growth and reduce poverty. A multitude of firms can become more profitable by using digital tools more productively and more intensively. In addition, a few innovators may uncover profitable ways to provide African businesses with needed and affordable digital products. As digitalization progresses, healthier and more modern businesses will generate jobs and incomes. At IFC, we are committed to supporting Africa's vision to connect every individual, business, and government by 2030. We recognize the transformative impact of the digital economy to generate incomes and jobs for the region's growing population, to empower women, and to improve governance and transparency. We are keen to contribute to this process by providing knowledge, policy advice, and financial support for businesses in developing countries. We are an active investor in the full digital value chain, from infrastructure to start-ups, providing financing and advisory services. Many of the insights in this book will shape IFC's future digital strategy.

Alongside researchers, academics, and institutions, IFC can answer the most pressing questions and design better solutions for meaningful impact. I am confident that our stakeholders, including entrepreneurs, policy makers, and development practitioners, will further engage in and benefit from these valuable interactions. We hope this book will contribute to this constructive process.

Makhtar Diop
Managing Director
International Finance Corporation

ACKNOWLEDGMENTS

This book was prepared under the guidance of Susan Lund, International Finance Corporation (IFC) vice president for Economics and Private Sector Development, and Paolo Mauro, director of IFC's Economic and Market Research Department. In addition, Sérgio Pimenta, IFC regional vice president for Africa; Roumeen Islam, senior economic adviser to the managing director; and Denis Medvedev, senior economic adviser, provided support and guidance.

This research was carried out by an IFC team led by Marcio Cruz, principal economist, in collaboration with World Bank colleagues and external researchers and academics. The core team of coauthors comprised Zineb Benkirane, Xavier Cirera, Yannick Djoumessi, Samuel Edet, Beliyou Haile, Georges Houngbonon, Maty Konte, Megan Lang, Florian Mölders, Mariana Pereira-López, Santiago Reyes Ortega, Edgar Salgado, Tarna Silue, Davide Strusani, and Trang Thu Tran.

Furthermore, Izak Atiyas, Paulo Bastos, Joel Cariolle, Lucio Castro, Mark Dutz, Leo Holtz, Murendi Madzhie, Sanghamitra Warrier Mukherjee, Florian Münch, Andrew Partridge, Ariane Volk, and Verena Wiedemann also made valuable contributions. Lucien Ahouangbe, Pablo Gordillo, Aman Mahajan, and Dimas Setyonugroho provided research assistance for specific chapters. Rui Costa, Kyung Min Lee, Justice Tei Mensah, Marko Rissanen, Antonio Soares Martins, and Nouhoum Traore provided support on data used in the analysis. Mark Dutz gave technical and editorial advice. Paolo Mauro and Denis Medvedev provided detailed suggestions on drafts.

The authoring team benefited from numerous interactions with academic researchers. Eric Verhoogen from Columbia University provided comments as an adviser. Emanuele Colonnelli from the University of Chicago, Diego Comin from Dartmouth College, and Jonas Hjort from University College London collaborated on background research for specific chapters and gave overall feedback. Mary Hallward-Driemeier from Georgetown University peer reviewed the book. Vivien Foster from Imperial College London reviewed the concept note. Juanita González-Uribe from the London School of Economics reviewed background papers.

The book also benefited from discussions with participants in IFC's 2nd Annual Research Conference on Digitalization and Development, hosted by Sciences Po. Tavneet Suri from the Massachusetts Institute of Technology, Folu Okunade from Hello Tractor, and Alison Gillwald from Research ICT Africa provided helpful comments and discussions as panelists in a session focused on digitalization of businesses in Africa.

Peer reviewers from IFC included German Cufre, Dahlia Khalifa, and Sarvesh Suri, with additional comments from Emmanuel Nyirinkindi. Mohamed Eissa and Linda Munyengeterwa reviewed the concept note. Shruti Chandrasekhar, Ami Dalal, Marieme Diop, Pablo Fajnzylber, Charlotte Kaheru, Elom Lassey, Ralf Martin, Cesaire Meh, Zeinab Partow, Carlo Rossotto, Matthew Saal, and Hoi Ying So contributed with additional discussions.

Peer reviewers from the World Bank included Gaurav Nayyar and Michel Rogy, with additional comments from Andrew Dabalen and Indermit Gill. Robert Cull, Mona Haddad, Mark Williams, and Albert Zeufack reviewed the initial concept note. Asya Akhlaque, Sebastien Dessus, Martha Martinez Licetti, and Christine Zhenwei Qiang also helped with additional discussions. Roberto Fattal, Leonardo Iacovone, and Marc Schiffbauer provided feedback on specific chapters.

We thank Brian Beary and Chris Vellacott from IFC's publications team for their editorial contributions, as well as Irina Sarchenko for help with graphic design. William Shaw contributed with detailed editorial suggestions. We are also grateful to the World Bank Group's editorial production team, including Jewel McFadden, acquisitions editor; Caroline Polk, production editor; and Melina Rose Yingling, designer, for the marketing, production, and design of this book, and to the IFC communications team, including Monica De Leon and Erik Churchill, for their creative energy in promoting the book. We also thank Adama Badji, Gleice De Marrocos, Sabrina Islam, Linette Malago, and Irina Tolstaia for their exceptional administrative support.

This book is a product of IFC's Economics and Private Sector Development Vice Presidency, with financial support from the Government of Japan through the Comprehensive Japan Trust Fund.

OVERVIEW

Digitalization presents investment opportunities for African firms and those who conduct business with them. Digital technologies are being adopted at a faster pace than previous waves of technological innovation. People and firms in Africa have embraced this transformation. By making fuller use of digitalization, African firms across all economic activities can become more productive, profitable, and integrated in global, regional, and local value chains. Likewise, people can benefit from the lower costs and learning that digital technologies can facilitate. Existing or new businesses can serve this rapidly expanding market—for example, by building digital infrastructure or providing appropriate software solutions. Previous studies suggest that digitalization can create opportunities for investment, growth, and jobs.[1] However, access to and utilization of digital technologies are uneven, with many firms in Africa being left behind.

This book analyzes the opportunities to increase productive use of digital technologies by businesses across Africa. Building on ongoing World Bank Group research initiatives,[2] it provides a novel analysis of the extent of digitalization across businesses. The analysis goes beyond country-level uptake gaps to understand the opportunities arising from using specific digital technologies more intensively. It also analyzes the cost and investments needed for digital upgrading by firms and the opportunities for digital business providers in Africa.

The book consists of two parts. Part 1 measures various aspects of incomplete digitalization of firms in Africa; assesses the main barriers to, and costs of, adoption; and analyzes the potential economic impact of digitalization. Part 2 explores what can be done to mobilize more private sector investment to boost digitalization and development. It focuses on three areas in which the World Bank Group, particularly the International Finance Corporation, has actively supported businesses in developing countries: infrastructure, tech start-ups and disruptive technologies, and access to finance. It concludes with a discussion of policies to unlock private investments. The book's findings can be summarized in the following main messages, organized by key topics addressed in this book.

State of Digitalization in African Businesses

African firms can reap opportunities by making fuller use of digitalization. Fewer than one in three firms that have adopted digital technologies make intensive use of them for business purposes, a phenomenon defined in this book as *incomplete digitalization* (refer to figure O.1). This new evidence, based on nationally representative data from Burkina Faso, Ethiopia, Ghana, Kenya, Malawi, and Senegal, shows that 86 percent of firms with five or more workers have access to one or more digital enablers (mobile phone, computers, or internet). Even so, 23 percent of firms are digitally enabled but do not adopt digital technologies for productive tasks, such as business administration, planning, sales, and payments. Moreover, 39 percent of firms adopt digital technologies for those functions, but not intensively—that is, as the most frequent technology used to perform a task. On average, only 24 percent of firms make intensive use of the most sophisticated digital technology they adopted in a business function. Only 11 percent make intensive use of advanced digital technologies for general business functions (such as enterprise resource planning).[3] The bulk of firms continue to regularly rely on manual methods. Additional novel data from Ethiopia, Ghana, Kenya, Nigeria, South Africa, Tanzania, and Uganda show that this gap follows similar patterns and is wider among microbusinesses (those with fewer than five employees).

FIGURE O.1

Degrees of Incomplete Digitalization

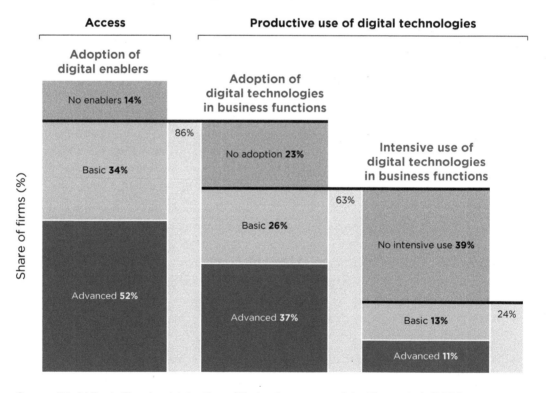

Source: World Bank, Firm-level Adoption of Technology survey data; Cirera et al. (2024).
Note: The left bar classifies adoption of enablers, namely the percentage of African firms with access to at least one digital enabler (mobile phone, computer, or internet). Computers with internet connection are classified as advanced enablers. The middle bar shows the average share of firms with digital enablers that adopt digital technologies across GBFs. *Basic* digital technologies refer to general applications (e.g., standard software, email). *Advanced* digital technologies refer to integrated systems or specialized software designed to perform specific functions (e.g., enterprise resource planning). The right bar shows the average share of firms that intensively use their most sophisticated digital technologies across GBFs. "No intensive use" estimates include 6 percent of firms that adopt advanced digital technologies but intensively use basic digital. GBFs = general business functions.

Africa is a diverse region with variation in adoption and use of digitalization across countries, mostly driven by differences in size of firms. In a group of middle-income countries (Ghana, Kenya, and Senegal), 57 percent (on average) of firms with five or more workers adopt computers and internet versus 44 percent of such firms in low-income countries (Burkina Faso, Ethiopia, and Malawi). Large and medium-size firms tend to make fuller use of digitalization and are more prevalent, relative to the working-age population, in the first group of countries. Firms in low-income countries are less likely to have access to digital enablers and to productively use digital technologies, but cross-country differences in business digitalization are driven mostly by the composition of firms, with a high prevalence of micro- and informal businesses in low-income countries. Cross-country differences also mask regional variations. For example, lower-income subnational regions in middle-income countries still face sizable gaps in uptake of digital enablers. Gaps in intensive use are especially relevant for middle-income countries in regions with better digital infrastructure.

Mobile phones and digital payments are important entry points to digitalization, but they do not necessarily lead to digitalization of other business functions performed by firms. As many as 86 percent of firms use mobile phones for business operations, and 61 percent have adopted advanced digital technologies for payment. These are by far the most common uses of digital technology by African firms. However, these firms are slow to digitalize beyond mobile and digital payments. Almost two-thirds of firms that adopted advanced digital payment systems in the region have not yet adopted a second advanced digital technology to perform business functions. Moreover, widespread adoption of digital payments does not translate into its intensive use as the most frequent payment method. Only 7 percent of firms that have adopted digital payment methods report using them intensively.

Economic Effects and the Potential for Digital Upgrading across Businesses

Digitalization of businesses can boost productivity, jobs, and growth. The arrival of high-speed internet in Africa has led to productivity gains in incumbent firms and further growth in output and employment, driven by both entry of domestic firms and greenfield foreign direct investment. Yet, further gains may be limited if internet availability does not translate into intensive use of digital technologies. Research presented in this book shows that each step in the process of digitalization matters. Firm-level productivity gains led by high-speed internet have hitherto been driven by adoption of digital technologies to perform general business functions (for example, administration, sales, or payment). The gains are potentially greater if such adoption is translated into more intensive use.

More than 600,000 formal firms with five or more workers and up to 40 million microbusinesses in Africa have high potential to benefit from digital upgrades. To shed light on the potential for digitalization across the continent, this book provides new estimates of the universe of firms and own-account businesses across all

54 countries in Sub-Saharan and North Africa, including characteristics such as the number of workers, registration status, and sector. Using statistical models to identify the type of firms that are more likely to adopt digital technologies, the analysis then identifies more than 600,000 formal firms with five or more workers (24 percent of all such firms) with high probability to adopt basic or advanced digital technologies for key business functions, based on similar characteristics of firms already using these technologies.[4] Similarly, about 10 percent of firms that have already adopted these technologies have the potential to use them more intensively. Among 230 million informal microfirms and owner–operator businesses, as many as 40 million could start using some form of digital technology for functions such as accounting, planning, sales, marketing, supply management, or payments.

The overall economic effects of firm digitalization might be limited if not expanded to microbusinesses and informal businesses, which account for most employment in Africa. Large formal firms play a disproportional role in moving workers to use more productive digital technologies. However, 7 in 10 African workers are self-employed, and the bulk of employment is informal. If all formal firms with the predicted market potential to upgrade to advanced digital technologies were to do so, this gain would be limited to 7 percent of all formal workers in Africa. If micro and informal businesses with high probability also were to upgrade, about 15 percent of all workers could gain access to some form of digital technology for productive tasks, switching from manual to digital technologies. This potential highlights the importance of expanding all workers' access to digital technologies, as well as facilitating entry of new formal firms and reallocating workers to larger, more digitally enabled firms.

Barriers to Digital Adoption

Incomplete digitalization results from several factors, including the following:

- Poor digital and complementary electricity infrastructure

- High prices of technology (high tariffs, lack of competition, insufficient continent-wide regulations supportive of market integration)

- Low levels of human capital and firm capabilities (which constrains the development of digital solutions and their adoption by firms)

- Limited access to finance (hindering investments in digitalization and innovations by digital adopters and providers).

These elements cover both demand and supply sides of digitalization. African countries lag other regions and developing countries of similar per capita income in most of these areas.

Digital equipment and software cost more, in terms of US dollars, in Africa than in other regions, thereby deterring firms from adoption. Using novel datasets with item-level information, this research finds that machinery and equipment, both digital and analog, are 35–39 percent more expensive in Sub-Saharan Africa, in absolute terms, than in the United States, and 13–15 percent more expensive in North Africa.

FIGURE O.2

Prices of Digital and Nondigital Products, by Region, Relative to the United States

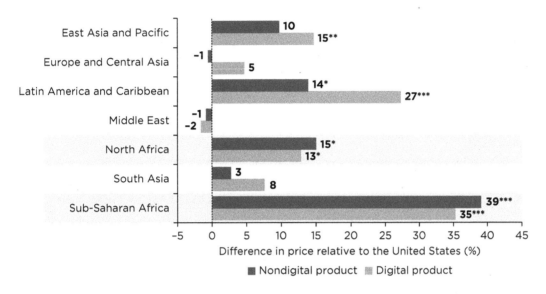

Sources: International Comparison Program (database), World Bank; Cruz et al. (2024).
Note: Percentage difference in the average price of digital versus nondigital products in the categories of machinery and equipment and other products from the International Comparison Program, relative to prices in the United States. Prices of digital and nondigital technologies are in US dollars at market price. The analysis is done on a sample of 160 countries, including 49 African countries. There are 107 products, of which 46 are digital, including software, and the remaining 61 are nondigital. Prices for machinery and equipment include the import duties and other taxes actually paid by the purchaser, the costs of transporting the asset to the place where it will be used, and any charges for installing the asset so that it will be ready for use in production. The coefficients reported are the percentage differences relative to the United States computed using the results of the ordinary least squares estimations, where we estimate the logarithm price of the products on region dummies and product dummies. The results are robust, with a sample restricted to products for which price data is available for more than 40 percent of countries and at least 25 percent of African countries.
*Significant at the 10% level. **Significant at the 5% level. ***Significant at the 1% level.

This research also finds that standard software is more expensive in Africa (refer to Figure O.2). Other factors that complement technology adoption, such as digital infrastructure, electricity, and specialized high-skilled workers, are also relatively scarce and expensive in Africa, compared to other regions in the world. Trade frictions—including high tariffs on imported digital goods, lack of infrastructure, and market concentration—hamper technology affordability and diffusion in the continent.

Opportunities and Policies to Unlock Private Investments

High costs of digital adoption can lead to opportunities for digital business providers and the financial sector. Part 2 of this book highlights the private investment opportunities that arise from the diagnostics presented in part 1 and points to policy areas to unlock these investments (refer to figure O.3). First, improving the coverage of digital infrastructure can enhance the quality of digital enablers (for example, internet connection, use of cloud computing) and facilitate access to advanced applications (for example, business administration software with a lower cost of implementation and maintenance). This can also increase the expected value of adopting computers and other devices. Second, digital tech providers, especially start-ups, can design novel applications and digital platforms that offer affordable, user-friendly solutions for performing specific business functions. Third, financial sector providers can expand their markets to fund these new digital solutions, as well as finance digital technologies that leverage information on businesses and reduce risks and transaction costs for their operations, improving coverage and reducing the cost of capital involved in digital upgrading.

The arrival of new submarine cables in Africa can reduce the price of connectivity, if regulatory reforms boost investment in middle- and last-mile digital infrastructure. The arrival of new submarine cables is projected to generate a sixfold increase in international internet bandwidth by 2027 (compared with 2022). Estimates in this book suggest that this expansion of connectivity could lead to a 10–11 percent annual drop in the price of broadband internet below the historical trend. Yet, to reduce prices and increase the number of connections among new users, more investment in middle- and last-mile infrastructure (up to $6 billion annually) is required. Regulatory reforms

FIGURE O.3

Incomplete Digitalization, Investment Opportunities, and Policies

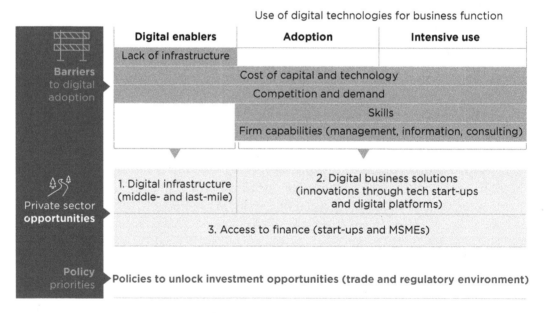

Source: Original figure for this publication.
Note: MSMEs = micro-, small, and medium-size enterprises.

to facilitate private investments in middle- and last-mile infrastructure include allowing foreign participation in digital infrastructure and providing connectivity services, liberalizing incumbents in broadband markets, facilitating competition in international gateways and leased-lines markets, and supporting or mandating infrastructure sharing.

Additional funding for tech start-ups can enable further innovation and diffusion of digital technologies. Disruptive start-ups can turn problems such as informality or lack of financial inclusion into profitable business opportunities, thereby enabling digitalization of micro-, small, or medium-size firms. The success of mobile payments in Africa shows the importance of innovation led by tech companies. Local digital solutions can be tailored to local needs, such as the use of artificial intelligence (AI)–driven speech recognition software to address communication costs in the presence of illiteracy or many local dialects, or user-friendly applications to improve accounting systems and reduce matching cost with suppliers and customers. Satellite imagery with AI-powered weather forecasts can improve the quality, timeliness, and productive use of data for agriculture and many other applications, with the promise of transforming rural livelihoods. Digital tech start-ups incorporating such disruptive technologies are more likely to succeed in terms of exit price or valuation growth, but they often struggle to attract funding—even more so in Africa, where these firms are younger and smaller and grow at a slower pace than in other regions. In Latin America, ventures with disruptive potential receive twice as much funding as nondisruptive ones, whereas in Africa they receive 40 percent more. Addressing market failures to facilitate financing of innovative early-stage disruptive businesses can strengthen the design and scaling of apps to boost firm digitalization and help low-income, low-skilled owners and workers to learn and meet their productive needs.

More private finance is needed to enable the generation and productive use of digital technologies addressing local demands. Digital infrastructure investments in Africa reached more than $32 billion between 2010 and 2021 (cumulative), with large participation of the private sector. Yet, to enable the productive use of digital technologies, it is critical to increase access to finance both for digital tech start-ups to provide innovative applications and for enterprises across all sectors, aiming to digitalize day-to-day operations. Firms in Africa experience a greater rejection when applying for loans to carry out technology upgrades than those in other regions. The financing gap for the digitalization of business administration among existing formal firms is $1.4–$2.7 billion, based on different scenarios. Moreover, the funding pipeline for digital tech firms in Africa is smaller and takes longer than in other regions, particularly for young firms, with only one-quarter of the funded firms receiving their first venture capital deal within the first five years.

Reducing tariffs on digital goods and facilitating market integration of digital business solutions would make technology more affordable. African countries have consistently imported nearly 70 percent fewer digital goods relative to other manufacturing imports than the rest of the world. Tariffs on digital goods are higher in Africa than elsewhere. The African Continental Free Trade Area (AfCFTA) is set to reduce tariffs on technology goods imported from member countries, but its impact might be limited because most imports of digital goods come from outside the region. Import-weighted tariffs on these products would decrease by only 0.3 percentage point, on average, across countries. Simulation exercises suggest the AfCFTA negotiations should consider including tariff concessions on digital goods imported from nonmember countries, potentially curbing costs more significantly, especially in countries that currently have the highest tariffs. Regional market integration may also provide opportunities for complementary policies to facilitate exports and intraregional trade on digital business solutions.

Notes

1. For example, using the time of and geographical variation in the rollout of submarine cables across the African continent, studies have shown that the arrival of high-speed internet has led to an increase in firm entry, greenfield foreign direct investment, employment, and productivity (refer to Hjort and Tian, forthcoming). Additional evidence indicates that the spread of mobile phones and banking have led to poverty reduction (refer to Suri and Jack 2016).

2. See Begazo, Blimpo, and Dutz (2023) on digitalization in Africa and Cirera, Comin, and Cruz (2022) for a broader discussion on firm adoption of technology, including the description of the methodology and data used in this book.

3. Chapter 1 provides the detailed classification of basic and advanced digital technologies across business functions. *Basic* refers to general-purpose digital technologies that are not specifically designed to perform a particular task (e.g., standard software, email). *Advanced* refers to digital integrated systems that rely on specialized software, applications, or platforms designed to perform specific business functions.

4. These estimates suggest that 28 percent of formal firms with five or more workers already adopt basic digital technologies, and 22 percent of them adopt advanced digital technologies for administration.

References

Begazo, Tania, Moussa P. Blimpo, and Mark A. Dutz. 2023. *Digital Africa: Technological Transformation for Jobs.* Washington, DC: World Bank. https://doi.org/10.1596/978-1-4648-1737-3.

Cirera, Xavier, Diego Comin, and Marcio Cruz. 2022. *Bridging the Technological Divide: Technology Adoption by Firms in Developing Countries.* Washington, DC: World Bank. https://doi.org/10.1596/978-1-4648-1826-4.

Cirera, Xavier, Diego Comin, Marcio Cruz, and Santiago Reyes. 2024. "The 'Incomplete' Digitalization of Firms in Africa." Background paper, World Bank, Washington, DC.

Cruz, Marcio, Samuel Edet, Maty Konte, and Mega Lang. 2024. "The Cost of Technology in Africa." Unpublished manuscript, International Finance Corporation, Washington, DC.

Hjort, Jonas, and Lin Tian. Forthcoming. "The Economic Impact of Internet Connectivity in Developing Countries." *Annual Review of Economics.*

Suri, Tavneet, and William Jack. 2016. "The Long-Run Poverty and Gender Impacts of Mobile Money." *Science* 354 (6317): 1288–92. https://doi.org/10.1126/science.aah5309.

ABBREVIATIONS

AfCFTA	African Continental Free Trade Area
AFR	Africa
agtech	agricultural technology
AI	artificial intelligence
ARPU	average revenue per user
AWS	Amazon Web Services
CAGR	compound annual growth rate
capex	capital expenditure
cleantech	clean technology
CRM	customer relationship management
DFI	development finance institution
EAP	East Asia and Pacific
ECA	Europe and Central Asia
ERP	enterprise resource planning
FAT	Firm-level Adoption of Technology
FDI	foreign direct investment
fintech	financial technology
FMCG	fast-moving consumer goods
GBF	general business function
GDP	gross domestic product
GPS	Global Positioning System
GSMA	Global System for Mobile Communications Association
HR	human resources
ICP	International Comparison Program (World Bank)
ICT	information and communication technology
IFC	International Finance Corporation
IoT	Internet of Things
IPO	initial public offering
IT	information technology
ITU	International Telecommunication Union
LAC	Latin America and the Caribbean
MENA	Middle East and North Africa
ML	machine learning

MSMEs	micro-, small, and medium-size enterprises
PE	private equity
RFID	radio-frequency identification
RIA	Research ICT Africa
SAR	South Asia
SMEs	small and medium enterprises
SRM	supplier relationship management
tech	technology
telecom	telecommunications
UNCTAD	United Nations Conference on Trade and Development
USF	Universal Service Fund
VC	venture capital
WBES	World Bank Enterprise Surveys

All dollar amounts are US dollars unless otherwise indicated.

Introduction

Background

The rapid diffusion of information and communication technology in Africa, particularly through mobile devices, has been remarkable. The spread of mobile phones across African countries, where many users bypassed the landline stage, is among the best examples of so-called leapfrogging in economic development. In 2000, North America reached the peak of 68 fixed telephone subscriptions per 100 people, whereas Sub-Saharan Africa still had 1.4 (refer to figure I.1, panel a). Yet, in that year, the number of mobile cellular subscriptions in Sub-Saharan Africa surpassed the

FIGURE I.1

Mobile Telephony Diffusion in Africa—A Rare Example of Leapfrogging

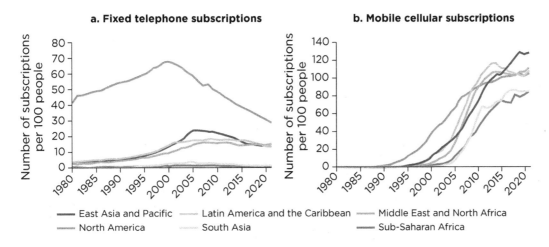

Source: World Bank (2023).

number of landlines and continued to increase at a rapid speed, reaching 84 subscriptions per 100 people in 2022 (figure I.1, panel b), whereas landline subscriptions never exceeded 2 per 100 people.

Mobile money (payment) has been another rare case of leapfrogging, with innovative solutions brought by digital tech firms in Africa. Many users make payment transactions through digital platforms before they have access to a bank account, but similar disruptions are not observed across the economy. Technology upgrading by firms has, for the most part, been gradual. Many African firms still face large gaps in accessing, adopting, and productively using digital technologies.

Most countries in Africa have a historic opportunity to narrow their digital gaps and boost investments, productivity, and jobs. On the international connectivity side, for example, the cable consortia 2Africa and Equiano will provide new high-capacity cables with multiple landing sites on the African continent. A wide range of complementary internet and data infrastructure investments are being made within and across countries. International internet bandwidth in the region is projected to increase sixfold between 2022 and 2027, the fastest growth in the world (TeleGeography 2023). In addition, a vibrant digital entrepreneurship ecosystem is emerging across Africa. As of 2021 (latest available data), the continent hosted more than 1,000 active tech hubs, defined as "organizations currently active with a physical local address, offering facilities and support for tech and digital entrepreneurs" (Briter Bridges 2023). These entrepreneurs provide digital services and applications, such as financial tech services, e-logistics, or connecting smallholder farmers to markets. Africa's venture capital landscape has expanded at an unprecedented rate. In 2022, it attracted more than $3 billion in venture capital investment, a steep increase from the $185 million observed in 2015.[1]

To reap the digital dividend from these investments, however, African firms need to turn improvements in digital infrastructure into productive use. Access to reliable and high-quality internet service, electricity, and other infrastructure is necessary but not sufficient for technology upgrading and its full productive use. Constraints may include finance, capabilities, or other barriers to complementary private investments needed to fully benefit from digitalization.

Several steps are involved in turning adoption of digital technologies into economic impact (refer to figure I.2). These include not only access to digital enablers, such as mobile devices, computers, and internet connectivity, but also productive use of these technologies. A full analysis requires understanding the business function in which technologies are adopted, the level of sophistication of the technology, and the intensity (or frequency) of its use. This framework is applied in the following chapters, drawing on granular information on the productive use of digital technologies from a new survey instrument and dataset put together by the World Bank.[2]

Most firms in Africa still rely on older, analog-based technologies to perform key tasks that can be digitalized, such as business administration and planning. New evidence from the World Bank's Firm-level Adoption of Technology survey for several countries in Africa, presented in this book, suggests that most formal businesses in Africa already benefit from the availability and use of a mobile phone, but the use of computers and internet varies dramatically across firm size groups. Among microbusinesses, fewer

FIGURE I.2

Reaping the Digital Dividend—From Availability to Productive Use

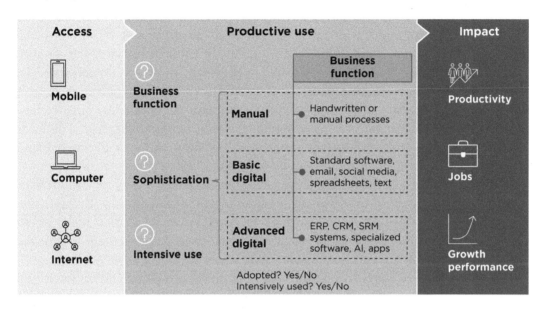

Sources: Adapted from Cirera, Comin, and Cruz (2022) and Begazo, Blimpo, and Dutz (2023).
Note: AI = artificial intelligence; CRM = customer relationship management; ERP = enterprise resource planning; SRM = supplier relationship management.

than 10 percent have adopted computers or internet for business. Sophisticated digital technologies such as specialized apps, specialized software, or enterprise resource planning are used for business administration tasks by about only 35 percent of formal firms with five or more workers. This share drops to 14 percent of such firms when considering intensive use, defined as the most frequently used technology for a task. Indeed, for more than half of these firms, "handwritten process" is the most frequently used method to perform business administration.

Three levels of firm digitalization are discussed in this book. First, a sizable share of firms are not digitally enabled, defined as lacking internet, computers, and mobile phones. Second, among digitally enabled businesses, a large share do not use these technologies to perform productive functions, such as business administration, planning, sales, and payments. Third, among firms already using digital technologies to perform these functions, only a small share intensively use them as the most frequent method to perform these tasks. These gaps between rapid expansion of digital connectivity and gradual conversion into the most productive uses lead to different levels of what we refer to as *incomplete digitalization.*

Incomplete digitalization is a market opportunity for the private sector in Africa. The region has dramatically improved connectivity in recent decades and has good prospects for attracting further investments in the future. However, there is still a large gap in the process of adoption and intensive use of more advanced digital technologies for business purposes, those that are likely to have the most significant impact in productivity, profit, and job creation. Incomplete digitalization can be seen as a business opportunity, namely, to close the remaining digital gaps through a process of adopting and making more productive use of these technologies to perform specific business functions.

Digital technology upgrading is currently expensive for African firms, making this market attractive for innovation and disruption led by the private sector. New evidence presented in this book shows that machinery, equipment, and software are, on average, significantly more expensive in Africa than elsewhere. Internet connectivity is also expensive, but its cost has been declining over time, with improvements in digital and electricity infrastructure. There is also evidence that lack of affordability of entry-level devices (for example, mobile phones, computers) is a barrier to further digital diffusion in developing economies, particularly at the household level. However, the use of digital technologies for business purposes can be embedded in different types of equipment and have diverse purposes for productive use. Further understanding the local ecosystem and the potential for digital entrepreneurs to create solutions that disrupt these markets would enable a pipeline of bankable projects that could channel more private capital toward the productive use of digitalization, which can scale up the economic and social returns on investments in digital infrastructure.

The potential, challenges, and limitations of productive use of digitalization on the continent depend on whether innovative solutions are developed to meet the needs of African firms and workers. Only 6 percent of workers are estimated to be employed by large firms (100 or more workers), and 9 percent are employed by small and medium-size enterprises (between 5 and 100 workers), with the remainder employed by micro-businesses, mostly informal own-account firms (many of which are "entrepreneurs by necessity"). To varying degrees, these firms face high costs from digital technology upgrades, beyond other constraints from lack of scale, lack of apps to meet local needs, managerial capabilities, or access to finance. To enhance the productive use of digital technologies across the continent, it is critical to enable innovative solutions from the private sector. These solutions are most likely to originate from tech entrepreneurs or start-ups offering products and services that address specific demands from local businesses—and provide them at affordable prices.

Turning Global Trends into Opportunities

Several factors have implications for the potential benefits of digitalization in the region:

- *Demographics.* With Africa poised to have the largest workforce in the world by 2100, investments in digital technologies offer opportunities both to upgrade the skill levels of its workforce and to generate the jobs needed to boost prosperity and living standards. This pattern is already evident through the increasing number of Africa-based digital tech developers.

- *Market integration.* African countries have started to open their markets under the African Continental Free Trade Area (AfCFTA), which took effect in 2021, and reductions in trade tariffs of goods and services across borders are now under way. The AfCFTA, coupled with the opportunities brought forth by submarine cables and complementary investments, harnesses the potential for further regional integration that can be spurred by digitalization. It provides the necessary scale for viable private sector investments in regional tech hubs that have spillover potential for users across neighboring economies.

- *Services growth.* With the ratio of trade in services to world output continuing to rise, African firms can participate virtually in a diverse range of services. In addition, the ongoing reshaping of existing supply chains creates opportunities for participation by African firms across sectors, supported by digital services.

- *Green growth.* As consumers worldwide shift their buying habits toward greener products, opportunities emerge to make profitable investments in greener power to support the types of production that rely on digital services as well as more energy-efficient and sustainable production across Africa.

Investments in digitalization channeled to productive use can leverage potential economic gains from these trends. To support their realization, the channels through which investments in digital infrastructure, along with other complementary investments, can enhance productive use need to be expanded. To do so, it will be important to understand both the purposes for which digital technologies are used by businesses across sectors and the extent of incomplete digitalization across businesses.

What Are the Main Contributions of This Book?

Previous studies by researchers in academia and organizations, including the World Bank Group, have analyzed various aspects of digitalization, including access, productive use, and impact. This agenda has been especially relevant to Africa, with specific targets for improving coverage and affordability of digital technology.[3] Most of the recent research has investigated specific layers of the digital economy, especially broadband infrastructure, with limited analysis of the potential for additional private investments by businesses across sectors.[4] Overall, rigorous evidence has pointed to digitalization's potential economic benefits, from an increasing volume of investments and entrepreneurship to job growth, depending on the enabling environment.

This book addresses a knowledge gap in the level of incomplete digitalization and how to mobilize private capital to increase productive use of digital technologies by businesses across Africa. It is organized in two parts. Part 1 focuses on where firms stand on digitalization and the main barriers they face to digital adoption. It addresses the following core questions:

- *Chapter 1.* Where do businesses in Africa stand on digitalization?

- *Chapter 2.* What are the economic effects and the potential for digital upgrade?

- *Chapter 3.* What are the main barriers to adoption, including the cost of technology?

To address these questions, this book relies on a comprehensive list of novel and rich datasets providing new evidence on the status of and prospects for firm digitalization in Africa. The analysis in chapter 1 relies on the World Bank Firm-level Adoption of Technology survey, based on nationally representative data at the establishment level for Burkina Faso, Ethiopia, Ghana, Kenya, Malawi, and Senegal. It also includes data from countries outside the Africa region, including Bangladesh, Brazil, India, the Republic of Korea, and Viet Nam, used for comparison purposes. In addition, it also uses new data from Research ICT Africa, covering micro- and informal businesses from Ethiopia, Ghana, Kenya, Nigeria, South Africa, Tanzania, and Uganda.[5] To further understand the level of firm digitalization and to gauge the potential for digital upgrade and implications for workers across the continent, chapter 2 provides new estimates of the total number of firms and own-account businesses across all countries in Africa, including Sub-Saharan and North Africa. It uses firm characteristics such as number of workers, formal status, and sector to estimate the potential market for and implications of digital upgrade. This approach builds on the finding that most variations in digitalization patterns across countries are driven by the size composition of firms. Chapter 3 presents new evidence on the cost of technology and other complementary factors for adoption, such as human capital. The analysis relies on novel datasets combining item-level prices from the World Bank's International Comparison Program dataset with global coverage and web-scraped data from e-commerce platforms, along with primary data collection led by the International Finance Corporation (IFC) on digital solution providers from Kenya.

Part 2 analyzes what can be done to mobilize more private sector investment to boost digitalization of businesses. It addresses the following questions:

- *Chapter 4.* What are the investment prospects and opportunities in digital infrastructure?

- *Chapter 5.* How can the productive use of digital technologies be boosted through tech start-ups, and how can the pipeline of meaningful entrepreneurs in the region be increased?

- *Chapter 6.* How can access to finance be improved and private capital investments be fostered?

- *Chapter 7.* What policies can unlock private sector investments in digitalization?

The analysis of infrastructure (chapter 4) is based on novel data on submarine cable attributes and internet prices assembled for this book, based on several sources, including TeleGeography, the International Telecommunication Union, and the Global System for Mobile Communications Association. The analysis of tech start-ups (chapter 5) relies on new methods and data sources, combining information from several platforms, including PitchBook, Crunchbase, Preqin, Refinitiv, and LinkedIn for all countries in Africa and drawing on new primary data collected by IFC from about 3,200 start-ups and more than 300 supporting organizations (for example, incubators, accelerators, and investors) across all African countries. The analysis of finance in chapter 6 combines the data sources used in chapters 1 and 5, including new evidence on the demand for finance from start-ups. Chapter 7 uses a novel approach to identify digital goods and assess the potential impact of the AfCFTA on the basis of trade data from World Integrated Trade Solution, as well as relying on an extensive literature review of the effect of cross-sectoral policies to unlock investment opportunities.

Notes

1. This figure from Disrupt Africa (2022) focuses only on venture capital. Partech (2022), which includes equity and debt, estimates around $6.5 billion in total (venture capital, equity, and debt) for 2022.

2. The World Bank's Firm-level Adoption of Technology survey covers more than 300 technologies across almost 60 business functions, including general tasks that are common to all firms and sector-specific functions. The survey was designed in consultation with industry experts, identifying the sophistication of technologies used in specific business functions and the intensity of use. The dataset includes nationally representative samples, totaling more than 20,000 firms, in 15 countries, with various levels of income across Africa, Latin America, Europe, and Asia. Further details about the survey and the data are provided by Cirera, Comin, and Cruz (2022).

3. The Broadband Commission for Sustainable Development (2019) summarizes the strategy targeting "A Digital Infrastructure Moonshot for Africa." Under the Digital Economy for Africa initiative, almost 40 country-level diagnostics providing analytical foundations and policy recommendations have been completed.

4. The 2023 World Bank report *Digital Africa: Technological Transformation for Jobs* (Begazo, Blimpo, and Dutz 2023) emphasizes the impact of digital and complementary technologies on jobs and poverty reduction. Rami and Gallegos (2023) discuss the importance of affordable devices for all and analyze the drivers of costs in the supply and demand for internet-enabled mobile devices for individuals in developing countries. Nayyar, Hallward-Driemeier, and Davies (2021) also emphasize the opportunities of service-led development, with a prominent role for digitalization. Hjort and Tian (forthcoming) provide a comprehensive review of this literature, focusing on the implications of internet for developing countries.

5. Further details on the Firm-level Adoption of Technology survey and Research ICT Africa data sources are available in the appendix. For other data sources, additional information is provided in the respective chapters.

References

Begazo, Tania, Moussa P. Blimpo, and Mark A. Dutz. 2023. *Digital Africa: Technological Transformation for Jobs*. Washington, DC: World Bank. https://doi.org/10.1596/978-1-4648-1737-3.

Briter Bridges. 2023. "Africa's Regional Innovation Ecosystem Mappings." https://briterbridges.com/regional-mappings.

Broadband Commission for Sustainable Development. 2019. *Connecting Africa through Broadband: A Strategy for Doubling Connectivity by 2021 and Reaching Universal Access by 2030*. Geneva: Broadband Commission. https://broadbandcommission.org/wp-content/uploads/2021/09/WG DigitalMoonshotforAfrica_Report2020-1.pdf.

Cirera, Xavier, Diego Comin, and Marcio Cruz. 2022. *Bridging the Technological Divide: Technology Adoption by Firms in Developing Countries*. Washington, DC: World Bank. https://doi.org/10.1596/978-1-4648-1826-4.

Disrupt Africa. 2022. *African Tech Startups Funding Report 2022*. Nairobi, Kenya: Disrupt Africa. https://disrupt-africa.com/wp-content/uploads/2023/02/The-African-Tech-Startups-Funding-Report-2022.pdf.

Hjort, Jonas, and Lin Tian. Forthcoming. "The Economic Impact of Internet Connectivity in Developing Countries: An Overview of the Evidence." *Annual Review of Economics*.

Nayyar, Gaurav, Mary C. Hallward-Driemeier, and Elwyn Davies. 2021. *At Your Service? The Promise of Services-Led Development*. Washington, DC: World Bank.

Partech. 2022. "2022 Partech Africa Report." Partech Partners, Paris. https://partechpartners.com /africa-reports/2022-africa-tech-venture-capital-report.

Rami, Amin, and Doyle Gallegos. 2023. *Affordable Devices for All: Innovative Financing Solutions and Policy Options to Bridge Global Digital Divides*. Washington, DC: World Bank.

TeleGeography (database). "Transport Networks," "GlobalComms," and "Data Centers" modules, Washington, DC (accessed 2022–23), https://www2.telegeography.com/.

World Bank. 2023. World Development Indicators (dataset). World Bank, Washington, DC. https:// databank.worldbank.org/source/world-development-indicators.

PART 1

Digitalization of Businesses in Africa

CHAPTER 1

Making Full Use of Digitalization
Where Do Businesses in Africa Stand?

Xavier Cirera, Marcio Cruz, and Santiago Reyes Ortega

Key Messages

- Businesses in Africa have made significant progress in digital uptake, but more needs to be done to adopt and make full use of digitalization in productive tasks. New evidence based on nationally representative data from Burkina Faso, Ethiopia, Ghana, Kenya, Malawi, and Senegal shows that 86 percent of firms have access to one or more digital enablers (mobile phone, computers, or internet), but only 52 percent of firms have computers with internet. In addition, novel data from Ethiopia, Ghana, Kenya, Nigeria, South Africa, and Uganda indicate that the gap is even larger for microbusinesses (those with fewer than five workers), with 5 percent having adopted computers.

- About 60 percent of firms face some level of incomplete digitalization. Twenty-three percent have not adopted digital technologies for productive use while having digital enablers, and 39 percent do not use their technologies intensively as the most frequent technology to perform a task, despite having adopted them. On average, only 37 percent of firms have adopted an advanced digital technology to perform a specific business function, and only 11 percent use them intensively.

- Mobile phones and digital payments are important entry points for firm digitalization in Africa, but they do not necessarily lead to digitalization across other business functions. Although 61 percent of firms have adopted digital payment options, they are the main payment method in only 7 percent of firms. Moreover, 2 out of 3 firms that use digital payments have not adopted a second digital technology for other uses within the firm.

- Service-sector firms rely on digital technologies more often than firms in other sectors, and a wide gap exists across firm size. For firms in manufacturing and agriculture, the use of digital technologies to perform sector-specific tasks usually requires a large technological leap, one beyond the current capabilities of most firms in Africa.

Introduction

Understanding firm digitalization entails examining not only the uptake of internet and devices, but also the specific purpose for and intensity with which firms use different types of digital technologies to perform productive tasks. This chapter examines the digitalization gaps in African firms at the business function level. This analysis supports subsequent chapters to identify investment opportunities and estimate the potential demand for innovative solutions and infrastructure that can help close those gaps.

This chapter addresses the following questions:

• What are the patterns of firm digitalization in Africa?

• What are the digitalization gaps across different types of firms?

• How do sectoral differences shape digitalization potential?

To address these questions, the analysis builds on new evidence on the use of digital technologies by businesses in Africa, disaggregated by size, sector, and formal status.[1] For firms with five or more workers, the chapter relies on the World Bank's Firm-level Adoption of Technology (FAT) survey,[2] which covers more than 6,000 firms in Africa using nationally representative samples for Burkina Faso, Ethiopia, Ghana, Kenya, Malawi, and Senegal, as well as other developing countries, including Bangladesh, Brazil, India, and Viet Nam. For microbusinesses, including own-account workers (businesses with one person), the chapter draws on data from the Research ICT Africa (RIA) think tank, covering more than 3,000 businesses in Ethiopia, Ghana, Kenya, Nigeria, South Africa, Tanzania, and Uganda.

Setting the Stage: What Is Firm Digitalization About?

Firm digitalization is a continuous process that varies across business functions. Whereas some firms may digitalize only payment methods, others digitalize their processes across all general business functions (GBFs) (refer to figure 1.1), and a few others digitalize their entire operation, including sector-specific functions, in a sophisticated and integrated way. Cirera, Comin, and Cruz (2024) show that such granular measures help in understanding what technologies are used, how they are used, and why they were chosen by firms—a critical step to understanding the process of technology diffusion and the overall technological progress of an economy. Building on that work, this chapter outlines new measures of digitalization by firms.

Digitalization varies in terms of technological sophistication, adoption across different business functions, and intensity of use by firms. Different sophistication levels of technology can be used to perform similar tasks, ranging from manual to advanced digital technologies. Basic digital technologies have general applications and can be used for digitizing information in a standard manner, whereas advanced digital technologies are more specialized to specific tasks and facilitate data integration into the firm's

FIGURE 1.1

Digitalization Is a Continuous Process across Business Functions

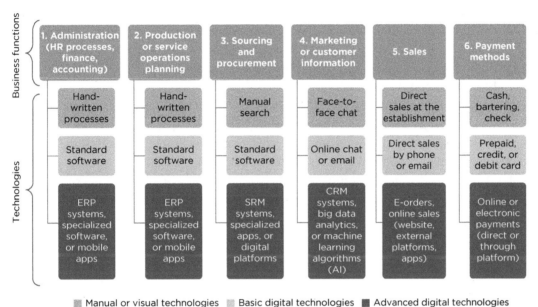

Manual or visual technologies   Basic digital technologies   Advanced digital technologies

Source: Adapted from Cirera, Comin, and Cruz (2024).
Note: Administration refers to tasks related to HR, finance, and accounting. *Manual or visual technologies* refers to processes that do not depend on digital technologies in any instance. *Basic digital technologies* refers to general-purpose digital technologies that are not specifically designed for a particular business function or rely indirectly on digital technologies. *Advanced digital technologies* refers to integrated systems that rely on specialized software, applications, or platforms to perform specific business functions. This category includes technologies in the technological frontier. AI = artificial intelligence; CRM = customer relationship management; ERP = enterprise resource planning; HR = human resources; SRM = supplier relationship management.

operation and decision-making processes. Figure 1.1 summarizes the key technologies used for performing GBFs, defined as tasks common across all firms, grouped into manual, basic, and advanced technologies.[3] The novel FAT dataset allows us to distinguish among a digital technology available at a firm, the purpose for which a business function is used, and the intensity of such use, based on the most frequent method used to perform a task. This unique feature of the data makes it possible to estimate the various stages of digitalization among African firms. The following sections rely on the FAT dataset, except the "Low Digital Use among Microbusinesses and Informal Businesses" section, which is based on the RIA dataset.[4]

Measuring Incomplete Digitalization

African firms have advanced significantly in the adoption of digital enablers, especially mobile phones, but they still lag in the adoption of computers with an internet connection. Most firms in the sample have some sort of digital enabler—mobile phones, computer, or internet connectivity. Many of these firms have not adopted computers with an internet connection, which are important enablers for the use of more advanced technologies, such as enterprise resource planning (ERP) or customer relationship management (CRM) software systems. In addition to this uptake gap, a large share of firms that have already accessed digital enablers are not adopting digital technologies or intensively using them as the most frequent technology to perform productive tasks, a phenomenon defined in this book as *incomplete digitalization*.

This chapter provides new measures of incomplete digitalization along two dimensions beyond having no access to digital technologies (no digitalization): adoption (across specific business functions) and intensive use for productive purposes (among technologies adopted in specific functions). As a prerequisite, firms must have access to digital infrastructure and must use a digital enabler in the form of a digital device such as a mobile phone or computer, or have connectivity to the internet. Firms that do not take up one or more digital enablers are characterized as not having any degree of digitalization. Digitally enabled firms that are not adopting digital technologies for a productive purpose, such as using computers with standard software (for example, spreadsheet software) or ERP systems for administrative tasks (for example, accounting), are characterized by a first level of incomplete digitalization—namely, having an adoption gap. In addition, firms that have already adopted these technologies to perform specific business functions may not use them as the most frequent technology to perform these tasks and thus have an intensive-use gap. These differences can lead to variation in the levels of digital sophistication and the specific productive purpose for which the technology is being used. Figure 1.2 summarizes the level of incomplete digitalization among African firms across GBFs and across these different dimensions.

Most formal firms with five or more workers are digitally enabled, but there is large variation across types of firms. On average, 86 percent of African firms covered by the FAT survey have access to one or more digital enablers (mobile phones, computers, or internet). Only 52 percent have access to computers with an internet connection, which would allow the use of more advanced digital technologies for business functions. The other 34 percent tend to rely only on mobile phones, a more common characteristic among small businesses. Fourteen percent of firms are not digitalized at all, a feature that is more common among smaller firms and those in low-income countries or regions outside the capital cities.

About 60 percent of African firms in the sample face some level of incomplete digitalization. Twenty-three percent do not make productive use of digital technologies despite having digital enablers, and 39 percent do not intensively use their most advanced digital technologies they have already adopted to perform specific business functions.[5] This means that 2 in 3 firms adopting any digital technologies for productive purposes do not use their most sophisticated technology intensively, relying instead on manual or basic digital technologies. Regarding advanced digital technologies, 37 percent of firms adopt them for a certain GBF, but only 11 percent use them intensively. The lack of intensive use of advanced digital technologies, among businesses that have adopted them, shows

FIGURE 1.2

Degrees of Incomplete Digitalization

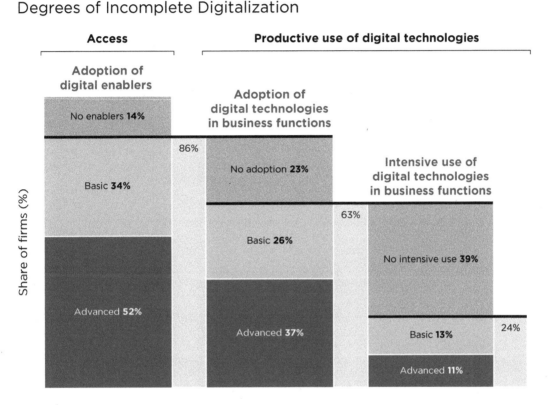

Sources: World Bank, Firm-level Adoption of Technology survey data; Cirera et al. (2024).
Note: The left bar classifies adoption of enablers, namely the percentage of African firms with access to at least one digital enabler (mobile phone, computer, or internet). Computers with internet connection are classified as advanced enablers. The middle bar shows the average share of firms with digital enablers that adopt digital technologies across GBFs. Basic digital technologies refer to general applications (e.g., standard software, email). Advanced digital technologies refer to integrated systems or specialized software designed to perform specific functions (e.g., enterprise resource planning). The right bar shows the average share of firms that intensively use their most sophisticated digital technologies across GBFs. "No intensive use" estimates include 6 percent of firms that adopt advanced digital technologies but intensively use basic digital. GBFs = general business functions.

that solutions for the region need to go beyond addressing barriers to adoption and help to facilitate their usage.

Completing digitalization is associated with higher levels of firm productivity. Firms with higher levels of advanced and intensive use of digital technologies have higher levels of productivity even after controlling for size, sector, and location differences. Figure 1.3 shows a gradual increase in productivity levels among African firms associated with the use of digital technologies for business administration, from no access to digital enablers, to intensive use of advanced digital technologies. This association does not necessarily mean that increasing the use of digital technologies would increase productivity—the figure does not infer a causal relationship—but previous studies have shown that improving access to digitalization can lead to higher levels of productivity.[6]

FIGURE 1.3

Completing Digitalization and Productivity

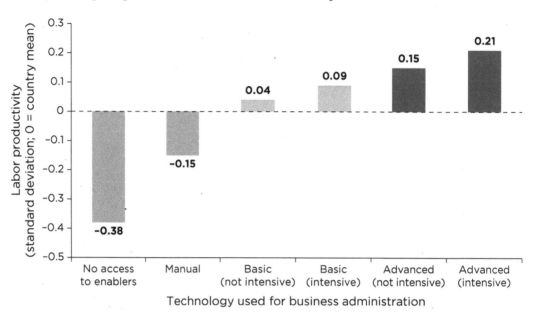

Source: World Bank, Firm-level Adoption of Technology survey data; Cirera et al. (2024).
Note: Estimated levels of a linear regression correlating labor productivity (measured as standard deviations from the country mean) with firms' size, sector, location, and the different levels of digitalization in business administration.

Africa is a diverse region with important variation in digitalization of firms across countries. Figure 1.4 summarizes some of these differences by displaying countries in the FAT sample in two groups. Group 1 (Burkina Faso, Ethiopia, and Malawi) consists of countries with lower income levels and larger digital gaps. Group 2 (Ghana, Kenya, and Senegal) has middle-income countries and is more advanced in digitalization by several measures (for example, infrastructure, share of the population with internet, concentration of tech start-ups). In addition, representative data from Viet Nam and the Republic of Korea are used as benchmarks.

The results highlight three key findings:

• For lower-income countries, lack of access to digital enablers is still an important challenge for digitalization, in particular access to the internet. In middle-income countries, connectivity is widespread across firms, but there are still regional disparities in regions outside of capitals.

FIGURE 1.4

Degrees of Incomplete Digitalization, by Country Group

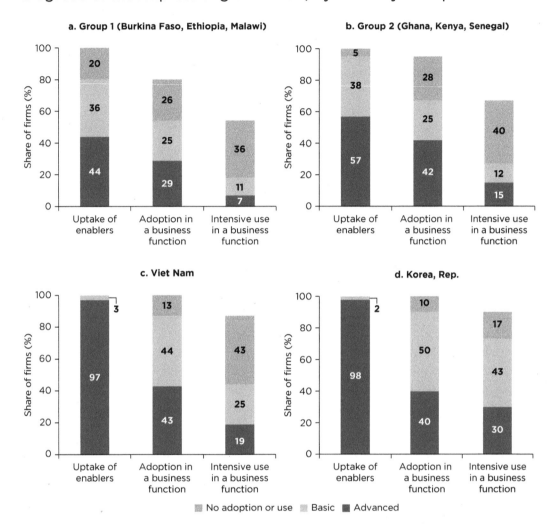

Source: World Bank, Firm-level Adoption of Technology survey data.
Note: In each panel, the left bar classifies adoption of enablers, namely the percentage of firms with access to at least one digital enabler. The middle bar shows the percentage of firms with digital enablers that do not adopt digital technologies, adopt basic digital technologies, or adopt advanced digital technologies to perform GBFs. The right bar shows the percentage of firms that do not intensively use digital technologies, intensively use basic digital technologies, or intensively use advanced digital technologies to perform GBFs, among those that already adopt digital technologies to perform these functions. Firms that adopt an advanced digital technology but use basic digital as their most widely used technology are classified under no intensive use. Estimates in the middle and right-hand bars represent averages across GBFs. Representative data from Viet Nam and the Republic of Korea are included in panels c and d, respectively, as benchmarks. GBFs = general business functions.

- In Africa, firms that are digitally enabled are less likely to adopt a digital technology in a GBF relative to Viet Nam. Although this is true for both groups of countries, firms in group 2 tend to adopt more advanced digital technologies than those in group 1.

- Converting the adoption of digital technologies into intensive use of them is a key challenge across all countries.

Thirty-six percent of all firms in group 1 and 40 percent of all firms in group 2 do not intensively use the most sophisticated digital technologies at their disposal, on average, across business functions. This challenge is also present in countries such as Viet Nam, and it is a contrast to the digitalization story of Korea, where most firms that adopt a digital technology use it intensively. Yet, the lack of adoption or intensive use of digital technology should not be an objective per se but rather a decision driven by the gains expected by the firm, such as profitability. Chapter 3 provides a broader discussion of barriers to digital adoption.

The World Bank report *Digital Africa: Technological Transformation for Jobs* (Begazo, Blimpo, and Dutz 2023) emphasizes the variation of digitalization across countries, but there is also sizable variation within countries (refer to figure 1.4), and even greater variation in technology sophistication within firms, as highlighted by Cirera, Comin, and Cruz (2024). Therefore, this chapter focuses on the average patterns across firms to highlight some key findings that are consistent within and outside Africa. Some common patterns across firms' characteristics suggest that detailed information on firm demographics (for example, the number of firms by size and formal status) can be informative as to the prospects of digitalization, and are further explored in chapter 2. The next sections of this chapter describe in detail the magnitude of incomplete digitalization across different dimensions among African firms.

Three Layers of Digital Gaps across Firms

The three layers of digital gaps across firms include the uptake gap for digital enablers, incomplete digitalization through adoption gaps, and incomplete digitalization through intensive-use gaps. This section provides more detailed measures across these dimensions.

Digital Enablers: The Uptake Gap regarding Devices and Connectivity

Mobile phone adoption is widespread across African firms, but there is large variation in adoption of other devices and connectivity, depending on firms' size, sector, and location. Firms located outside major urban areas, smaller firms, and agricultural-sector firms have lower levels of adoption of digital enablers (refer to figure 1.5). Such variation can partly be explained by the role of technology across different business models. For example, for many service-sector firms, smartphones and computers are their main way of connecting with their clients and providing services. For agricultural firms, digital enablers might mean a higher level of access to information, but they are still able to offer their products in the absence of those enablers.

FIGURE 1.5

Percentage of Firms Adopting Digital Enablers

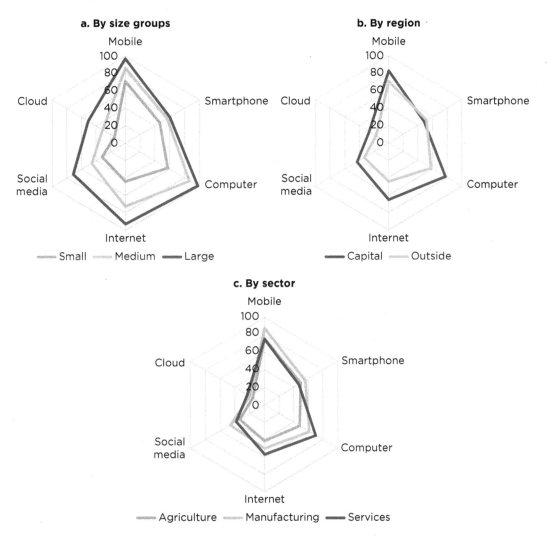

Source: World Bank, Firm-level Adoption of Technology survey data; Cirera et al. (2024).

Despite recent progress in the availability of digital infrastructure and widespread adoption of mobile phones, African firms lag in their uptake of digital enablers such as computers or internet. Figure 1.6 shows that this uptake gap persists for firms in Africa compared with other regions (including Latin America, Asia, and Europe), controlling for income differences, which points to barriers to digitalization beyond the region's stage of development.

FIGURE 1.6

African Firms' Mobile Phone, Computer, and Internet Uptake Gap as Compared to Other Regions

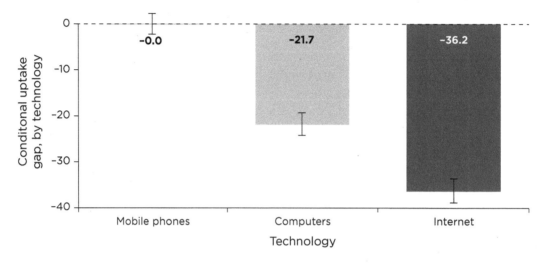

Source: World Bank, Firm-level Adoption of Technology survey data; Cirera et al. (2024).
Note: Estimated margins of a dummy variable for African countries in a linear regression controlling for size, sector, and income differences. Countries outside of Africa include Bangladesh, Brazil, Chile, Georgia, India, Poland, and Viet Nam.

Uptake of digital devices and connectivity is a prerequisite for digitalization. The gap in the uptake of different digital enablers in Africa exists even across groups of firms that tend to have higher access to digital infrastructure, such as large firms, service-sector firms, and firms located in capital cities. Results show that even after controlling for income, African firms tend to lag in the usage of computers and internet relative to similar firms in other global regions. These same gaps are larger for firms in agriculture, small firms, and firms outside of major cities, underscoring how the traditional digital uptake divide in Africa is larger and is not solely explained by differences in income across countries.

Incomplete Digitalization through Adoption Gaps for Productive Use

Digitalization goes beyond the adoption of digital enablers. African firms exhibit low levels of productive use of digital technologies in most GBFs, with the exception of digital payments. For most GBFs, adoption of advanced digital technologies has been low among firms with five or more workers (refer to figure 1.7). Manual processes are the typical technology used by African firms for most business functions.

FIGURE 1.7

Adoption of Digital Technologies Varies across Business Functions

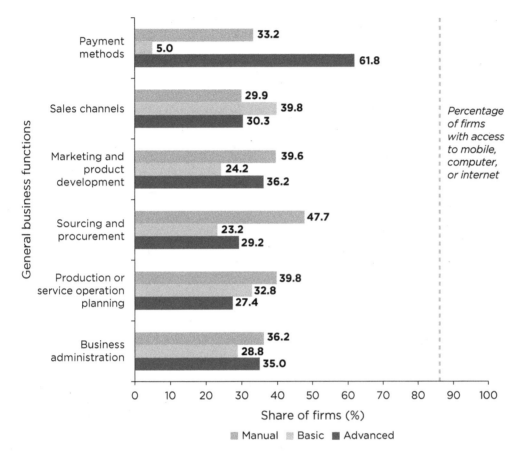

Source: World Bank, Firm-level Adoption of Technology survey data; Cirera et al. (2024).

Firms' adoption of digital enablers does not automatically translate into productive use for business purposes to perform specific tasks that could rely on digital tools. These tasks, such as business administration or planning, are information intensive and could benefit from various applications of digital technologies, from basic spreadsheet files for accounting all the way to more automated systems, such as ERP. Indeed, when looking at the average across GBFs, between 30 percent and 48 percent of firms do not adopt any digital technology to perform a specific GBF. A large share of those already have access to computers and internet.

Despite significant variation across firms linked to characteristics including size, sector, and region, only in payment methods and among large firms does adoption of advanced digital technologies exceed 50 percent. Digital payments are widespread even in groups less inclined to digitalize, such as small or agricultural firms and firms outside capital cities. At the same time, half of medium-size firms and 20 percent of large firms still rely on manual or basic digital technologies to perform business administration tasks.

Differences across size, sector, or location might reflect differences in the net benefits of digitalization by different types of firms. However, African firms have lower adoption of advanced digital technologies for almost all GBFs than do similar firms outside the region, particularly for business administration. These results hold after controlling for income levels or focusing only on firms with access to computers. This first level of incomplete digitalization suggests adoption barriers specific to Africa, such as the costs of technology that are assessed in the next chapters. The adoption gap is more concentrated in internal business functions, with business administration standing out for having the largest gap. More important, these are functions that usually require further investments to use integrated digital technologies, and their use is less dependent on economies of network (for example, customers and suppliers also need to use the technology for interactions). The adoption and use gaps are also larger outside capital cities and in small and medium-size enterprises.

Incomplete Digitalization through Intensive-Use Gaps

Low uptake of enabling technologies and low adoption of digital technologies for productive use within firms are only part of the digitalization challenge in Africa. This section presents evidence of African firms' lack of intensive use of available digital technologies in their day-to-day operations. Although many firms have adopted digital payment technologies and about one-third have adopted advanced digital technologies for business administration, intensive use of such digital technologies is very low even in large firms (refer to figure 1.8). For most GBFs, the majority of firms in Africa still rely on manual processes, including for payment methods, for which cash and checks are the most frequently reported. For sales, as well as for customer relationships for marketing and product development purposes, the use of manual methods—that is, those that involve face-to-face interactions, without any use of digital technologies—is also predominant. These functions (payments, sales, and marketing) each involve direct interaction with individuals and other businesses that are external to the firm, such as customers and suppliers, requiring their adoption for intensive use. For these external-to-firm functions, the gap between use and intensive use is larger than for those functions that are internal to the firm, such as administration and planning.

Even in large firms, cases of incomplete digitalization are widespread. Between 40 percent and 55 percent of large firms that have adopted advanced digital technologies for business administration, production planning, sourcing, or marketing use manual or basic digital technologies intensively in their day-to-day operations rather than the

FIGURE 1.8

Intensive Use of Digital Technologies Varies across Business Functions

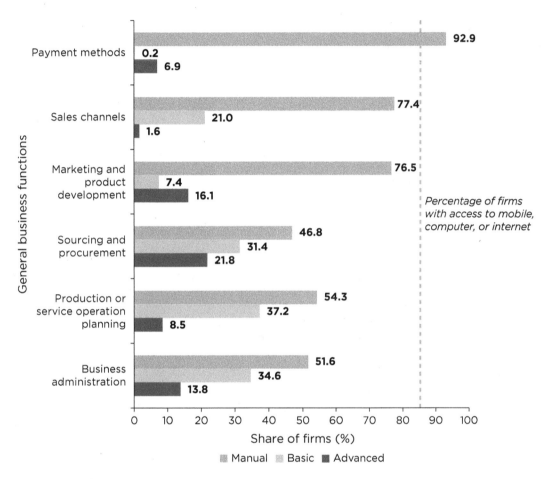

Source: World Bank, Firm-level Adoption of Technology survey data; Cirera et al. (2024).
Note: Intensive use refers to the technology most frequently used to perform the business function.

advanced digital technologies at their disposal. These gaps are even larger in other types of firms and are widespread in sales and payment methods (refer to figure 1.9, panel a).

In summary, 2 out of 3 firms that have adopted advanced digital technologies for internal business functions do not use them intensively in their day-to-day operations,[7] instead using analog or basic digital technologies. On average, firms tend to adopt basic digital technologies but still rely mostly on manual procedures when considering the most frequently (or intensively) used digital technologies to perform GBFs (refer to figure 1.9, panel a). In contrast to external business functions, which depend

FIGURE 1.9

Incomplete Digitalization in Productive Use of Advanced Digital Technologies

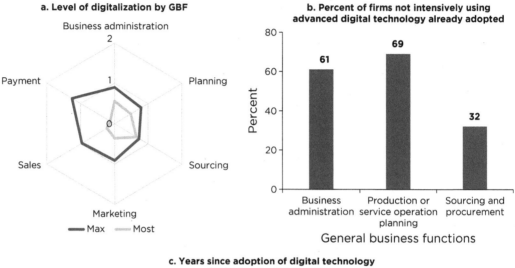

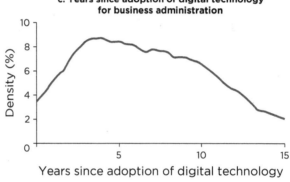

Source: World Bank, Firm-level Adoption of Technology survey data; Cirera et al. (2024).
Note: Panel a shows the average digitalization index by GBF. The index takes a value of 2 if the technology used is a sophisticated digital one, 1 if it is basic, and 0 if it is manual. Panel b shows the share of firms that do not use the sophisticated digital technology intensively, conditionally on having adopted it. Panel c shows the distribution of the number of years of adoption of a sophisticated digital technology for firms with incomplete digitalization. GBF = general business function; max = maximum level of sophistication of the technologies adopted; most = level of sophistication of the most intensively (frequently) used technology.

further on interaction with customers,[8] the intensive use of digital technologies in internal functions (for example, business administration and planning) relies more on management decisions. These functions also show a large share of firms not intensively using advanced digital technologies already adopted to perform these tasks (refer to figure 1.9, panel b). These cases of incomplete digitalization are not driven by firms having recently switched to using digital technologies. On average, these firms have had advanced technologies at their disposal for more than eight years yet still rely intensively on less advanced technologies (refer to figure 1.9, panel c).

Digital Payments as Entry and End Points

The digital divide across firms is less evident in the use of digital payments, an important entry point of digitalization in Africa. Half of the firms with low levels of digitalization have implemented digital payment methods.[9] After assigning firms (by using cluster analysis) to digitalized (leading) or low-digitalization (laggard) groups, the data show that larger gaps between leading and laggard firms are associated with functions that are internal to the firm, namely, business administration and planning (refer to figure 1.10).

Although the typical entry point to more advanced digitalization is through digital payments, only a small share of firms in Africa progress to using a second digital technology in other business functions. In many African firms, digitalization seems to start and end with digital payments (refer to figure 1.11). Most firms that adopt advanced digital technologies for payments do not adopt a second digital technology. Outside Africa, more firms tend to proceed to implementing more advanced digital technologies for

FIGURE 1.10

Digitalization Classification by Adoption of Advanced Digital
Technologies in Each GBF

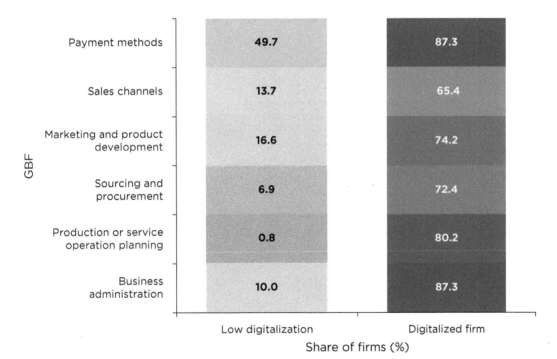

Source: World Bank, Firm-level Adoption of Technology survey data; Cirera et al. (2024).
Note: Classification of firms into low-digitalization or digitalized groups is the result of a k-means cluster analysis across firms. The cluster analysis groups firms on the basis of the similarity of selected indicators. In this case, the digitalization status in each GBF is used. The optimal number of clusters was two. The figure shows the percentage of firms that use advanced digital technologies by GBF and group. GBF = general business function.

FIGURE 1.11

Digital Payments as the Entry and End Points for Digitalization

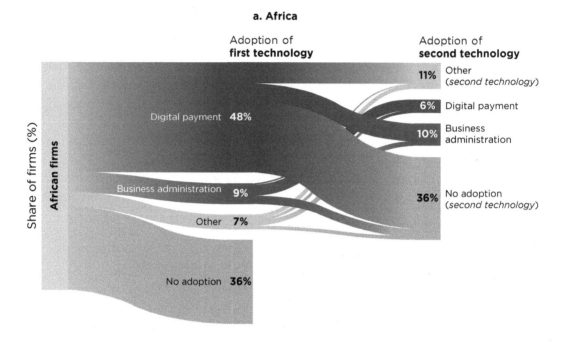

a. Africa

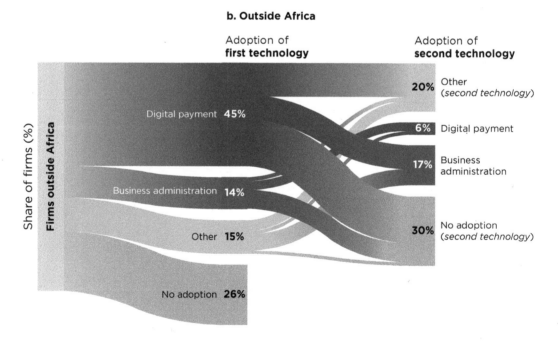

b. Outside Africa

Source: World Bank, Firm-level Adoption of Technology survey data; Cirera et al. (2024).
Note: Figure shows the percentage of firms that adopt advanced digital technology in chronological order. For presentation purposes, only the first two technologies are shown.

business administration or online sales channels after starting using digital payments. The typical firm outside the region also starts using more advanced digital tools for business administration earlier in its life cycle.

Patterns of digitalization are consistent along firm size, with large firms being more likely to adopt and intensively use more advanced technologies. Large firms tend to be earlier adopters of digital technology for several reasons, including economies of scale, allowing them to make more investments, and having a larger expected value because of their greater specialization of workers compared with small firms. Yet, there is a smaller gap between small and large firms in adoption of digital payments (refer to figure 1.12) and in intensive use (refer to figure 1.13).

FIGURE 1.12

Use of Digital Technologies by Business Function across Size Groups in African Businesses

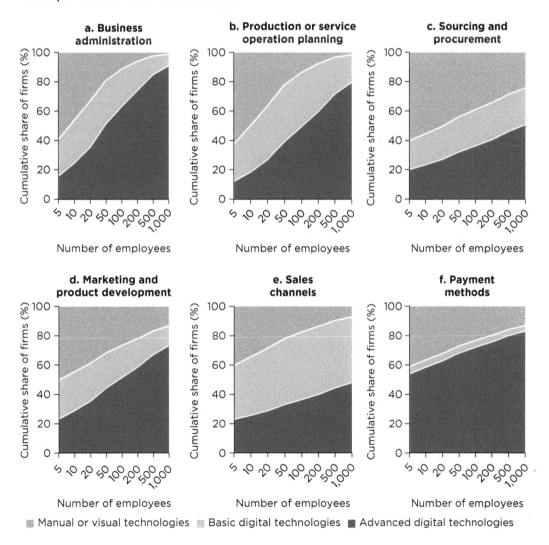

Source: World Bank, Firm-level Adoption of Technology survey data; Cirera et al. (2024).

FIGURE 1.13

Intensive Use of Digital Technologies by Business Function across Size Groups in African Businesses

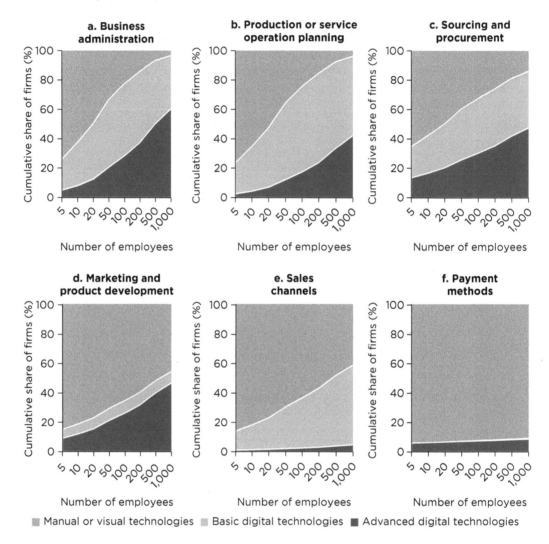

Source: World Bank, Firm-level Adoption of Technology survey data; Cirera et al. (2024).

Although most firms adopt digital technologies for payments and business administration once they attain a certain size, this is not the case for other business functions. Between 25 percent and 50 percent of African firms with more than 100 employees do not adopt any advanced digital technology for production planning, sourcing and procurement, marketing, or sales (refer to figure 1.12). Digital payment constitutes an atypical case of leapfrogging, where even smaller firms jump from manual to advanced digital technologies, skipping the adoption of intermediary (basic) digital technologies, which can be explained by significant reductions in cost of adoption. Yet, we observe that this does not translate into broader diffusion of digital technologies in other functions across similar-size groups.

Low Digital Use among Microbusinesses and Informal Businesses

To understand the full context of digitalization by firms in Africa, it is important to recognize digitalization patterns in informal and microbusinesses (those with fewer than five workers). About 70 percent of Africa's labor force is employed by microbusinesses (including self-employment activities). In Sub-Saharan Africa alone, this represents about 400 million workers, which reinforces the importance of understanding this group of firms in Africa. Although microbusinesses will generally have less need to digitalize across all business functions—for example, there is less information and fewer workers to manage within the firm—digital technologies provide them with opportunities to obtain information, learn skills to increase productivity, connect with suppliers and customers, and expand markets.

Lower levels of digitalization are more prevalent among microbusinesses in Africa. Fewer than 20 percent of microbusinesses report having a working internet connection through enabling devices such as mobile phone or computer (refer to figure 1.14, panel a). Advanced digital technologies are largely absent, except for digital payments. When these firms adopt digital technologies for productive use, they tend to choose basic applications such as spreadsheet, email, or social media largely enabled through smartphones. Low levels of digitalization in other business functions are consistent across both own-account and employer business units (those with at least one employee). Box 1.1 explores the urban–rural divide in access to and adoption of digital technologies.

Despite low levels of digitalization among microbusinesses, some similarities emerge among formal firms with five or more workers, including the use of advanced digital payments. Digital payment is also the most common entry point, with 31 percent of microbusinesses using advanced digital technologies (refer to figure 1.14, panel b).

Evidence of incomplete digitalization in terms of the adoption and productive use gap is also present in informal firms. Of the few informal and microbusinesses that do use computers, a sizable share still perform accounting and operation planning tasks manually (refer to figure 1.14, panel c). Around 2 in 3 informal and microbusinesses that have access to digital enablers such as mobile phones or internet still rely mostly on manual processes. This usage gap may be limiting these firms' growth as well as their potential transition into the formal market.

FIGURE 1.14

Adoption of Digital Technologies in GBFs by Informal and Microbusinesses

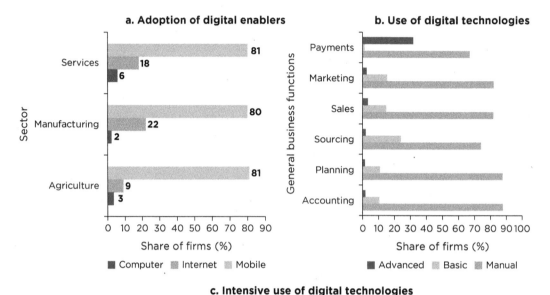

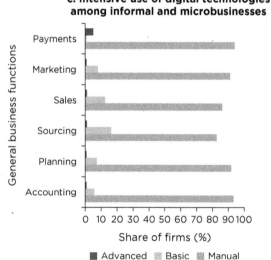

Sources: Research ICT Africa data; Atiyas et al. (2024).
Note: GBFs = general business functions.

BOX 1.1

The Digital Gap among Rural Microbusinesses

Despite progress over the years, the use of information and communication technology (ICT)-enabling tools and digital services remains limited in rural Africa. Although the rural-urban divide in the use of enablers by microbusinesses is relatively small for any type of mobile phone (79 percent versus 84 percent), the gaps are larger for the use of smartphones (28 percent versus 43 percent), computers (3 percent versus 7 percent), and the internet (12 percent versus 23 percent) (refer to figure B1.1.1, panel a). A significant rural-urban gap also exists in the use of digital technologies for business functions.

FIGURE B1.1.1

Use of Digital Enablers and Digital Technologies by African Microbusinesses

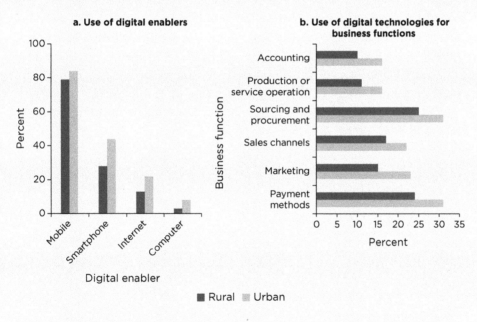

Source: RIA 2022-23 microbusiness data from seven African countries (Atiyas et al., 2024).
Note: Digital technologies combine basic and advanced technologies used for business purposes. RIA = Research ICT Africa.

continued

BOX 1.1 *(Continued)*

Relative to microbusinesses in rural areas, those in urban areas are 29 percent more likely to use digital technologies for payments, 57 percent more likely to use them for accounting, and 35 percent more likely to use them for marketing (refer to figure B1.1.1, panel b).[a] Other studies also show that smallholders in rural Africa either do not use available digital solutions or use them minimally (Abdulai et al., 2023; GFAR 2023).

Despite lower use of digitally enabled services among rural communities in Africa, evidence shows that adoption of agricultural technology by agricultural households improves economic outcomes. For example, deploying digital technology in agriculture has a positive impact on inputs and yields and helps lower transaction and rental costs for tractors. Similarly, mobile money has a positive impact in areas including inputs use, profits, and commercial orientation, and digitally enabled output market information helps farmers both in the prices they receive and in their commercial orientation. Meanwhile, digital trading platforms help them increase trade volumes and sales revenue (Arouna et al., 2020; Daum et al., 2021; Fabregas, Kremer, and Schilbach 2019; Falcao Bergquist and McIntosh 2021; Kikulwe, Fischer, and Qaim 2014; Riley 2018; Suri, Bharadwaj, and Jack 2021), reinforcing the importance of enabling further digitalization among microbusinesses in rural areas.

a. The data reported are unconditional averages. Rural–urban differences in conditional averages (controlling for size, sector, and country) are statistically significant.

Digitalization of Sector-Specific Technologies

Businesses are more likely to connect with digital technologies for sector-specific business functions in services rather than in agriculture and manufacturing. About 80 percent of the technologies used to perform GBFs are digital, according to the World Bank's FAT survey. This is because GBFs are typically intensive in the processing of information to which digital technologies are well suited. Across sectors, digital technologies are more prevalent in services such as retail, finance, and transport than in agriculture and manufacturing activities. Although 60 percent of available technologies for services are digital, that figure is only 30 percent or 40 percent for agriculture and mining.[10]

Digital technologies in service-specific functions tend to be available at lower levels of sophistication, which usually facilitates adoption. In agriculture and manufacturing (production of goods), digital technologies tend to be embedded in frontier non-digital technologies, such as GPS-enabled tractors for harvesting or drones used in irrigation. Digital technologies in services are more similar to GBFs in this regard. In services, most of the core functions tend to be more information intensive, enabling a wider variety of digital technologies to perform each function. As in the case of GBFs, basic digital technologies such as a computer with standard software can be widely applied to perform many sector-specific tasks. Thus, African businesses operating in service sectors—including accommodation, land transport, financial services, whole-sale, and retail—tend to use digital technologies more intensively, with digitalization being available and used at a lower level of technological sophistication than in agri-cultural or manufacturing activities, for example, apparel and food processing (refer to figure 1.15).

Use of digital technologies to perform sector-specific functions in agriculture and food processing is relatively limited, with only a small share of firms in those sectors

FIGURE 1.15

Digital Diffusion across Large Firms in Africa, by Sector

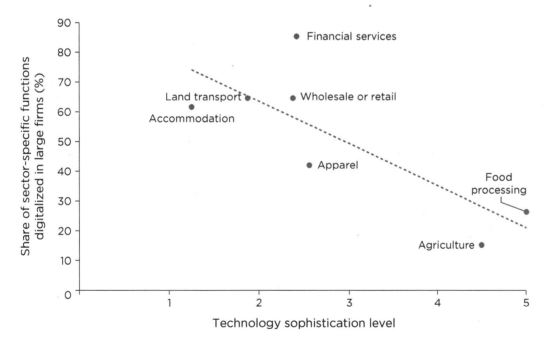

Source: World Bank, Firm-level Adoption of Technology survey data; Cirera et al. (2024).
Note: Technology sophistication level measures how close the first digital technology (which signifies less complexity) is to the frontier technology (which signifies higher complexity). A value of 5 means that the first digital technology is equal to the frontier technology in complexity, and a value of 1 means that the first digital technology is further from the frontier (less complex). The analysis is restricted to large firms to highlight adoption at the top of the distribution.

FIGURE 1.16

Sector-Specific Digital Technologies Adopted in Agriculture and Food Processing

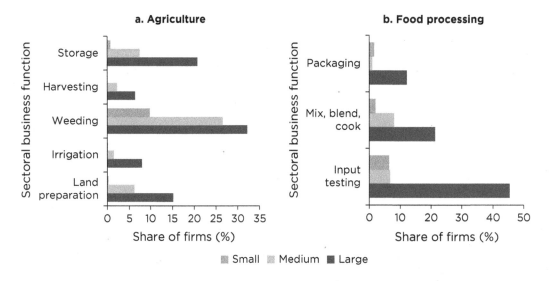

Source: World Bank, Firm-level Adoption of Technology survey data.

adopting them. Still, there are significant variations across business functions. In agriculture, for example, digitalization is more prevalent for weed monitoring and control. In food processing, digital technologies tend to be more frequently adopted for input testing. In both cases, these technologies are more prevalent among large firms (refer to figure 1.16).

Most African agricultural and manufacturing firms are significantly far from the technology frontier—meaning they are not using the most complex digital technologies (Cirera, Cruz, and Reyes 2024). The low prevalence of digital adoption in these sectors suggests that most of these firms are not adopting frontier technologies, but it does not indicate where an average firm stands in terms of technology sophistication in these countries.

Service-sector firms of all sizes are adopting digital technologies for their operations. The lower costs of adoption and the closeness between digital technologies and the business model for service-sector firms make them more likely to adopt digital technologies (refer to figure 1.17). Business functions such as maintaining inventory records, point-of-sale systems, and connecting with customers are some of the digital technologies most associated with retail.

As with what is observed in GBFs, a large share of firms that adopt sector-specific technologies do not use them intensively. This aspect is marked in manufacturing and services firms. These sectors tend to use multiple technologies, and their intensive use requires multiple workers and processes to be in place. In retail, for example, about

FIGURE 1.17

Sector-Specific Digital Technologies Adopted in Services

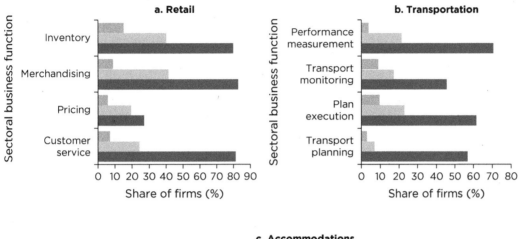

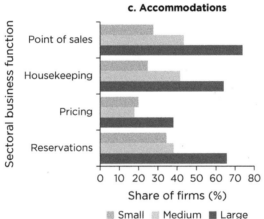

82 percent of firms that adopted digital enablers do not use digital technologies to perform tasks related to inventory. Similarly, about 68 percent of food processing firms do not use digital technologies for input testing, and 55 percent of firms in accommodation do not use their point-of-sale system intensively.

Summing Up

Despite recent advances in infrastructure and uptake of digital enablers, several opportunities to increase digitalization in firms remain. A large share of firms with access to mobile phones, computers, or internet are still manually performing productive tasks that could benefit from digitalization. Among those firms, many are not using these advanced technologies intensively as the most frequent way to perform productive tasks, even if they are at their disposal. The adoption of advanced digital payments across businesses is remarkable. Learning from the leapfrogging case in digital payments could be a guide to developing simple and low-cost solutions for firms to adopt advanced digital technologies for other business functions.

Informal microbusinesses still make up the majority of firms in the region. Digital technologies, including new user-friendly applications of artificial intelligence, can provide new opportunities to obtain information, acquire skills, and expand markets. Nevertheless, the digitalization levels of these microbusinesses are low in all dimensions. Most microbusinesses still lag in access to computers and internet. The urban–rural divide highlights disparities that need to be addressed.

Notes

1. This chapter is based on new evidence from two background papers (Atiyas et al., 2024; Cirera et al., 2024). Firm-level incomplete digitalization findings in this chapter are based on firms with five or more workers covered in the World Bank's Firm-level Adoption of Technology (FAT) survey, except for those in the "Low Digital Use among Microbusinesses and Informal Businesses" section and box 1.1 that explicitly focus on microbusinesses, which use the Research ICT Africa (RIA) dataset. For more information on the FAT and RIA surveys, see appendix A.

2. For more information, see Cirera, Comin, and Cruz (2024).

3. The World Bank's FAT dataset covers more than 60 business functions and 300 technologies, including those that are sector specific. The rank of sophistication was designed in collaboration with more than 50 sector experts. For more details, see appendix A.

4. As part of the collaboration between RIA and the World Bank on a new wave of data collection in 2022–23, the questionnaire was preharmonized with some questions and technologies included in the World Bank's FAT survey.

5. Among firms grouped as "no intensive use," an average of 6 percent adopt both basic and advanced digital technologies but use only basic digital technology intensively.

6. Arouna et al. (2020) show a positive effect of digital technologies on agriculture yields. Gal et al. (2019) find that a 10-percentage-point increase in the adoption of digital technologies such as ERP, CRM, or cloud computing is associated with increases in firms' productivity between 0.8 percent and 1.9 percent per year. Further discussion on this topic is covered in chapter 5.

7. Refers to GBFs that tend to involve processes within the firm: business administration, production planning, and sourcing.

8. Refers to GBFs that tend to involve processes outside the firm: marketing, sales, and payment methods.

9. A cluster analysis was performed to group firms on the basis of their digitalization patterns. The optimal number of groups was two. Figure 1.10 shows each group, where digitalized firms are defined as those clustered in the second group.

10. See Cirera, Comin, and Cruz (2022) for a more detailed discussion on the prevalence of digital technologies by business functions.

References

Abdulai, Abdul-Rahim, Philip Tetteh Quarshie, Emily Duncan, and Evan Fraser. 2023. "Is Agricultural Digitization a Reality among Smallholder Farmers in Africa? Unpacking Farmers' Lived Realities of Engagement with Digital Tools and Services in Rural Northern Ghana." *Agriculture and Food Security* 12: 11. https://doi.org/10.1186/s40066-023-00416-6.

Arouna, Aminou, Jeffrey D. Michler, Wilfried G. Yergo, and Kazuki Saito. 2020. "One Size Fits All? Experimental Evidence on the Digital Delivery of Personalized Extension Advice in Nigeria." *American Journal of Agricultural Economics* 103 (2): 596–619. https://doi.org/10.1111/ajae.12151.

Atiyas, Izak, Marcio Cruz, Mark A. Dutz, Justice Mensah, and Andrew Partridge. 2024. "Digital Technology Choices among Microenterprises in Africa." Background paper, International Finance Corporation, Washington, DC.

Begazo, Tania, Moussa P. Blimpo, and Mark A. Dutz. 2023. *Digital Africa: Technological Transformation for Jobs.* Washington, DC: World Bank. https://doi.org/10.1596/978-1-4648-1737-3.

Cirera, Xavier, Diego Comin, and Marcio Cruz. 2024. "Anatomy of Technology and Tasks in the Establishment." NBER Working Paper 32281, National Bureau of Economic Research, Cambridge, MA. https://www.nber.org/papers/w32281.

Cirera, Xavier, Diego Comin, and Marcio Cruz. 2022. *Bridging the Technological Divide: Technology Adoption by Firms in Developing Countries.* Washington, DC: World Bank. https://doi.org/10.1596/978-1-4648-1826-4.

Cirera, Xavier, Diego Comin, Marcio Cruz, and Santiago Reyes. 2024. "The 'Incomplete' Digitalization of Firms in Africa." Background paper, World Bank Group, Washington, DC.

Daum, Thomas, Roberta Villalba, Oluwakayade Anidi, Sharone Masakhwe Mayienga, Saurabh Gupta, and Regina Birner. 2021. "Uber for Tractors? Opportunities and Challenges of Digital Tools for Tractor Hire in India and Nigeria." *World Development* 144: 105480. https://doi.org/10.1016/j.worlddev.2021.105480.

Fabregas, Raissa, Michael Kremer, and Frank Schilbach. 2019. "Realizing the Potential of Digital Development: The Case of Agricultural Advice." *Science* 366 (6471): eaay3038. https://doi.org/10.1126/science.aay3038.

Falcao Bergquist, Lauren, and Craig McIntosh. 2021. "Search Cost, Intermediation, and Trade: Experimental Evidence from Ugandan Agricultural Markets." CEGA Working Paper WPS-173, Center for Effective Global Action, University of California, Berkeley. https://doi.org/10.26085/—C3759K.

Gal, Peter, Giuseppe Nicoletti, Christina von Rüden, Stéphane Sorbe, and Théodore Renault. 2019. "Digitalization and Productivity: In Search of the Holy Grail—Firm-Level Empirical Evidence from European Countries." *International Productivity Monitor* 37 (Fall): 39–71.

GFAR (Global Forum on Agricultural Research). 2023. "Collective Action on Inclusive Digital Transformation of Agriculture." https://gfair.network/content/gfar-collective-action-inclusive-digital-transformation-agriculture.

Kikulwe, Enoch M., Elisabeth Fischer, and Matin Qaim. 2014. "Mobile Money, Smallholder Farmers, and Household Welfare in Kenya." *PLoS One* 9: e109804. https://doi.org/10.1371/journal.pone.0109804.

Riley, Emma. 2018. "Mobile Money and Risk Sharing against Village Shocks." *Journal of Development Economics* 135: 43–58. https://doi.org/10.1016/j.jdeveco.2018.06.015.

Suri, Tavneet, Prashant Bharadwaj, and William Jack. 2021. "Fintech and Household Resilience to Shocks: Evidence from Digital Loans in Kenya." *Journal of Development Economics* 153: 102697. https://doi.org/10.1016/j.jdeveco.2021.102697.

CHAPTER 2

Economywide Effects of Digitalization

Marcio Cruz, Edgar Salgado, and Trang Thu Tran

Key Messages

- The arrival of high-speed internet in Africa has led to sizable gains in employment, productivity, and economic growth. Existing evidence suggests that this stems from various channels, including higher entry of domestic and foreign firms as well as productivity improvements within existing firms. New evidence in this chapter points to the adoption of digital technologies in general functions, such as business administration, as a driver of firm-level productivity gains from better access to internet. Additional gains may be expected once digital technologies are used more intensively.

- About 600,000 firms in Africa (among the estimated 2 million formal firms with five or more workers across the continent) can potentially benefit from fuller use of digitalization by investing in basic or advanced digital technologies. The potential is especially strong for small and medium-size enterprises. Moreover, of the almost half-million formal firms estimated to have adopted advanced digital technologies without using them intensively, about 10 percent are likely to become intensive users. Additionally, among 204 million microbusinesses (those with fewer than five workers), as many as 40 million (20 percent) could upgrade to some digital technologies. These estimates are based on firms having characteristics similar to those already adopting these digital technologies.

- The prevalence of employment in micro- or informal businesses underscores the need to adapt and shape technologies for the local productive needs of these businesses and for new entrants. Currently, 7 in 10 African workers are self-employed, operating own-account businesses relying largely on manual technologies.[1] Moreover, it is important to ensure that the prevailing business environment facilitates the reallocation of workers to larger, more digitally enabled and growing firms, because such firms play a disproportional role in pairing workers with more advanced technologies, thereby boosting productivity, output, and jobs.

Introduction

This chapter assesses the potential economywide impact of digitalization and the market prospects for digital upgrade. It documents evidence of the impact of digitalization and takes stock of country-specific findings in Africa, with a focus on entrepreneurship, productivity, and jobs. It also discusses the scope for further impacts in the context of regional trends such as increased market integration and improvements in digital infrastructure, which could facilitate digital adoption among firms that are relatively similar to those already adopting these technologies. The aim is to show the implications for firms and workers in the continent.

This chapter addresses the following questions:

- How does digitalization affect productivity and jobs?
- What is the potential market for digital upgrading among businesses in Africa?
- How many workers might benefit from digital upgrades by firms across the continent?

The analysis builds on a summary of evidence on the impact of digitalization and new estimates of the market prospects for digital upgrade among firms in Africa. First, it provides a brief review of the literature along with new evidence of the channels through which firms benefit from improvements in digital infrastructure to upgrade and grow. Second, the market prospect analysis is based on a background study for this book estimating the number of firms with various characteristics and patterns of digitalization (described in chapter 1), combined with statistical modeling to estimate the probability of digital upgrade across firms for all countries in the region. Third, the implications for workers of digital upgrading of firms also build on simple scenario analyses based on the number of workers associated with firms of different types.

Economic Impact of Digitalization: What Are the Channels?

The potential economic benefits of greater digitalization in Africa emerge through different channels within and across firms using the technologies. Economic growth, poverty reduction, and boosted shared prosperity in developing and emerging markets rely on increasing the number and quality of jobs through new firm entry and expansion, productivity gains, and sustained higher profits. Because digitalization reduces various economic costs, it affects how firms process information, organize production, and access markets.[2] Evidence suggests that digital technologies can improve business practices and encourage innovation.[3] Addressing the constraints on digitalization in African economies can expand demand for new and existing products, allow small and medium-size enterprises to enter existing and new markets, reduce the cost of production and trading, and further integrate into global value chains (Banga and te Velde 2018).

Digital Upgrading and Firm Productivity

Access to digital enablers and adoption and intensive use of digital technologies are associated with firm-level productivity gains in developing countries. Evidence from the World Bank's Firm-level Adoption of Technology (FAT) survey further suggests that more productive regions have a larger number of firms intensively using more advanced digital technologies (figure 2.1). It also suggests that differences in technology sophistication account for 31 percent of cross-establishment dispersion in productivity (Cirera, Comin, and Cruz 2024a). Adoption of simple technologies such as website and email is associated with modest improvements in manufacturing productivity and significant increases in both employment and fixed assets in 82 developing countries (Cusolito, Lederman, and Pena 2020). New evidence for Senegal suggests that the adoption of technologies for general business functions may underlie this internet-enabled productivity gain (box 2.1). The effect seems to be present among

FIGURE 2.1

Firm-Level Digitalization Is Associated with Higher Productivity

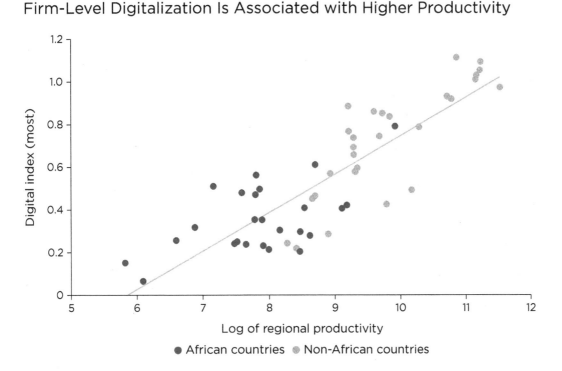

Source: World Bank, Firm-level Adoption of Technology survey; Cirera et al. (2024b).
Note: Regional firm productivity is the average value added per worker in each subnational region, controlling for sectoral differences, and adjusted by purchasing power parity. The digital index reflects the average use of digital technology across six general business functions: administration, planning, sourcing, marketing, sales, and payments. It refers to the most frequently used technology to perform each of these tasks. It takes the value of 2 if the technology used is advanced digital, 1 if it is basic digital, and 0 if it is manual.

BOX 2.1

How Does Digitalization Occur in the Firm When Internet Access Improves?

Several studies find that internet connectivity can make firms, workers, and other input factors in developing economies more productive. Yet, to understand how this mechanism works and the potential spillover effects throughout the economy, it is critical to study how improvements in digital infrastructure, which facilitate access to high-speed internet, change the way firms perform specific tasks.

What specific business functions within firms benefit most from improvements in digital infrastructure? To help answer this question, an ongoing study (Berkes et al., forthcoming) combines information on the GPS location of the firms that participated in the World Bank's Firm-level Adoption of Technology survey in Senegal with the location of the node of the Senegalese internet backbone. It then explores the contribution of digital infrastructure to the adoption of technologies through the effects of proximity to the nodes, which translates into having access to better-quality internet service, improved by the arrival of submarine internet cables in 2011. The key findings are the following:

First, new evidence for Senegal shows that improving internet access significantly increases the likelihood of technology adoption, with positive effects on productivity. On average, doubling the distance from an access node to internet reduces the likelihood of having an internet connection by 5 percentage points. This effect is about 10 percent of the sample mean (0.47) and hence economically relevant. When restricting the sample to firms established for more than 10 years—or before the rollout of improvements on submarine cables in Senegal—the results are even stronger, with high-speed internet connections increasing by about 40 percent. Both formal and informal firms made significant productivity gains.

Second, internet access increases the sophistication of digital technology in firms. However, in line with the incomplete digitalization pattern described in chapter 1, this happens through selected business functions, and only a subset of firms end up using these

continued

BOX 2.1 *(Continued)*

technologies intensively. Better access to internet explains adoption of more advanced technologies for general business functions, but not the adoption of technologies for sector-specific business functions. Moreover, the increase in intensive use of these technologies is driven by a subsample of formal and older firms.

even the smallest firms. Digital technologies such as smartphones and inventory control or point-of-sale software may foster labor productivity, sales, and employment among microbusinesses in Senegal (Atiyas and Dutz 2021).

Effect of Digitalization on Entrepreneurship and Foreign Direct Investment

Beyond its impact on incumbent enterprises, improved access to digital technologies can affect aggregate productivity and employment through its effects on business entry. Better internet access can increase demand for digital services and lower entry cost, which may in turn increase the expected returns from entry for both local and foreign firms. High-speed internet has triggered an increase in entrepreneurship and greenfield foreign direct investment (FDI) in Africa, particularly in services (figure 2.2). The arrival of fast internet is associated with an increase in net entry of formal firms in South Africa (Hjort and Poulsen 2019) and an increase in the rate at which households transition to operating a nonfarm business in the Africa region, with the strongest effects in services (Houngbonon, Mensah, and Traore 2022). Similarly, high-speed internet stimulated FDI, with benefits concentrated in finance, technology, health, and retail (Mensah and Traore 2023).

Spillover and Distributional Effects of Digitalization

Firms' use of digital technologies also appears to help other firms, other markets, and their workers. Early adopters can reduce experimental costs for later adopters. As a result, individual firms' decisions to generate or adopt technologies benefit other firms in the same location or customers down the supply chain (McElheran et al., 2023). Even for informal firms with lower levels of technology use, proximity to formal firms may

FIGURE 2.2

Arrival of Fast Internet Improves Firm Entry and Greenfield FDI

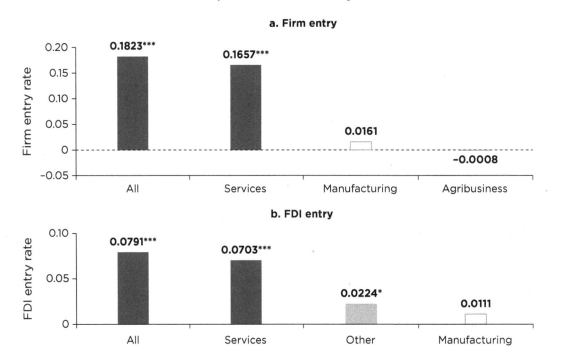

Sources: Houngbonon, Mensah, and Traore (2022); Mensah and Traore (2023).
Note: Results on the impact of the availability of high-speed internet summarized from Houngbonon, Mensah, and Traore (2022) (Living Standards Measurement Study–Integrated Surveys on Agriculture) for firm entry (panel a) and from Mensah and Traore (2023) (fDi Markets data on greenfield FDI projects) for FDI entry (panel b). Both studies exploit the staggered arrival of submarine internet cables to the coast of Africa and the subsequent rollout of terrestrial fiber networks across the continent. FDI = foreign direct investment.
*Significant at the 10% level. **Significant at the 5% level. ***Significant at the 1% level.

spur digital adoption among them (refer to box 2.2). Moreover, digitalization can promote entry of informal firms into the formal sector. Improved access to finance through financial technology solutions, for example, may tilt the benefits of formalization to outweigh the costs from increased transparency and regulation (Bussolo et al., 2023; Klapper, Miller, and Hess 2019).

To the extent that digital technologies can raise the productivity and income of workers, these spillover benefits will not be fully captured by firm investments. Evidence across countries at different income levels shows that broadband access not only is associated with higher firm productivity but also increases workers' wages on average (Almeida, Corseuil, and Poole 2017; Chen 2021; Tian 2018). Results from the FAT survey also suggest that average wages are higher in firms that use more advanced digital technologies, conditional on other firm characteristics.

BOX 2.2

Digitalization Spillovers from Formal to Informal Firms

Jolevski et al. (2024) examine spillovers in the use of digital technologies from formal to informal businesses. Using a unique set of geocoded data from the 2019 World Bank Enterprise Surveys in Zambia, the findings indicate that closer geographic proximity to formal firms is associated with a significantly higher likelihood of digital adoption by informal businesses. The finding holds for various types of digital technologies (refer to figure B2.2.1). For most of the digital technologies under consideration, the technology spillover effect from formal firms is greater for informal businesses with a highly educated owner, a permanent location, and younger firm age.

FIGURE B2.2.1

Closer Proximity to Formal Firms Increases Digital Adoption among Informal Firms

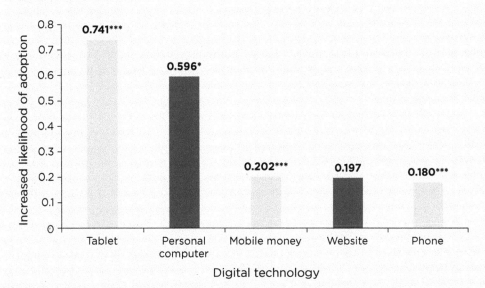

Source: Jolevski et al. (2024).
Note: Estimates on the impact of distance from (the closest) formal firms on informal firms' likelihood of adopting different digital technologies. Results are conditional on firm size, age, sector fixed effects, and owner characteristics.
*Significant at the 10% level. **Significant at the 5% level. ***Significant at the 1% level.

Moreover, fast internet appears to considerably increase employment in developing countries (Hjort and Tian, forthcoming). The increase in employment does not appear to be at the expense of less connected areas. Although the effect is higher for skilled workers, it is also positive for those with only primary school education and tends to lead to more job opportunities in services (Caldarola et al., 2023). Additional studies have shown positive effects on economic growth (Calderon and Cantu 2021; Goldbeck and Lindlacher 2023) and poverty reduction (Bahia et al., 2020; Masaki, Ochoa, and Rodriguez-Castelan 2020).

Potential Effects of Digital Upgrading in Africa

The interaction between firms' technology adoption and their employment composition determines workers' access to technology and, in turn, their productivity and income. Gains from digitalization are ultimately the result of productive use of these technologies by businesses and workers. To get a sense of how much potential there is, it is important to estimate the size of the market in Africa. Recent work by the International Finance Corporation suggests that Africa has about 244 million businesses, broadly defined. Of these, a large majority are own-account businesses, and 98 percent of these are informal (box 2.3, figure B2.3.2). Excluding own-account activities but keeping microbusinesses that employ workers, Africa has approximately 12.7 million firms, with 2 million of those being formal businesses employing five or more workers. This section uses estimates on firm and worker distribution across African countries to build a scenario analysis of the potential implications of digital upgrades across different type of businesses.

New Regional Trends May Speed Up the Diffusion of Digital Technologies in Africa

New developments in the region may speed up digital diffusion, which, as discussed further in chapter 3, has hitherto been hampered by high technology costs and other factors such as uncertain returns on adoption. The increased capacity created by the submarine cables can reduce the price of broadband internet (refer to further discussion in chapter 4), which could in turn boost uptake in fixed broadband and other digital solutions. Indeed, as discussed in box 2.1, results from Senegal show that proximity to internet infrastructure increases digital adoption. Moreover, greater trade integration from the African Continental Free Trade Area may reduce tariffs for digital goods and further improve the net gains from more intensive use of digital technologies.[4]

BOX 2.3

How Many Firms Are There in Africa?

Answering this deceptively simple question is harder than it seems for two reasons: defining what constitutes a firm and limited data availability. Background research for this project provides a novel methodology that combines multiple data sources to estimate the number of firms in Africa, considering their size and formal status.

Given the proliferation and relevance of informal businesses in Africa, these estimates distinguish between own-account businesses (many of which exist because their proprietors cannot find alternative employment) and those that employ workers. The total number of own-account businesses is disproportionately high in Africa, whereas the number of firms with at least 20 workers (medium and large firms) is disproportionately low (figure B2.3.1). Own-account businesses' density (ratio of number of own-account businesses to working age population) declines with gross domestic product per capita (panel a). Conversely, the density of firms employing 20 or more workers is positively associated with economic development.

Data on registered firms are scarce in Africa, a challenge compounded by the lack of harmonization across datasets. Countries generally differ in the definition of a firm or the sectors covered by the establishment census (a census focused on assessing businesses rather than individuals). To overcome this challenge, These estimates use as the starting point harmonized data from the International Labour Organization on the number of employers. Under the assumption that every employer constitutes a firm, it then breaks this number down by size and formal status, by combining data from the World Bank Enterprise Surveys (WBES) and microdata from the few available establishment censuses and surveys (censuses for Burkina Faso, Cameroon, Ghana, and Rwanda and micro-, small, and medium-size enterprises survey for Kenya). Combining this information with a statistical model that links the proportion of micro-, small, medium-, and large-size firms to different moments of the firm size distribution (mean and 25th, 50th, 75th, and 90th percentiles), the analysis predicts the size composition for every country using adjusted firm size moments from WBES and complementary data sources. Because data from WBES are not representative of the whole universe of firms in a country, the methodology adjusts

continued

BOX 2.3 *(Continued)*

FIGURE B2.3.1

Correlation of Firm Density and GDP per Capita

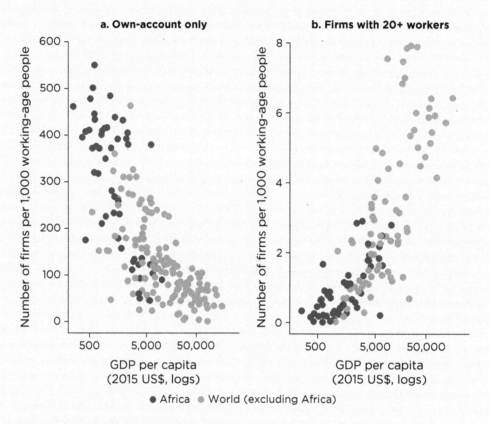

Source: Castro et al. (2024).
Note: Own-account businesses are individuals engaged in own-account activities with no employees. GDP = gross domestic product. Firm density is measured by the total number of firms per 1,000 working-age people in each country.

for differences in formal and informal distribution using representative datasets from establishment censuses and surveys from Burkina Faso, Cameroon, Ghana, Kenya, and Rwanda.

The result of this exercise is an estimate of the number of firms in each African country, distinguished by size and formal status. This allows the definition of a further subset of firms: those that are formal and have at least five employees. This group is associated with better economic outcomes where entrepreneurial activity booms.

continued

BOX 2.3 *(Continued)*

FIGURE B2.3.2

Market Size: The Universe of Businesses in Africa

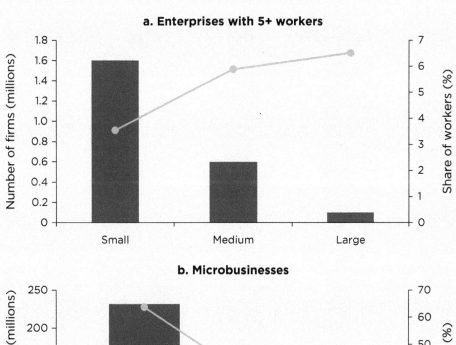

a. Enterprises with 5+ workers

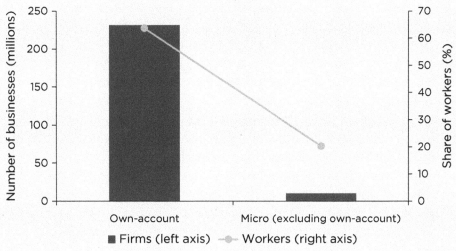

b. Microbusinesses

■ Firms (left axis) ●— Workers (right axis)

Source: Castro et al. (2024).
Note: Own-account firms are individuals engaged in own-account activities with no employees, as reported by the International Labour Organization. The density of firms with different sizes results from the breakdown of total employers.

continued

BOX 2.3 *(Continued)*

The estimates suggest that Africa has 12.7 million enterprises with more than one employee (2.3 million with 5 or more workers) and 231 million own-account businesses for which the proprietor constitutes the sole employee (refer to figure B2.3.2). Regarding labor, only 6.5 percent of workers are estimated to be employed by large firms (100 or more workers), 9.5 percent by small and medium-size enterprises (5–100 workers), and 84 percent in microbusinesses, mostly informal own-account businesses.

Moving Up the Digitalization Ladder: Estimating Potential Demand

In view of these regional developments, which firms can be expected to move up the digitalization ladder? This section provides a back-of-the-envelope calculation focused on business administration, because its digitalization level can serve as a better proxy than other functions for the overall technological sophistication of firms.[5] Of 2.3 million formal firms with five or more workers in Africa, 1.3 million are estimated to have adopted manual technologies, 728,000 to have adopted basic technologies, and 575,000 to use advanced technologies for business administration (map 2.1).[6]

To better understand the market potential for digital upgrade among businesses, this chapter combines detailed measures of technology adoption in selected countries with estimates of firm characteristics across Africa. More specifically, the analysis relies on estimates of the number of firms by size, sector, and formal status in Africa and evidence of digital adoption by firms from the FAT and Research ICT Africa (RIA) surveys. The potential market for digital upgrade is estimated on the basis of the probability of digital adoption according to firms' characteristics across countries (box 2.4).

Potential Market Size from New Adoption and More Intensive Use of Digital Technologies

Of the 2 million formal firms in Africa, 23 percent—more than half a million firms—stand to gain from digitalizing their business administration technologies. This estimation is based on the characteristics they share with firms that have already adopted

MAP 2.1

Current Market Size of Technology Adoption for Business
Administration

Thousands of businesses

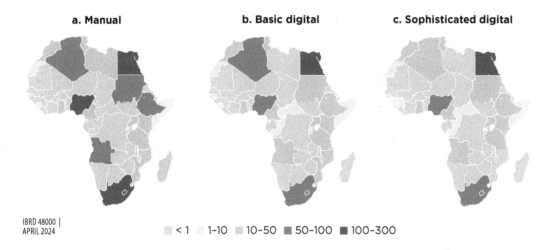

a. Manual   **b. Basic digital**   **c. Sophisticated digital**

IBRD 48000 |
APRIL 2024

░ < 1   ░ 1–10   ▒ 10–50   ▓ 50–100   ■ 100–300

Source: Original calculations based on the methodology described in box 2.4.
Note: Estimates per country are calculated using the number of formal firms with at least five workers
multiplied by the average adoption by firm size (small, medium, and large) for two income groups, as
reported by the World Bank's Firm-level Adoption of Technology survey.

digital technologies in business administration. As reported in figure 2.3, panel a,
520,000 firms are estimated to have the potential to move from using manual technologies to using basic digital technologies (83 percent are small firms). Similarly, 98,000
firms that are already users of basic technologies have the potential to use advanced
digital technologies (71 percent are small firms).

Digital upgrading does not automatically lead to intensive use of digital technologies. Of 575,000 firms already adopting advanced digital technologies for business
administration, we estimate that 23 percent use them intensively as the most frequent
technology to perform the task. This leaves about 444,000 that are using advanced technologies, but not intensively, as reported in figure 2.3, panel b. Using the methodology
outlined in box 2.4, we estimate that about 11 percent (47,000 firms) of these firms have
high potential to switch from nonintensive to intensive use, based on similar observed
characteristics.

About 5 percent of firms have high probability to upgrade either from manual
to basic or from basic to advanced digital technologies, with large variation across
countries. Map 2.2 shows the geographic dispersion of these two levels of upgrading, namely, those that could benefit from upgrading from manual to basic digital
technologies, and those that are likely to benefit by upgrading from basic to advanced
digital technologies, expressed as the percentage of all firms in each country.

BOX 2.4

Estimating the Potential Market for Digital Adoption
across African Firms

The estimates of the proportion of firms' users of one type of technology (manual or basic) who are more likely to upgrade to the next
level (basic or advanced) are based on similarities to firms that have
already upgraded. Because the availability of technology does not
necessarily mean that every firm can adopt it, it is important to filter
out those firms that have real potential from those with a low probability of moving up the digital ladder. To account for this, a two-step
statistical procedure was implemented. In the first step, using multi-
nomial probability models, we regress technology choices (manual,
basic digital, and advanced digital) on a group of firm characteristics (index of management practices,[a] sector, location, age, and size).
With this model, we predict the probability (or propensity) of having
any of the three types of digital technology. The model allows the
prediction of technology adoption for both types of firms, the ones
that already adopted the technology and those that did not.

The second step consists of assuming a rule of thumb to estimate the
number of firms that could upgrade from basic to advanced digital. This
exercise is based on the observed characteristics used in the estimation
model. Because the model predicts the probability of adoption for both
firms that adopted the technology and those that did not, the median
predicted probability among adopters is used as the threshold to identify firms with the higher probability of adoption among those who are
not using such technology.

Figure B2.4.1 illustrates the exercise. Panel a suggests that 13 percent
of firms have the potential to upgrade from basic to advanced use of
digital technologies. These are the firms with an estimated probability
of adoption higher than the threshold described earlier (marked with
the vertical dashed line). A similar exercise (panel b) suggests that
the percentage of firms already users of advanced technologies that
could become intensive users of the technology is 11 percent. Similar
exercises are conducted to estimate the probability of adopting basic
digital technologies among nondigitalized businesses and to estimate
the potential for digital upgrade among microbusinesses.

The result itself is conservative because, among all firms with the
potential to upgrade, these estimates consider only the top 10 percent
of firms with the highest probability of adoption.

continued

BOX 2.4 *(Continued)*

FIGURE B2.4.1

Estimated Propensity Scores for Adoption and Intensive Use of Digital Technology

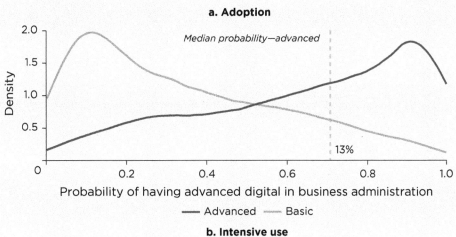

a. Adoption

Median probability—advanced

13%

— Advanced ----- Basic

b. Intensive use

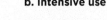

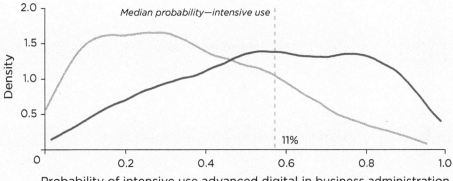

Median probability—intensive use

11%

— Has advanced digital—intensive use
----- Has advanced digital—no intensive use

Source: Original calculations based on data from World Bank, Firm-level Adoption of Technology survey.
Note: Firm density is measured by the total number of firms per 1,000 working-age people in each country. In panel a, the propensity score is calculated using an ordered probit estimation in which the dependent variable has three categories (manual, basic, and advanced). Covariates are age, size (number of employees), region, and management score. In panel b, the propensity score is calculated using a logit estimation in which the dependent variable is a dummy to identify whether the firm uses advanced technologies intensively. Covariates are age, size (number of employees), region, and management score. Regression is constrained to users of advanced technologies only.

a. Management practices are found to explain technology adoption (Bloom, Sadun, and Van Reenen 2012).

FIGURE 2.3

Market Potential for Digital Upgrading and More Intensive Use for Business Administration Technology

Thousands of firms

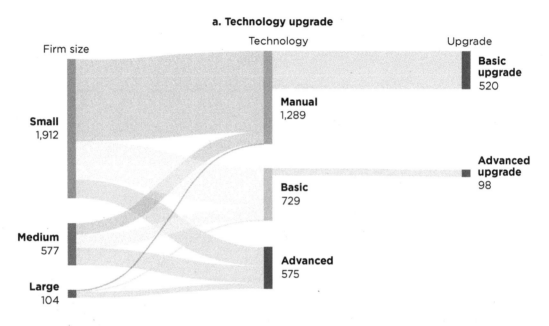

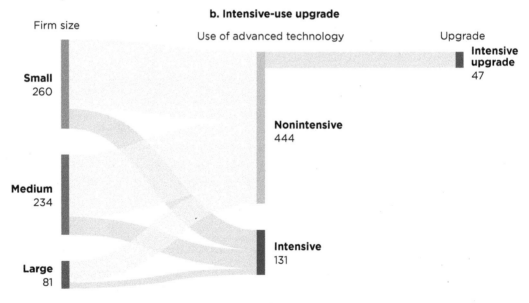

Source: Original calculations based on the methodology described in box 2.4.
Note: The number of firms per country is calculated using the estimated number of formal firms with at least five workers multiplied by the average proportion of firms with the potential to adopt a new technology by firm size (small, medium, and large) in two income groups as reported in the Firm-level Adoption of Technology survey. Panel a shows the number of firms with the potential to upgrade from one technology to the next. Panel b focuses on users of advanced technologies and shows the number of nonintensive users who could become intensive users of advanced digital technologies.

MAP 2.2

Percentage of Firms Using One Type of Business Administration
Technology That Could Upgrade to the Next Level

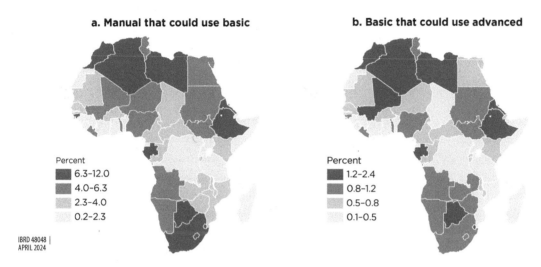

a. Manual that could use basic

b. Basic that could use advanced

Percent
- 6.3–12.0
- 4.0–6.3
- 2.3–4.0
- 0.2–2.3

Percent
- 1.2–2.4
- 0.8–1.2
- 0.5–0.8
- 0.1–0.5

IBRD 48048 |
APRIL 2024

Source: Original calculations based on the methodology described in box 2.4.
Note: The number of firms per country is calculated using the estimated number of formal firms with
at least five workers and the average proportion of firms with the potential to adopt a new technology by firm size (small, medium, and large) and country income group as reported by the Firm-level
Adoption of Technology survey. Percentage calculated as the number of firms that could upgrade
over the total number of firms (including microbusinesses).

Potential Market Size of Digital Upgrade among Own-Account Businesses

The market potential for own-account and microbusinesses is much larger in number,
although smaller in proportion and magnitude of potential investments. Of 241 million
own-account and microbusinesses in Africa, 204 million are estimated to use manual
technologies, of which as many as 40 million, or 18 percent, could upgrade to some
digital technologies. These estimates are based on the RIA data on informal firms, which
provides the proportion of own-account and microbusinesses that use manual technologies but have the potential to adopt some form of digital technology for accounting,
planning, managing supplies, sales, marketing, and payments.[7]

Digital Technology and Workers

The potential economywide impact of digital upgrading, particularly for workers in
Africa, hinges on the characteristics of their employers. The presence of more advanced
technologies in large firms will disproportionally allow workers to benefit from these
technologies. However, as discussed earlier, more than 70 percent of workers in the
region are still employed in own-account or microbusinesses, characterized by largely
manual technologies. In most African countries, counting these microbusinesses

and own-account businesses shifts the share of workers using advanced technology significantly downward and reveals how workers' lack of access remains a major issue.

Across Africa, the predicted level of technology sophistication, as measured by workers' access to an advanced digital technology, increases with a country's income level. This result is partially driven by higher average firm-level technology sophistication in higher-income countries. However, most of the variation reflects the share of workers employed in large firms increasing with a country's income level.

Improved Worker Access to Advanced Technologies through Upgrading of Existing Businesses

The share of African workers with the potential to gain greater access to advanced digital technology through upgrading of formal firms is limited. Assuming formal firms with five or more workers with high potential to upgrade would do so, the estimated gain in the share of African workers accessing advanced digital technology is just 7 percent of all formal workers. When one includes workers in own-account businesses—a category that captures most workers in Africa—the gain without any entry and reallocation of labor toward more technologically advanced firms is even more limited. These estimates vary across countries, but they tend to be a small share of workers across all (figure 2.4). Assuming micro-, informal, and own-account businesses with potential will also upgrade, then 17 percent of their workers can gain access to some form of digital technology. In total, upgrading among formal and informal firms with high probability to do so would result in about 15 percent of all workers switching from manual to digital technologies.[8] These estimates ignore the fact that further advanced digitalization could lead to reductions in demand for jobs.

Improved Access through Workers' Transition into Larger Firms

The prevalence of informal and own-account businesses in Africa underscores the need to not only adopt digital technologies for current businesses but also to support the transitioning of workers to larger, more digitally enabled firms. Figure 2.5 presents the estimated gains in workers' access to digital technology through different channels. Taking Burkina Faso as an example, where most workers are employed in micro-size and own-account businesses, shifting the firm size distribution to a level similar to that of Kenya would generate the highest gain in access. An entry shock of a magnitude similar to estimates from Houngbonon, Mensah, and Traore (2022), triggered by the arrival of high-speed internet, has a smaller effect because of the small size of most entrants but has more impact than that achieved by incumbents' upgrading only. Even combined, the cumulative effect of all three channels would result in a share of workers accessing advanced digital technology that is behind Kenya's level.

FIGURE 2.4

Estimated Gains in Workers' Access to Digital Technology for Business Administration in Africa, through Upgrading of Potential Firms

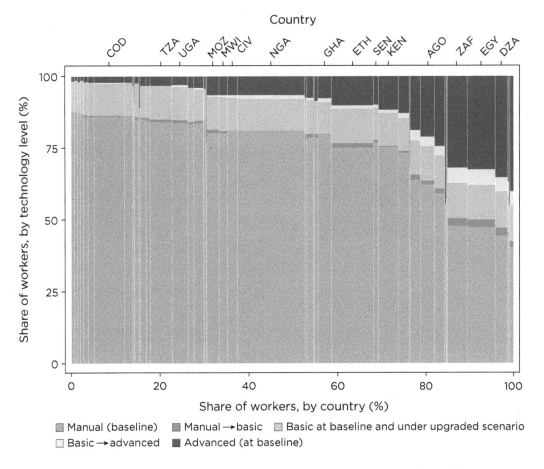

Legend:
- Manual (baseline)
- Manual → basic
- Basic at baseline and under upgraded scenario
- Basic → advanced
- Advanced (at baseline)

Sources: Original calculations based on the methodology described in boxes 2.4 and 2.5.
Note: The y axis presents the share of workers by technology level within each country. The x axis presents a country's workers as a share of all workers in Africa. Countries are sorted by the estimated level of worker access to advanced digital technology. Labels refer to the top 15 countries in terms of population share, among those with available data. Estimates are based on firm size projections in Castro et al. (2024) and firm-level digital technology level using FAT and Research ICT Africa data. The upgrading potential by different levels of technology sophistication is based on FAT data and is calculated for formal firms with at least five workers only. See further explanations in boxes 2.4 and 2.5. For a list of country codes, go to https://www.iso.org/obp/ui/#search/code. FAT = Firm-level Adoption of Technology.

FIGURE 2.5

Estimated Gains in Worker Access to Advanced Business
Administration Technology, Burkina Faso

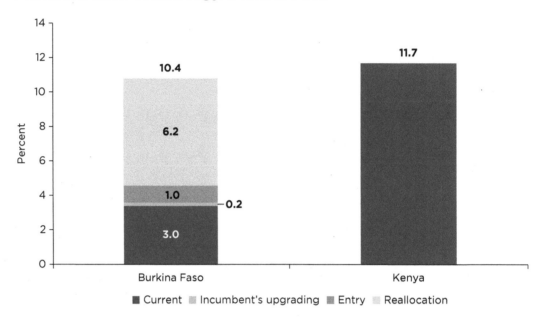

Sources: Original calculations based on the methodology described in boxes 2.4 and 2.5.
Note: Cumulative effect of incumbent upgrading, market entry, and shift in firm size distribution
on the share of workers with access to advanced digital technology. Estimates are based on firm
size projections in Castro et al. (2024) and firm-level digital technology level and upgrading potential using Firm-level Adoption of Technology and Research ICT Africa data. See further explanation
in boxes 2.4 and 2.5. Under the entry scenarios, workers are assumed to move from own-account
businesses to firms with employees. Assumptions on entry are based on an entry shock, following
estimates from Houngbonon, Mensah, and Traore (2022), and the size distribution of entrants using
Ghana's census data for firms. Assumptions on reallocation of workers are based on Kenya as a
benchmark country. That is, countries with an estimated share of workers in medium and large firms
lower than that of Kenya are assumed to have the firm size distribution in Kenya under the reallocation of workers scenario.

BOX 2.5

Estimating Firm and Worker Access to Technology in Africa

This analysis combines findings from the Firm-level Adoption of Technology (FAT) and Research ICT Africa (RIA) surveys on digital use in firms with estimates of firm demographics (refer to box 2.4) to project firm and worker access to digital technology in Africa. The focus is on technology adopted for business administration because its level of sophistication can be considered a representative technology level for African firms (chapter 1).

More specifically, the level of technology adopted—manual, basic digital, or advanced digital—is assumed to vary by country income level and by firm size and formal status, where assumptions are drawn from the FAT and RIA surveys. For firms with five or more workers, the analysis applies the averages from group 1 (Burkina Faso, Malawi, and Ethiopia) to low-income countries and those from group 2 (Ghana, Kenya, and Senegal) to middle-income countries. For microbusinesses, the analysis applies the averages from the RIA data. For each country, the share of firms and number of workers by firm size and formal status will thus determine the aggregate share of firms and workers that have access to technology at each level. Although a strong assumption, evidence from chapter 1 nevertheless suggests that firm size distribution and income level capture a large share of the variations in firm-level technology adoption.

Under the upgrading scenario, formal firms with market potential, that is, those with observable characteristics that predict a higher level of technology sophistication than their current technology, are assumed to adopt the next level of technology sophistication (refer to box 2.4 for further description of market potential). That is, high-potential firms that are currently using manual or basic digital technology will adopt basic or advanced digital technology, respectively. For countries without FAT data, the actual share of firms defined as having market potential is not known. We assume these shares are similar for the same income level and by firm size and formal status, extrapolating these shares from the FAT survey.

Summing Up

Digitalization of businesses in Africa provides several opportunities to enhance productivity and job growth. This chapter provides new estimates of the potential market for digital upgrading across businesses in African countries, accounting for up to 600,000 formal firms and 40 million microbusinesses with characteristics similar to those already benefiting further from digitalization. It also provides estimates of the share of workers in Africa who can directly benefit from digital upgrading of firms, based on their association with different types of firms.

These estimates demonstrate how challenging it is to boost the number of workers benefiting from productive digital technologies in Africa. Structural transformation, which enables workers to move from informal microbusinesses to large modern firms, is a gradual process. Closing the digital gap for African workers will require fostering long-term sectoral shifts as the number and size of formal firms grow over time. Concurrently, it requires conducive business environments and accessible finance to enable digital entrepreneurs to more effectively adapt digital technologies to the current skill sets and productive needs of informal microbusinesses.

Notes

1. For the purposes of this book, an *own-account business* refers to a self-employed individual with no employees.

2. See Goldfarb and Tucker (2019) for a review of how digitalization reduces economic costs such as search, tracking, verification, and transportation.

3. For example, US firms using a communication technology are more likely to contract out production across locations, often at lower coordination cost with suppliers (Fort 2017). In Kenya's transport sector, the use of real-time monitoring devices led vehicle owners to modify contracts to induce higher effort and lower risk taking, which lowered firm costs (Kelley, Lane, and Schönholzer 2021). Access to digital technologies can also boost product demand through e-commerce platforms (Jin and Sun 2021) or export markets (Hjort and Poulsen 2019). Liberian firms with access to the internet can more easily convert knowledge of how to bid for contracts from large buyers into actual sales (Hjort, Iyer, and de Rochambeau 2021). Another channel is access to finance. Evidence suggests a positive association between use of mobile money apps and firms' access to finance in Africa (Gosavi 2018). Informal entrepreneurs in Kenya who use mobile money for business-related payments are more likely both to receive goods and services on credit from suppliers and to grant credit to customers (Tetteh et al., 2021).

4. See chapter 6 for further discussion on the potential effects of the African Continental Free Trade Area on prices of digital goods.

5. Cirera, Comin, and Cruz (2024a) show that firms with a higher level of technology sophistication use more advanced technology in business administration than in other general business functions.

6. Assumptions based on Firm-level Adoption of Technology data are used to estimate the total number of firms with such technology levels across countries, based on the characteristics of these firms, following similar definitions described in chapter 1.

7. Because of data constraints in the Research ICT Africa data, it is not feasible to estimate digital upgrading potential with three levels of technology (manual, basic digital, advanced digital).

8. Several caveats are needed to interpret these estimates. First, the estimates still represent an upper bound of workers' exposure to technologies because they do not consider the intensity of use within firms and the share of workers within firms that use any specific technologies. Second, the population of workers here excludes those working in household agricultural enterprises. Third, these estimates abstain from the fact that further advanced digitalization could lead to reductions in demand for jobs in Africa. Most African firms are far from the frontier of using automated technologies, and only a small share of workers are associated with those firms. Analysis of the potential effects of further automation abroad on African jobs goes beyond the scope of this book.

References

Almeida, Rita, Carlos Henrique Leite Corseuil, and Jennifer Poole. 2017. "The Impact of Digital Technologies on Routine Tasks: Do Labor Policies Matter?" Policy Research Working Paper 8187, World Bank, Washington, DC. https://ssrn.com/abstract=3034542.

Atiyas, Izak, and Mark A. Dutz. 2021. "Digital Technology Uses among Informal Micro-Sized Firms: Productivity and Jobs Outcomes in Senegal." Policy Research Working Paper 9573, World Bank, Washington, DC.

Bahia, Kalvin, Pau Castells, Genaro Cruz, Takaaki Masaki, Xavier Pedros, Tobias Pfutze, Carlos Rodriguez Castelan, and Hernan Winkler. 2020. "The Welfare Effects of Mobile Broadband Internet: Evidence from Nigeria." Policy Research Working Paper 9230, World Bank, Washington, DC.

Banga, K., and D. W. te Velde. 2018. *Digitalisation and the Future of Manufacturing in Africa*. London: Overseas Development Institute.

Berkes, E., X. Cirera, D. Comin, and M. Cruz. Forthcoming. "Infrastructure, Productivity, and Technology Adoption." Background paper, World Bank, Washington, DC.

Bloom, Nicholas, Raffaella Sadun, and John Van Reenen. 2012. "Americans Do IT Better: US Multinationals and the Productivity Miracle." *American Economic Review* 102 (1): 167–201. https://doi.org/10.1257/aer.102.1.167.

Bussolo, Maurizio, Akshay Dixit, Anne Golla, Aananya Kotia, Jean N. Lee, Prema Narasimhan, and Siddhart Sharma. 2023. "How Selling Online Is Affecting Informal Firms in South Asia." Policy Research Working Paper 10306, World Bank, Washington, DC.

Caldarola, Bernardo, Marco Grazzi, Martina Occelli, and Marco Sanfilippo. 2023. "Mobile Internet, Skills and Structural Transformation in Rwanda." *Research Policy* 52 (10): 104871. https://doi.org/10.1016/j.respol.2023.104871.

Calderon, Cesar, and Catalina Cantu. 2021. "The Impact of Digital Infrastructure on African Development." Policy Research Working Paper 9853, World Bank, Washington, DC.

Castro, L., M. Cruz, F. Molders, A. Volk, and E. Salgado. 2024. "Firm Demographics in Africa." Background paper, International Finance Corporation, Washington, DC.

Chen, Rong. 2021. "A Demand-Side View of Mobile Internet Adoption in the Global South." Policy Research Working Paper 9590, World Bank, Washington, DC. http://hdl.handle.net/10986/35302.

Cirera, Xavier, Diego Comin, and Marcio Cruz. 2022. *Bridging the Technological Divide: Technology Adoption by Firms in Developing Countries*. Washington, DC: World Bank. https://doi.org/10.1596/978-1-4648-1826-4.

Cirera, Xavier, Diego Comin, and Marcio Cruz. 2024a. "Anatomy of Technology and Tasks in the Establishment." NBER Working Paper 32281, National Bureau of Economic Research, Cambridge, MA. https://www.nber.org/papers/w32281.

Cirera, Xavier, Diego Comin, Marcio Cruz, and Santiago Reyes. 2024b. "The 'Incomplete' Digitalization of Firms in Africa." Background paper, World Bank Group, Washington, DC.

Cusolito, Ana Paula, Daniel Lederman, and Jorge Pena. 2020. "The Effects of Digital-Technology Adoption on Productivity and Factor Demand: Firm-Level Evidence from Developing Countries." Policy Research Working Paper 9333, World Bank, Washington, DC.

Fort, Teresa C. 2017. "Technology and Production Fragmentation: Domestic versus Foreign Sourcing." *Review of Economic Studies* 84 (2): 650–87. https://doi.org/10.1093/restud/rdw057.

Goldbeck, M., and V. Lindlacher. 2023. "Digital Infrastructure and Local Economic Growth: Early Internet in Sub-Saharan Africa." Job market paper, University of Munich, Munich, Germany.

Goldfarb, Avi, and Catherine Tucker. 2019. "Digital Economics." *Journal of Economic Literature* 57 (1): 3–43.

Gosavi, Aparna. 2018. "Can Mobile Money Help Firms Mitigate the Problem of Access to Finance in Eastern Sub-Saharan Africa?" *Journal of African Business* 19 (3): 343–60. https://doi.org/10.1080/15228916.2017.1396791.

Hjort, Jonas, Vinayak Iyer, and Golvine de Rochambeau. 2021. "Informational Barriers to Market Access: Experimental Evidence from Liberian Firms." Working Paper 27662, National Bureau of Economic Research, Cambridge, MA. https://doi.org/10.3386/w27662.

Hjort, Jonas, and Jonas Poulsen. 2019. "The Arrival of Fast Internet and Employment in Africa." *American Economic Review* 109 (3): 1032–79. https://doi.org/10.1257/aer.20161385.

Hjort, Jonas, and Lin Tian. Forthcoming. "The Economic Impact of Internet Connectivity in Developing Countries." *Annual Review of Economics*.

Houngbonon, Georges Vivien, Justice Tei Mensah, and Nouhoum Traore. 2022. "The Impact of Internet Access on Innovation and Entrepreneurship in Africa." Policy Research Working Paper 9945, World Bank, Washington, DC.

Jin, Y., and Z. Sun. 2021. "Lifting Growth Barriers for New Firms: Evidence from an Entrepreneurship Training Experiment with Two Million Online Businesses." Job market paper. https://scholar.harvard.edu/files/zsun/files/sun_jmp.pdf.

Jolevski, Filip, Gaurav Nayyar, Regina Pleninger, and Shu Yu. 2024. "Spillovers in ICT Adoption from Formal to Informal Firms: Evidence from Zambia." Policy Research Working Paper no. WPS 10757, World Bank Group, Washington, DC. https://doi.org/10.1596/1813-9450-10757.

Kelley, Erin M., Gregory Lane, and David Schönholzer. 2021. "Monitoring in Target Contracts: Theory and Experiment in Kenyan Public Transit." Working Paper WPS-150, Center for Effective Global Action, University of California, Berkeley. https://doi.org/10.26085/C36C7K.

Klapper, Leora, Margaret Miller, and Jake Hess. 2019. *Leveraging Digital Financial Solutions to Promote Formal Business Participation.* Washington, DC: World Bank. http://hdl.handle.net/10986/31654.

Masaki, Takaaki, Rogelio Ochoa, and Carlos Rodriguez-Castelan. 2020. "Broadband Internet and Household Welfare in Senegal." Policy Research Working Paper 9386, World Bank, Washington, DC. https://hdl.handle.net/10986/34472.

McElheran, Kristina Steffenson, Jianqiu Bai, Wang Jin, and Ryan Williams. 2023. "The Effects of Technology Adoption on Firms, Supply Chains, and Rivals." *Academy of Management Proceedings* 2023 (1): 19351. https://doi.org/10.5465/AMPROC.2023.19351abstract.

Mensah, Justice Tei, and Nouhoum Traore. 2023. "Infrastructure Quality and FDI Inflows: Evidence from the Arrival of High-Speed Internet in Africa." *World Bank Economic Review* 38 (1): 1–23. https://doi.org/10.1093/wber/lhad021.

Tetteh, Godsway, Micheline Goedhuys, Maty Konte, and Pierre Mohnen. 2021. "Mobile Money Adoption and Entrepreneurs' Access to Trade Credit in the Informal Sector." Working Paper 2021-043, United Nations University–Maastricht Economic and Social Research Institute on Innovation and Technology, Maastricht, the Netherlands.

Tian, Lin. 2018. "Division of Labor and Productivity Advantage of Cities: Theory and Evidence from Brazil." INSEAD working paper, Institut privé d'enseignement supérieur, Singapore. https://lin-tian.github.io/files/JobMarketPaper.pdf.

CHAPTER 3

Drivers of Adoption and the Cost of Technology

Marcio Cruz, Yannick Djoumessi, Samuel Edet, Maty Konte, and Megan Lang

Key Messages

- Upgrading technology is expensive for African firms. Machinery and equipment, both digital and analog, are 35–39 percent more expensive (in US dollar terms) in Sub-Saharan Africa and 13–15 percent more expensive in North Africa than in the United States. These higher costs also apply to standard software and general technologies in agriculture in the form of machinery and equipment, which are required for sector-specific digital applications.

- Factors that complement technology adoption, such as digital infrastructure, electricity, and specialized high-skilled workers, are also relatively scarce and expensive in Africa. The cost of fixed broadband internet in Sub-Saharan Africa is 20 percent of per capita gross national income, compared with less than 6 percent in other developing regions.

- More than 30 percent of firms identify market competition as a major driver of technology adoption. Likewise, trade frictions—including high tariffs of imported digital goods; lack of infrastructure; and market concentration hamper technology affordability and diffusion.

Introduction

This chapter examines the factors influencing digital adoption by firms in Africa.[1] Chapter 2 documented various economic gains from digitalization and many firms with high probability for digital upgrade in Africa. If these firms can become more productive through digital upgrading, what constrains them from doing so? It is well known that infrastructure, skills, market regulation, competition, and management practices influence firms' technology adoption decisions. However, previous studies have provided limited evidence on why these factors contribute to incomplete adoption of digital technologies more specifically, or why firms adopting digital technologies end up underutilizing them for business functions. Likewise, existing research has gathered little information on the costs of adoption, including the cost of explicit technology upgrading, paying for complementary skills and capabilities upgrading, and implementation and opportunity costs. This is particularly relevant for Africa, where trade costs, capital constraints, and other barriers faced by local firms are more stringent than in other regions. This chapter presents new evidence to address the following questions:

- What are the key drivers of digital adoption by firms in Africa?

- How expensive is digital technology in Africa compared with other regions?

- What are the trade costs for digital goods in Africa?

The chapter is organized as follows. First, it provides a brief overview of factors underlying digital technology adoption by firms. Second, it analyzes how these factors may become important obstacles to digitalization across African firms. Third, it provides new evidence on the cost of digital technologies (for example, machines, equipment, software, and digital services), combining several novel data sources, including item-level prices drawn from the World Bank's International Comparison Program (ICP), or obtained through web scraping for more than 50 countries in Sub-Saharan and North Africa. Fourth, it analyzes the trade costs for digital technologies in Africa.

Drivers of Digital Adoption by Firms

Incomplete digitalization results from several complementary factors:

- Poor digital and complementary electricity infrastructure

- High prices of technology

- Low levels of human capital and firm capabilities

- Low access to finance

- Lack of competition.

These elements cover both demand and supply sides of digitalization and may jointly explain why many firms are not adopting or intensively using digital technologies for productive purposes. Many African countries lag other peers of similar per capita income in several of these areas. This lack of complementary factors usually translates into the fact that technology upgrade is expensive for African businesses, even though the underlying reality is more complex—with, for instance, the insufficient development and scaling of affordable skill-appropriate apps to meet the productive needs of low-income farmers and other firms driven by a combination of all the preceding factors.

On the basis of a production function approach and taking available technologies as given, the drivers of technology adoption can be grouped into input- and output-side factors and firm capabilities (refer to figure 3.1). The literature provides comprehensive evidence on how these factors are associated with levels of technology adoption,[2] but less attention has been given to the high cost of technology adoption and use for businesses. This is a critical element for Africa, given the prevalence of businesses with small scale, low demand, and high uncertainty. The high cost of acquiring and operating these technologies may lead to low net benefits of digitalization (refer to box 3.1). The following sections analyze how some of these factors may act as barriers to digitalization of businesses in Africa.

FIGURE 3.1

Drivers of Technology Adoption

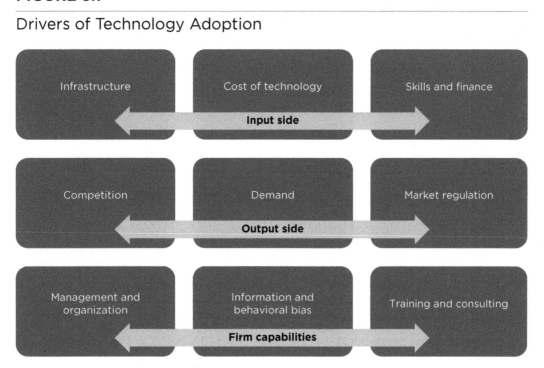

Source: Original figure for this publication based on Verhoogen (2023).

BOX 3.1

Is Digital Upgrading by Firms in Africa an Optimal Decision?

Are firms in Africa "leaving money on the table" because of low and incomplete digitalization? The expected return on investing in a digital device or software may not warrant the costs, or there may be too much uncertainty regarding the benefits of intensive use of a digital platform. Specific reasons why it may not be profitable for a firm to invest further in digitalization include the following:

- *Supply conditions.* Digital technologies may be expensive or require the use of other complementary technologies that might be expensive to adopt or involve additional variable cost for frequent use.
- *Lack of capabilities.* Operating digital technologies requires know-how that is costly to acquire or build through training.
- *Cost structures.* Other technological combinations might produce a better cost-benefit relation—for example, substituting labor for digital technology or outsourcing more advanced digital solutions to external service providers rather than investing in within-firm digital solutions.
- *Asymmetric or incomplete information.* Uncertainty may exist about the costs versus benefits of a technology, including implementation costs and expected benefits.

Digital Infrastructure and Electricity

Although internet coverage rates have been increasing, only 50 percent of the population of Africa has access to 4G mobile coverage compared with a world average of 88 percent. Africa remains the region with the lowest coverage rates overall. Limited availability of high-quality internet combined with limited and unreliable electricity coverage poses major challenges to African firms' investment in digital technologies.[3]

The cost of internet connection is high in Africa with respect to the average income, making it unaffordable for many individuals and microbusinesses. Fixed broadband in Sub-Saharan Africa costs more than 20 percent of per capita income, on average, compared with less than 6 percent in other regions, such as North Africa, South Asia, and Latin America and the Caribbean (refer to figure 3.2). Although the relative cost is driven by low income levels across African countries, it shows that the

FIGURE 3.2

Cost of Mobile and Broadband Internet as a Percentage of
Per Capita Gross National Income

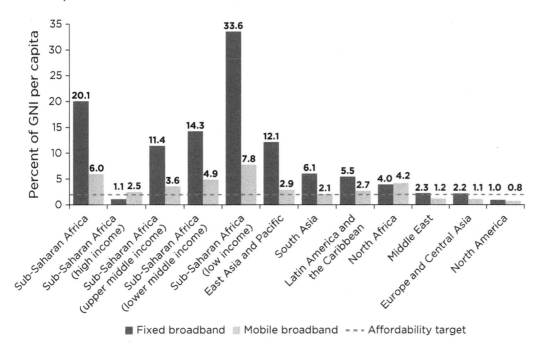

Source: International Finance Corporation calculations based on data from ITU (2022).
Note: Dashed line indicates the Broadband Commission for Sustainable Development affordability
target. GNI = gross national income.

price of connectivity is still very high for an average person in Africa, and it is significantly far from the "affordability target" (2 percent of per capita income) defined by
the Broadband Commission for Sustainable Development, a high-level public–private
partnership fostering digital cooperation.[4] Chapter 4 provides further information on
coverage and new evidence on the implications of improving digital infrastructure for
reducing the cost of connectivity.

The electricity infrastructure gap is also an important barrier across African countries. An estimated 600 million Africans have no access to power. Considering countries
with per capita incomes between $1,000 and $2,500 in 2021 (current US dollars), there
is a striking difference in access to electricity in rural areas between Sub-Saharan Africa
and non–Sub-Saharan Africa, estimated at 39 percent and 84 percent of the population,
respectively (Atiyas and Dutz 2023). The gap in access to electricity in urban areas is
narrower, at 86 percent for Sub-Saharan Africa versus 94 percent for non–Sub-Saharan
Africa. Box 3.2 shows a strong correlation between electricity access and digitalization. Evidence from the Firm-level Adoption of Technology surveys suggests that 3 in 4
firms suffer from recurrent electricity outages, which disproportionately affect small
and medium-size firms, which are less likely to adopt generators.

BOX 3.2

Digitalization and Access to Electricity

The relevance for digitalization of access to electricity, still limited in many African countries, and the cost of mobile broadband, generally higher in poorer countries, is corroborated by patterns in the data. Figure B3.2.1 shows the association between internet use and access to electricity in Africa. Circle sizes represent the price of a data-only mobile broadband basket that provides at least 2 gigabytes of monthly data, expressed as a share of gross national income per capita.

FIGURE B3.2.1

Internet Use and Access to Electricity in Africa

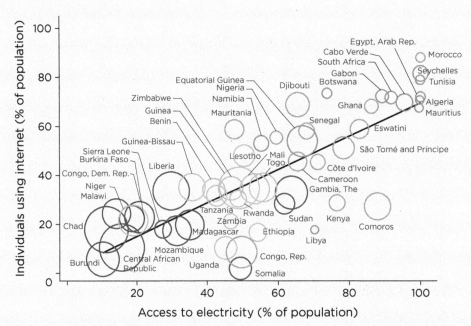

Sources: International Finance Corporation calculations based on data from the World Bank and ITU (2022).
Note: The solid line shows predicted internet use based on a linear unconditional regression. Circle sizes represent the price of a data-only mobile broadband basket that provides at least 2 gigabytes of monthly data, with larger circles indicating higher broadband prices. The four circle colors represent four groups of African countries ranked by per capita gross national income, from the lowest (dark blue) to the highest (green).

continued

BOX 3.2 *(Continued)*

These findings highlight the potential benefits of investing in business models that simultaneously tackle broadband connectivity and energy constraints to promote digitalization, especially in rural Africa. Despite ample renewable energy sources, Africa attracted only 2 percent of global investments in renewable energy in the past two decades (IRENA and AfDB 2022). Off-grid and minigrid energy solutions may promote digitalization by enhancing access to clean electricity in underserved areas of Africa where traditional grid connections may not be economical or feasible.[a]

a. For an analysis of the challenges and opportunities for private finance in clean energy, see IEA and IFC (2023).

In many countries in Africa, another major challenge is the absence of a functioning physical address system. This makes it difficult to deliver goods in a timely and accurate manner, especially for online transactions. Customers are often deterred by cumbersome requirements, such as the need to be present for delivery or the need for proof of identification upon receipt. It also makes it more difficult for start-up entrepreneurs to understand their potential market for new technologies.

Cost of Technology Upgrade in Africa

If digital technologies are too expensive, it will not be profitable for firms to adopt them. This section presents new evidence on differences in costs across countries. Data are from three data sources: the World Bank's ICP, web scraping from the Microsoft online store and Desertcart e-commerce platform, and primary data collection by International Finance Corporation staff. ICP data are used to calculate price-level indices for different categories of goods. The analysis considers aggregates as well as item-level comparisons of prices across countries. Because the restricted ICP item-level data have a limited time coverage, the analysis is supplemented with more recent item-level data scraped from various websites.

The ICP data suggest that cost may be a barrier to adoption for firms in Sub-Saharan Africa. As illustrated in figure 3.3, the price-level indices for machinery and equipment and other products in Sub-Saharan Africa are above the world average. The machinery and equipment category includes digital hardware, and other products includes software. This is striking given that the prices for all other categories of goods in Sub-Saharan Africa are substantially below the world average.

FIGURE 3.3

Price-Level Indices for Goods and Services, in Sub-Saharan Africa and North Africa, Relative to the World Average

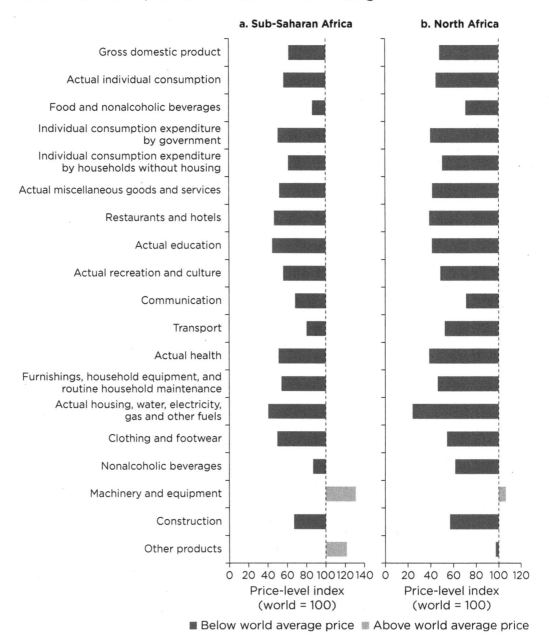

Source: International Comparison Program (database), World Bank; Cruz et al. (2024).
Note: Price-level indices for each category of good are calculated using purchasing power parity–adjusted prices for 2017 for 49 Sub-Saharan African and four North African countries. The world average price is denoted by 100.

Prices for digital products in Africa are high compared with those in other regions, not only in relative terms, but also in absolute terms, measured in US dollars.[5] Figure 3.4 shows the percentage difference in average prices relative to the United States for digital versus nondigital products included in the machinery and equipment and other products categories in the ICP data. Prices for both digital and nondigital goods are substantially higher in Africa than in any other region, confirming that high prices for digital technologies are not limited to the specific items used in the direct item-level comparisons.

Item-level data suggest that software is particularly expensive in Sub-Saharan Africa relative to other regions in the world. Examining item-level data from the ICP to identify digital versus nondigital goods in the categories of machinery and equipment and other products allows the development of a more detailed understanding of prices for digital goods. Item-level direct price comparisons also reduce concerns about bias that might arise from changes in the composition of available products between countries. Figure 3.5 reveals a negative relationship between per capita gross domestic product (GDP)

FIGURE 3.4

Prices of Digital and Nondigital Products, by Region, Relative to the United States

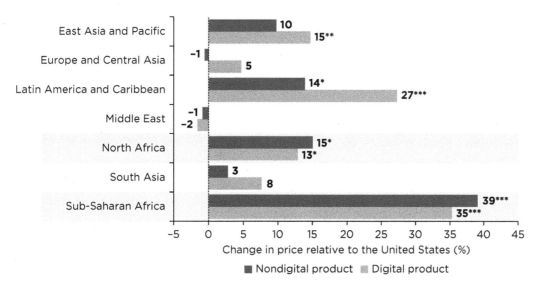

Sources: International Comparison Program (database), World Bank; Cruz et al. (2024).
Note: Percentage difference in the average price of digital versus nondigital products in the categories of machinery and equipment and other products from the International Comparison Program, relative to prices in the United States. Prices of digital and nondigital technologies are in US dollars at market price. The analysis is done on a sample of 160 countries, including 49 African countries. There are 107 products, of which 46 are digital, including software, and the remaining 61 are nondigital. Prices for machinery and equipment include the import duties and other taxes actually paid by the purchaser, the costs of transporting the asset to the place where it will be used, and any charges for installing the asset so that it will be ready for use in production. The coefficients reported are the percentage changes relative to the United States computed using the results of the OLS estimations, where we estimate the logarithm price of the products on region dummies and product dummies. The results are robust, with a sample restricted to products for which price data is available for more than 40 percent of countries and at least 25 percent of African countries.
*Significant at the 10% level. **Significant at the 5% level. ***Significant at the 1% level.

FIGURE 3.5

Correlation between Per Capita GDP and Price for Standard Software

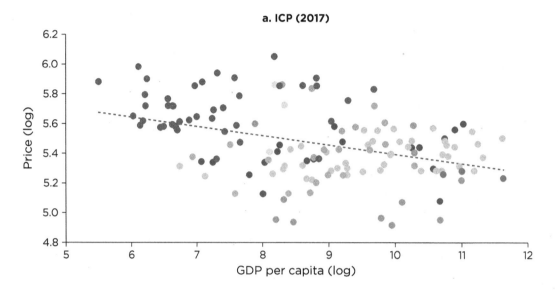

a. ICP (2017)

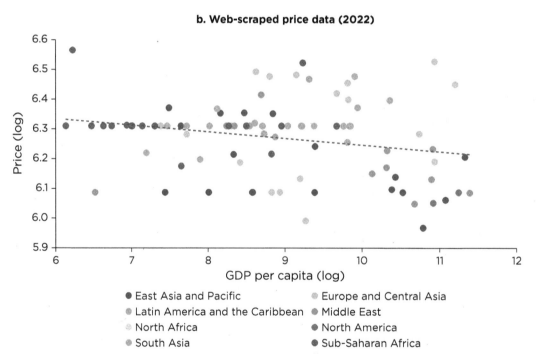

b. Web-scraped price data (2022)

- East Asia and Pacific
- Europe and Central Asia
- Latin America and the Caribbean
- Middle East
- North Africa
- North America
- South Asia
- Sub-Saharan Africa

Source: International Comparison Program (database), World Bank; Cruz et al. (2024).
Note: IFC calculations based on 2017 ICP data on software, 2022 web-scraped software price data from Microsoft online store, and World Bank data on GDP per capita for 2017 and 2022. The 2022 web-scraped software price data are obtained for 91 countries, which include 16 in Sub-Saharan Africa. The 2017 ICP software price data are obtained for 147 countries, which include 42 Sub-Saharan African countries. Prices are in US dollars at market prices. GDP = gross domestic product; ICP = International Comparison Program; IFC = International Finance Corporation.

and the price of the standard software products included in the ICP. The negative relationship observed in ICP is consistent with the negative relationship between per capita GDP and the price of standard software observed in the data web-scraped from the Microsoft online store. It also shows that prices for standard software are higher in nearly all countries in Sub-Saharan Africa than in other countries. Given the importance of standard software products for general business functions, these patterns suggest that cost may be an important factor explaining the low adoption of digital technologies designed for such functions among firms in the region.

Although prices are higher in Sub-Saharan Africa than in other regions for many digital goods, price levels alone do not fully capture the barriers that costs may pose to African firms. To better understand how affordable digital technologies are for firms in Sub-Saharan Africa, we can normalize price levels by average revenue of firms or per capita income. The prices for digital goods as a share of per capita GDP are substantially higher in Sub-Saharan Africa, given the lower average income compared with other regions, suggesting that cost and affordability are plausible first-order constraints to digital adoption in Africa.

Moreover, the cost of digital upgrade by businesses goes well beyond standard software. A recent supplier survey conducted in Kenya indicates that the cost of an enterprise resource planning system is three times as much as a basic computer (refer to box 3.3). Given the low affordability of basic digital technologies, more sophisticated software is simply out of reach for many African firms.

BOX 3.3

Digital Investment Escalator in Kenya

A background study conducted for this book presents evidence on the costs of digital upgrades. The study conducted a survey with a small number of Kenyan suppliers of digital technologies designed for customer relations, supplier relations, and enterprise resource planning. Combining survey responses with price data on less sophisticated technologies shows that there are steeply increasing costs to technological sophistication.

The average price of a computer in Kenya is $1,555. Equipping a computer with standard software brings the total cost to $2,059, a 32 percent increase. For firms in Kenya that want to upgrade to specialized software applications, the total investment cost is $9,370, more than three times the cost of a computer with standard software. The cost of digital upgrade increases sharply as technologies become more sophisticated.

continued

BOX 3.3 *(Continued)*

The training costs for upgrading to sophisticated software range from 5 percent to 50 percent of the total project budget, indicating that firms with lower capabilities may face disproportionately higher costs for technological upgrades. In addition, qualitative information from a supplier of sophisticated technologies indicates that cost can directly contribute to incomplete digitalization. The supplier notes that, to reduce the cost of upgrade, many clients opt to share licenses between employees or opt for a cheaper but less customized solution than would be optimal. Doing so prevents firms from fully realizing the benefits of digital technologies.

The high cost of technology adoption in Africa is not restricted to digital technologies applied to general business functions. For instance, the average prices in US dollar absolute terms of solar panels and thermostats correlate negatively with GDP per capita, being 47 percent and 96 percent higher, respectively, in Sub-Saharan Africa relative to the United States. In agriculture, the use of digital technologies applied to sector-specific tasks usually relies on machines and equipment that are not digital, such as the tractors or harvesters required to enable the use of GPS for harvesting or irrigation systems to make better use of precision agriculture. The costs of these technologies are also relatively higher in Africa (refer to box 3.4). Having established that cost and affordability pose plausible constraints to adoption, the next step is to consider potential drivers of such price differences.

Human Capital and Access to Finance

The ability of local technology firms to design and scale digital technologies and of all enterprises to adopt and use them is constrained by various levels of human capital. The overall low level of human capital across most Sub-Saharan Africa countries, with average learning-adjusted years of schooling of only 5.0 years (World Bank Human Capital Index 2020 dataset), means that only a small share of the overall population possesses the mathematics and critical reasoning skills required for new digital technology development and ongoing within-firm digital programming.

The scarcity of high-skilled workers is further exacerbated by the talent migration from Africa to advanced economies. For example, the top four African countries for digital

BOX 3.4

Barriers to Technology Adoption in Agriculture

There are large benefits to using digital technology for agricultural operations. An example is the Third Eye project in Mozambique, which deployed flying sensors to support farmers' decision-making. The project generated information for 2,800 smallholder farmers (mostly women) covering 1,800 hectares of land. It helped farmers make more informed decisions on when to plant, fertilize, and irrigate. Farmers recorded a 41 percent increase in crop production and a 55 percent increase in water productivity from using the flying sensors (Zacharenkova 2022).

Despite these benefits, the adoption of digital technologies by small-scale farmers in Sub-Saharan Africa is constrained by the high cost of these technologies. On average, the cost of an agricultural drone and an irrigation pump is 53 percent and 141 percent higher, respectively, than in North America, and harvesters and tractors are 562 percent and 251 percent more expensive, respectively, in Sub-Saharan Africa than in the United States (refer to figure B3.4.1). As discussed in chapter 1, for sector-specific applications of digital technologies in agriculture, complementary machinery and equipment, such as tractors and irrigation systems, are needed.

The relatively low literacy and skills levels and adaptive capacity found in rural agricultural communities are also important barriers. In the agriculture sector, which still employs more people than any other sector in Africa, most of the workforce lacks the skills necessary to consistently perform core tasks (Maïga and Kazianga 2017), and digital skills are no exception (Wiley 2021). Low digital literacy is shown to negatively affect the adoption and utilization of digital agricultural solutions in Africa (Tsan et al., 2019). Research ICT Africa survey data show that 18 percent of rural residents without a phone and 25 percent of rural households without internet cited lack of know-how as the main barrier to access.

Moreover, lack of agricultural technology solutions tailored to the needs and preferences of local agricultural communities can discourage adoption (Abate et al., 2023). For example, mobile lending in Africa mostly focuses on small, short-term loans for urban customers rather than on larger, longer-term loans that farmers may need (Parizat and Strubenhoff 2018).

continued

BOX 3.4 *(Continued)*

Even with successful digital platforms such as M-Pesa, only 15 percent of smallholders report that they have secured agricultural loans and made agriculture-related payments through the platform, according to one study (Parlasca, Johnen, and Qaim 2022). A study of Kenya's M-Shwari finds a preference for promotional ads in the local language rather than in English (Kiiti and Hennink 2016). Low levels of trust about the accuracy, quality, and source of the product (for example, digital advisory products) as well as perceived or real fears about the security and confidentiality of digitally exchanged data may also discourage adoption of agricultural technology (Adesina and Zinnah 1993; Jha et al., 2020; Thompson et al., 2018).

FIGURE B3.4.1

Agricultural Technologies Are More Expensive for Firms in Sub-Saharan Africa

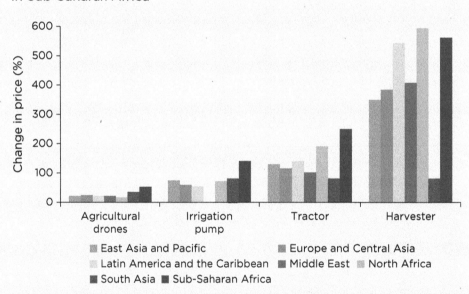

Sources: International Finance Corporation calculations based on International Comparison Program 2017 data (for tractor and harvester) and price data on Desertcart as of August 2023 (for agricultural drones and irrigation pumps).
Note: The percentage change in price for agricultural drones and irrigation pumps is relative to North America, whereas for tractors and harvesters, it is relative to the United States. Price data from Desertcart are listed prices. Actual prices paid by firms can some-times be based on informal negotiations.

talent—with expertise in areas such as software development life cycle, software testing, artificial intelligence, and mobile application development—mostly lost talent to advanced economies in 2019 (refer to box 3.5). Although the supply of advanced human capital in Africa has increased in recent years, Africa still lags behind other regions in per capita terms. For example, the 2021 *Africa Developer Ecosystem* report by Google and Accenture shows that the talent in Africa is young and growing fast, with 0.7 million professional developers. However, this is significantly less than the estimated 2.2 million professional developers in Latin America as of 2019 (EDC 2020).

High-skill human capital is expensive in Africa (refer to map 3.1). The cost of professional occupations that involve high digital skills such as information technology, telecommunications, business planning, science and technical services, and accounting and finance is 2.2 times higher in Sub-Saharan Africa than in the United States, relative to the average income. Previous studies have identified the importance of human capital—such as the use of the services of consultants—and has shown that provision of these services is correlated with technology sophistication (Cirera, Comin, and Cruz 2022). The high cost of human capital could explain why many firms, particularly local firms in Sub-Saharan Africa, do not employ highly trained professionals with the relevant digital skills.

MAP 3.1

High-Skill Human Capital in Sub-Saharan Africa Is Expensive

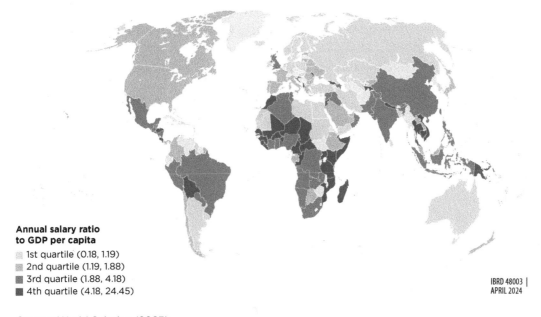

**Annual salary ratio
to GDP per capita**

1st quartile (0.18, 1.19)
2nd quartile (1.19, 1.88)
3rd quartile (1.88, 4.18)
4th quartile (4.18, 24.45)

IBRD 48003 |
APRIL 2024

Source: World Salaries (2023).
Note: Annual salary as a share of GDP per capita in job functions related to information technology. Annual salary dataset is based on WorldSalaries.com. GDP = gross domestic product.

In terms of basic human capital, high levels of illiteracy and fluency only in local languages limit the willingness and ability of many businesses to adopt and use available digital technologies. The ability of workers, managers, and owners to extract value from digital technologies is affected by the level and quality of basic education and follow-on technical and vocational education and training as well as experiential know-how. Averaged across Sub-Saharan Africa, literacy rates for adults and for youth (ages 15–24 years) are only 69 percent and 80 percent, respectively (World Bank 2021). The African continent is also the most linguistically diverse in the world, with more than 2,000 distinct languages, equating to one-third of all languages in global terms. Digital technologies could serve as a means of knowledge diffusion to improve the quality of education and bridge skills shortages. This likely requires the design and scaling of more attractive digital solutions geared to people's existing skill level (for example, voice-activated tools in the local language). However, Sub-Saharan Africa has seen a rapid increase in out-migration of technical talent (refer to box 3.5).

BOX 3.5

Tech Talent Migration

Skills training may have limited effects if firms in developing countries cannot retain their talent. Table B3.5.1 shows the percentage difference between the net migration of tech skills and other skills. Tech skills include general tech skills, such as software testing, web development, computer networking, and mobile application development, and disruptive tech skills such as data science, genetic engineering, artificial intelligence, and robotics. Other skills include business skills, so-called soft skills (communications and teamwork, for example), and specialized industry skills, such as national security, interior design, and mining.

Generally, tech talent has migrated to (in net terms) North America, East Asia and Pacific, and, recently, Europe and Central Asia. For developing regions such as South Asia, Sub-Saharan Africa, Latin America and

continued

BOX 3.5 *(Continued)*

the Caribbean, and the Middle East and North Africa, net migration of tech talent has consistently been negative. In addition, the outflow of tech talent relative to other talents has increased over time for all developing regions except Latin America and the Caribbean. In 2019, the loss of tech talent relative to other talent was 54 percent in Sub-Saharan Africa, higher than every other developing region except South Asia, where it was 64 percent.

TABLE B3.5.1

Migration of Tech Skills
Per 10,000 LinkedIn members with tech skills

Region	Net migra-tion of tech skills, 2015	Relative net migration of tech skills, 2015 (%)	Net migra-tion of tech skills, 2019	Relative net migration of tech skills, 2019 (%)
East Asia and Pacific	60	15	40	177
Europe and Central Asia	−30	−83	53	25
Latin American and the Caribbean	−125	−99	−230	−35
Middle East and North Africa	13	197	−113	−31
North America	45	236	138	113
South Asia	−271	−39	−299	−64
Sub-Saharan Africa	43	−5	−93	−54

Source: International Finance Corporation calculations, based on World Bank LinkedIn Digital Data for Development.
Note: Net migration of tech skills = inflow of tech skills − outflow of tech skills. Relative net migration of tech skills = [(net migration of tech skills − net migration of other skills)/|net migration of other skills|] × 100.

As in other sectors, access to finance is an important barrier to digital technology adoption, especially for small and medium-size enterprises. Figure 3.6, panel a, shows a positive association between digitalization and access to finance. Firms that take loans to purchase machines are significantly more likely to adopt more advanced digital technologies. Panel b shows that in Africa the probability of purchasing machinery and equipment using loans is less than 20 percent for small firms, 30 percent for medium-size firms, and about 50 percent for large firms.

Although further access to finance may facilitate digitalization of firms, adoption of digital technologies can also unlock new sources of financing. The data generated by digital platforms can form the basis for a credit history or provide more comprehensive data for lenders to assess risk. Conversely, firms that do not adopt digital payment platforms may fall further behind because lenders increasingly rely on data generated by digital technologies. Chapter 6 discusses policies to improve access to finance and ways to enhance private capital mobilization to support the digitalization of businesses.

FIGURE 3.6

Access to Finance and Digitalization

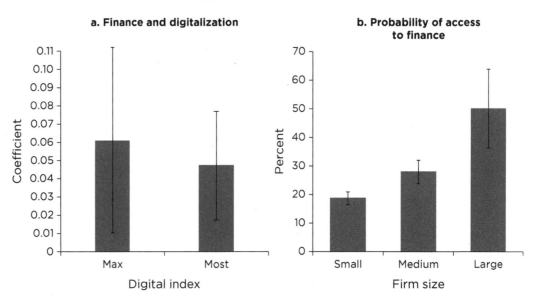

a. Finance and digitalization

b. Probability of access to finance

Source: World Bank, Firm-level Adoption of Technology survey.
Note: Panel a reports the association between digitalization and finance. The digital index takes the value of 0 (not digitalized), 1 (basic digitalization), and 2 (advanced digitalization), following the concept described in chapter 1. Panel b shows the predicted probability of firms purchasing machinery and equipment using loans. The 95 percent confidence intervals are reported. Max = maximum level of sophistication of the technologies adopted; most = level of sophistication of the most intensively (frequently) used technology.

Competition, Demand, and Trade Costs

Competitive pressure to upgrade technologies and increase productivity is an important driver for digital adoption. Although depreciation of existing equipment is a top driver of technology adoption for firms in Africa, competition is a close second, regardless of firm size (refer to figure 3.7). Firms operating in highly localized markets with limited competition may face insufficient incentives to adopt technology or to use it intensively. These firms may also be able to survive longer, despite low productivity levels. As such, higher competition can push firms to adopt new technologies. Furthermore, aside from the structural barriers that make Africa a challenging place for businesses and investors to thrive, firms must contend with the continent's fragmented market, with different countries adopting different policies. Thus, firms find it difficult to organize their activities or scale them across different markets. In addition, key sectors are often controlled by large business groups or state monopolies regarded as national champions. Such enterprises may use their market power to erect barriers against new entrants with disruptive business models (Maher et al., 2021).[6]

Limited competition can also lead to high costs for firms whose businesses rely on supplies or services from the incumbents. For example, before Wave's disruptive entrance into the Senegal and Côte d'Ivoire mobile money market in 2018, firms using

FIGURE 3.7

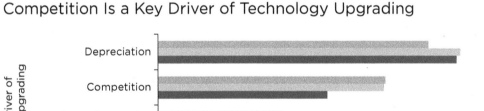

Competition Is a Key Driver of Technology Upgrading

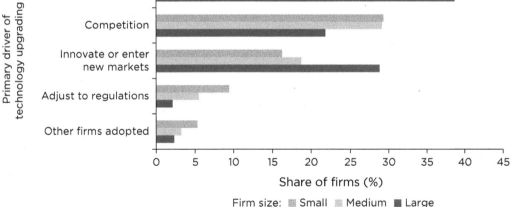

Source: World Bank, Firm-level Adoption of Technology survey.

mobile money services for payment of wages and business transactions were charged a transaction fee of 5–10 percent for money sent or received. After Wave imposed a flat fee of 1 percent for sending funds, competitors like Orange reduced their fees by four-fifths. This is an example of how competition can lower the cost of digital payment (refer to Kobo 2022). Digital markets often evolve faster than policies. When policies ensuring fair competition lag technological progress, new digital technologies may find it difficult to enter the marketplace. This is partially because many digital technologies naturally foster monopolies through network effects, requiring more effective regulations and competition policies.

Trade costs not only restrict competition but also serve as barriers to importing inputs. Imports of digital goods have consistently been lower (relative to other manufacturing imports) and tariffs on digital goods higher in Africa than in the rest of the world. On average, the share of digital goods in manufacturing imports is one-third lower than in the rest of the world, whereas tariffs are about three times higher. There is large variation in the region, with some countries reaching up to 15 percent in digital tariffs; large economies such as Ethiopia and Nigeria on average have tariffs of around 10 percent, significantly larger than the import-weighted tariff outside Africa, below 1 percent. When accounting for quality differences in unit value of trade, digital manufacturing goods are sourced at broadly similar prices abroad (Bastos, Castro, and Cruz 2024), suggesting that high prices in Africa are driven mostly by domestic factors, such as import tariffs, taxes, transport cost, installation cost, and lack of competition. These patterns are consistent with high prices for digital goods being driven in part by frictions impeding the flow of digital goods across borders in Africa.

Trade frictions and market concentration explain a significant share of the cross-country variation in the relative price of computers and software. Market frictions such as trademarks, electricity access, and internet connectivity have a negative association with the relative price of both computers and software. Conversely, market concentration and tariffs are associated with higher relative prices of these digital technologies. A decomposition exercise suggests that the combined influence of the propensity to trade (that is, trade openness) and market concentration can account for up to 30 percent of the cross-country variation in the prices of computers and software.

Beyond tariffs, differential protection for intellectual property rights may contribute to high technology prices in Sub-Saharan Africa. The World Trade Organization's rules governing trade in services and intellectual property date back to the establishment of the Trade-Related Aspects of Intellectual Property Rights agreement in the 1990s, which led to reforms in copyright, patent, and trademark regimes (Shadlen, Schrank, and Kurtz 2005). Although many high-income countries have aligned their intellectual property rights systems with these standards, many low-income countries have not, resulting in starkly different practices. This disparity inflates the cost of licensing, an important barrier to the adoption of essential standard software in the region. Trade frictions and the high costs of the technologies associated may also restrict firms from importing higher-quality digital goods. The most-imported digital goods in Africa are generally of lower quality than the global average (Bastos, Castro, and Cruz 2024).

Firm Capabilities

Advanced digital know-how within enterprises is a key ingredient in the adoption and intensive use of advanced technologies.[7] Figure 3.8 shows that a firm's digital index on both adoption and intensive use is positively and significantly associated with managerial skills and the share of workers with college degrees. These indices are

FIGURE 3.8

Digitalization and Firm Capabilities in Africa

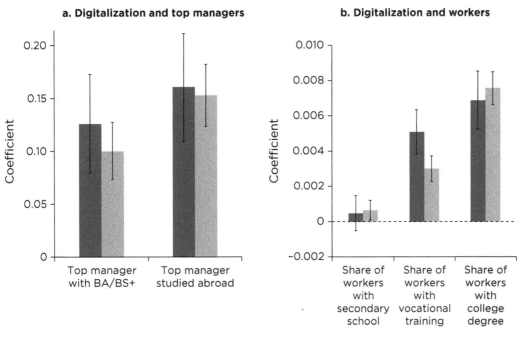

Source: World Bank, Firm-level Adoption of Technology survey.
Note: Panel a reports the association between digitalization and management skills. The digital index takes the value of 0 (not digitalized), 1 (basic digitalization), and 2 (advanced digitalization), following the concept described in chapter 1. Panel b shows the relationship between digitalization and share of workers with secondary education, vocational training, and a college degree. BA/BS+ = bachelor's degree or more; max = maximum level of sophistication of the technologies adopted; most = level of sophistication of the most intensively (frequently) used technology. 95% confidence intervals are shown.

higher by 12–16 percent if the top manager earned at least a bachelor's degree or was schooled abroad. Also, compared with non–high-skilled management, high-skilled management increases the probability of adopting sophisticated general business functions by around 10 percent. Such evidence aligns with Boyd and Curtis (2014), who find that higher managerial quality is associated with the adoption of more efficient technologies.

Given that the decision to invest in new technology hinges on how well the firm can estimate the returns, managerial skill may play a critical role in technology adoption. Managerial skills are positively associated with technology adoption and a wide range of firm performance indicators that may themselves alter the returns on a given technology. Good management practices are positively correlated with firm productivity, profits, research and development spending, and patents (Bloom and Van Reenen 2010; Scur et al., 2021). Managerial quality is also positively associated with human capital, suggesting that firms may need to pay a premium to hire managers who can effectively identify and adopt productive technologies. As such, human capital at the level of both workers and managers is closely linked.[8] Yet, evidence from the World Management Survey suggests that firms in Africa lag in the adoption of good managerial practices relative to other countries.

In addition to complementary factors, there is also the cost of learning and using digital technologies. Box 3.6 describes the results of an experiment based in India that suggests that learning costs can also be an important barrier to adoption and intensive use, followed by other components that potentially dissuade firms from continuing to use digital technologies for business administration, even after they reap short-term gains from them.

BOX 3.6

Digital Technology Adoption: Subsidizing Learning Costs for Firms in India

Microbusinesses represent a large share of the workforce in most low- and middle-income countries. Innovation through adopting new technologies can be a pathway to growth for microbusinesses. However, low adoption rates continue to hinder this growth potential.

An ongoing study (Mukherjee 2023) suggests that these low firm adoption rates are partly due to the high learning costs that deploying

continued

BOX 3.6 *(Continued)*

these technologies entails. The study focuses on a specific digital technology: a financial management app that helps firms view key financial statistics and manage cash flow. Although this technology offers firms a potentially profitable opportunity, it has several hidden costs. First are the additional costs of usage associated with entering data into the digital platform. Second are learning costs. The analysis draws from randomized visits to the firm by trained staff who help them enter transactions and use the digital platform and data from real-time app usage.

The study finds that temporarily reducing learning costs through visits from trained staff increases adoption in the short run, with improved financial planning and marketing practices observed. However, the effects taper off 7 or 8 months after the intervention. A potential explanation is associated with short-term returns (for example, firms quickly learn about their financial operations and improve business practices) and persistence of costs.

To sustain adoption, the study suggests that such interventions need to be complemented with policy interventions. The study structurally estimates a stylized model of dynamic adoption choice that allows adoption outcomes to be compared under four alternative interventions: monetary transfers over time to incentivize adoption, repeated reminders, improving human capital, and updating firms' beliefs about their profitability. Each of these counterfactual interventions alone is not sufficient to have a meaningful or sustained impact on adoption. However, the study finds that bundling any of these counterfactuals (except for the monetary transfer counterfactual) with supportive treatments leads to large and sustained increases in adoption outcomes.

Summing Up

This chapter shows that the digital gap among businesses in Africa may be driven by several complementary factors. To start, digital connectivity and electricity are still relatively scarce and expensive across African countries. Second, digital technologies used by businesses in the form of machinery, equipment, and software are significantly more expensive in Africa than in other parts of the world. Not only are digital technologies more expensive in the region, but so too are other machinery and equipment complementary to use in sector-specific digital applications. These high prices seem to be driven by various domestic factors, such as import tariffs, taxes, transport cost, installation cost, and lack of competition.

Although the high cost of digital adoption may explain the lack of digital adoption for productive tasks, other relevant factors, such as human capital and firm capabilities, may play a key role in explaining the gap in the intensive use of these technologies. The findings of this chapter suggest significant room to reduce the cost of technology adoption and improve firms' human capital, managerial, and technological capabilities. Moving forward, a better understanding of causal relationships between specific policies and the costs of digital technology adoption is central to addressing cost as a driver of incomplete digitalization.

Notes

1. Xavier Cirera and Jonas Hjort provided detailed suggestions and input for the preparation of this chapter and contributed to the background research.

2. Verhoogen (2023) provides a literature review of drivers of technology upgrade by firms in developing countries. Cusolito (2021) delves into the regulatory bottlenecks for digital adoption. Cirera, Comin, and Cruz (2022) show how these barriers are associated with lower levels of technology adoption.

3. Further evidence on digital infrastructure and the challenge of affordability is provided in chapter 4.

4. The Broadband Commission for Sustainable Development, which has the participation of several multilateral and private sector organizations, has declared as an advocacy target that by 2025, entry-level broadband services should be made affordable in low- and middle-income countries at less than 2 percent of monthly gross national income per capita.

5. Although the ICP is designed to provide rigorous cross-country price comparisons, it necessarily considers a limited bundle of goods, limiting the number of digital technologies that can be studied. Web-scraped data collected for this book provide validation of the results with ICP data and allow examination of a wider range of digital technologies. Results from the web-scraped data generally align with those from the ICP data.

6. Refer also to figure 4.8 in Begazo, Blimpo, and Dutz (2023), highlighting the extent of competitive constraints in market structures across the digital value chain.

7. Harrigan, Reshef, and Toubal (2021) show that increasing the number of workers who are engineers and technicians with skills and experience in science, technology, engineering, and mathematics has a positive effect on productivity that goes beyond investment in research and development.

8. Although many of these factors, particularly lack of firm capabilities, have been emphasized in previous work using evidence from the World Bank's Firm-level Adoption of Technology data (refer to Cirera, Comin, and Cruz 2022), less emphasis has been placed on the cost of digital adoption.

References

Abate, Gashaw T., Kibrom A. Abay, Jordan Chamberlin, Yumna Kassim, David J. Spielman, and Martin Paul Jr. Tabe-Ojong. 2023. "Digital Tools and Agricultural Market Transformation in Africa: Why Are They Not at Scale Yet, and What Will It Take to Get There?" *Food Policy* 116: 102439. https://doi.org/10.1016/j.foodpol.2023.102439.

Adesina, Akinwumi A., and Moses M. Zinnah. 1993. "Technology Characteristics, Farmers' Perceptions and Adoption Decisions: A Tobit Model Application in Sierra Leone." *Agricultural Economics* 9 (4): 297–311. https://doi.org/10.1111/j.1574-0862.1993.tb00276.x.

Atiyas, Izak, and Mark A. Dutz. 2023. "Digital Technology Uses among Microenterprises." Policy Research Working Paper 10280, World Bank Group, Washington, DC.

Bastos, P., L. Castro, and M. Cruz. 2024. "The Quality and Price of Africa's Imports of Digital Goods." Policy Research Working Paper 10718, World Bank, Washington, DC.

Begazo, Tania, Moussa P. Blimpo, and Mark A. Dutz. 2023. *Digital Africa: Technological Transformation for Jobs.* Washington, DC: World Bank. https://doi.org/10.1596/978-1-4648-1737-3.

Bloom, Nicholas, and John Van Reenen. 2010. "Why Do Management Practices Differ across Firms and Countries?" *Journal of Economic Perspectives* 24 (1): 203–24.

Boyd, Gale A., and E. Mark Curtis. 2014. "Evidence of an 'Energy-Management Gap' in US Manufacturing: Spillovers from Firm Management Practices to Energy Efficiency." *Journal of Environmental Economics and Management* 68 (3): 463–79. https://doi.org/10.1016/j.jeem.2014.09.004.

Cirera, Xavier, Diego Comin, and Marcio Cruz. 2022. *Bridging the Technological Divide: Technology Adoption by Firms in Developing Countries.* Washington, DC: World Bank.

Cruz, Marcio, Samuel Edet, Maty Konte, and Megan Lang. 2024. "The Cost of Technology in Africa." Unpublished manuscript, International Finance Corporation, Washington, DC.

Cusolito, A. P. 2021. "The Economics of Technology Adoption." Unpublished manuscript.

EDC (Evans Data Corporation). 2020. *Worldwide Developer Population and Demographic Study 2020.* Santa Cruz, CA: EDC. https://evansdata.com/reports/viewRelease.php?reportID=9.

Google and Accenture. 2021. *Africa Developer Ecosystem.* Mountain View, CA, and Dublin, Ireland: Google and Accenture.

Harrigan, James, Ariell Reshef, and Farid Toubal. 2021. "The March of the Techies: Job Polarization within and between Firms." *Research Policy* 50 (7): 104008.

ICP (International Comparison Program). 2020, October. Database. World Bank, Washington, DC. https://databank.worldbank.org/source/icp-2017.

IEA (International Energy Agency) and IFC (International Finance Corporation). 2023. *Scaling Up Private Finance for Clean Energy in Emerging and Developing Economies.* Paris: IEA.

IFC (International Finance Corporation). 2022. *Banking on SMEs: Driving Growth, Creating Jobs—Global SME Finance Facility Progress Report.* Washington, DC: IFC.

IRENA (International Renewable Energy Agency) and AfDB (African Development Bank). 2022. *Renewable Energy Market Analysis: Africa and Its Regions.* Abu Dhabi: IRENA and AfDB.

ITU (International Telecommunication Union). 2022. "ICT Prices." https://www.itu.int/en/ITU-D/Statistics/Pages/ICTprices.

Jha, Srijna, Harald Kaechele, Marcos Lana, T. S. Amjath-Babu, and Stefan Sieber. 2020. "Exploring Farmers' Perceptions of Agricultural Technologies: A Case Study from Tanzania." *Sustainability* 12 (3): 998. https://doi.org/10.3390/su12030998.

Kiiti, Ndunge, and Monique Hennink. 2016. *The Use and Impact of M-Shwari as a Financial Inclusion Banking Product in Urban and Rural Areas of Kenya.* Irvine, CA: University of California.

Kobo, Kingsley. 2022. "How Wave Rose to Become Francophone Africa's First Unicorn." *Quartz*, July 18, 2022. https://qz.com/africa/2189528/how-wave-rose-to-become-francophone-africas -first-unicorn.

Maher, Hamad, Anas Laabi, Lisa Ivers, and Guy Ngambeke. 2021. "Overcoming Africa's Tech Startup Obstacles." Boston Consulting Group, Boston.

Maïga, Eugenie W. H., and Harounan Kazianga. 2017. *The Role of Agricultural Skills Development in Transforming African Agriculture*. Accra, Ghana: African Center for Economic Transformation.

Mukherjee, Sanghamitra Warrier. 2023. "Digital Technology Adoption and Firm Productivity: Subsidizing Learning Costs for Micro-Firms in India." Job market paper, Department of Economics, University of Oxford, Oxford, UK.

Parizat, Roy, and Heinz-Wilhelm Strubenhoff. 2018. *Using Big Data to Link Poor Farmers to Finance*. Washington, DC: Brookings Institution.

Parlasca, Martin C., Constantin Johnen, and Matin Qaim. 2022. "Use of Mobile Financial Services among Farmers in Africa: Insights from Kenya." *Global Food Security* 32: 100590. https://doi .org/10.1016/j.gfs.2021.100590.

Scur, Daniela, Raffaella Sadun, John Van Reenan, Renata Lemos, and Nicholas Bloom. 2021. "World Management Survey at 18: Lessons and the Way Forward." *Oxford Review of Economic Policy* 37 (2): 231–258. https://doi.org/10.1093/oxrep/grab009.

Shadlen, Kenneth C., Andrew Schrank, and Marcus J. Kurtz. 2005. "The Political Economy of Intellectual Property Protection: The Case of Software." *International Studies Quarterly* 49 (1): 45–71. doi.org/10.1111/j.0020-8833.2005.00334.x.

Thompson, Nathanael M., Courtney Bir, David A. Widmar, and James R. Mintert. 2018. "Farmer Perceptions of Precision Agriculture Technology Benefits." *Journal of Agricultural and Applied Economics* 51 (1): 142–63.

Tsan, Michael, Swetha Totapally, Michael Hailu, and Benjamin K. Addom. 2019. *The Digitization of African Agriculture Report 2018–2019*. Wageningen, the Netherlands: CTA/Dalberg Advisers.

Verhoogen, Eric. 2023. "Firm-Level Upgrading in Developing Countries." *Journal of Economic Literature* 61 (4): 1410–64. https://doi.org/10.1257/jel.20221633.

Wiley. 2021. "Digital Skills Gap Index 2021." New York: Wiley. https://dsgi.wiley.com/.

World Bank. 2021. "World Development Indicators." Washington, DC: World Bank. https://databank .worldbank.org/source/world-development-indicators.

World Salaries. 2023. https://www.worldsalaries.com.

Zacharenkova, Julia. 2022. "How Drones Are Revolutionizing Agriculture." Vienna, Austria: OPEC Fund for International Development. https://opecfund.org/news/how-drones-are -revolutionizing-agriculture.

PART 2

Mobilizing Private Investment to Boost Digitalization and Development

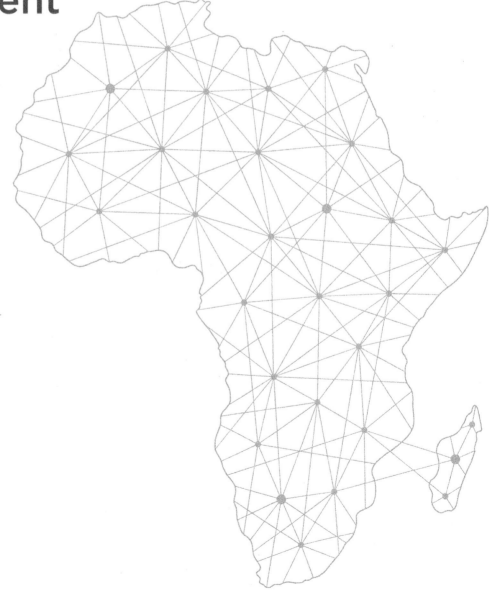

CHAPTER 4

Investment Opportunities in Digital Infrastructure

Georges Houngbonon, Tarna Silue, and Davide Strusani

Key Messages

- Africa hosts 2 percent of global digital infrastructure capacity with 14 percent of global internet users. However, the arrival of new submarine cables in recent years is expected to alleviate this gap. Digital infrastructure capacity is expected to increase sixfold between 2022 and 2027.

- The analysis presented in this chapter suggests that the expansion of submarine cables by 2027 may generate up to $6 billion in annual investment needs for middle-mile infrastructure (connecting a country's cities or communities to the internet) and last-mile infrastructure (connecting people and firms to the internet). These investment needs are twice the historical average, driven by the expected arrival of new submarine cables and the associated annual drop in the price of broadband of between 14 percent and 21 percent, more pronounced than it has been historically.

- Regulatory reforms can unlock investment opportunities in digital infrastructure by allowing greater competition. Potential measures include allowing foreign firms to participate in developing digital infrastructure and providing internet connectivity services, liberalizing incumbent fixed-line operators, facilitating competition in international gateways and leased lines, and supporting or mandating infrastructure sharing. The chapter reports new estimates of the impact of such measures, which would reduce prices and bring in more internet users.

Introduction

Digital infrastructure provision is poised to accelerate in Africa. This calls for new estimates of the status of existing gaps and prospects for narrowing them in the years ahead. To that end, it is important to extend the analysis beyond submarine cable connectivity and to trace how its interaction with rising demand by users will bring investment opportunities—particularly in middle- and last-mile digital infrastructure. Such infrastructure improvements would make digital services more affordable and help firms in Africa put digitalization to full productive use. This chapter addresses the following questions:

- What are the gaps in digital infrastructure in Africa?

- How will the expansion of submarine cables ameliorate affordability and foster demand for connectivity?

- How large would the resulting investment needs be for middle- and last-mile digital infrastructure?

- What regulatory reforms would amplify digital infrastructure's beneficial effects, measured by affordability?

To address these questions, a new dataset was assembled to capture submarine cables' attributes, internet access price, telecommunications (telecom) market competition, and regulation for more than 150 countries over 14 years (2008–21). The dataset was built from primary sources such as TeleGeography, the International Telecommunication Union (ITU), and the Global System for Mobile Communications. The price data cover both fixed and mobile broadband technologies, and the regulatory data cover 50 interventions, enabling an assessment of how such interventions can shape the influence of submarine cables on internet access prices.

Addressing Gaps in Digital Infrastructure in Africa

Digital infrastructure is the backbone of the digital economy. It consists of the undersea, underground, and above-ground cables; the tower sites, data centers, and satellites, as well as the spectrum assets and rights; and the active equipment that interconnects people globally through the internet and facilitates the delivery of products and services in all sectors (refer to figure 4.1). The digital infrastructure value chain is often considered as three segments: a "first mile" connecting countries; a "middle mile" of domestic connectivity, connecting cities and communities; and a "last mile" through which end users such as individuals, households, and businesses connect to the internet.

Submarine fiber optic cables are a crucial element of the first mile. On average, 15–20 new submarine cables have been deployed across the globe annually over the past 30 years, creating a global network. A similar trend is expected to continue over the next decade (TeleGeography 2023). Each new submarine cable typically requires several million dollars of investment and often calls for additional investments in middle- and last-mile digital infrastructure such as terrestrial fiber optic cables, data centers, and towers to benefit end users.

Africa has experienced a faster expansion in digital infrastructure over the past few years than any other region. The international internet bandwidth used, a measure of the

FIGURE 4.1

Digital Infrastructure

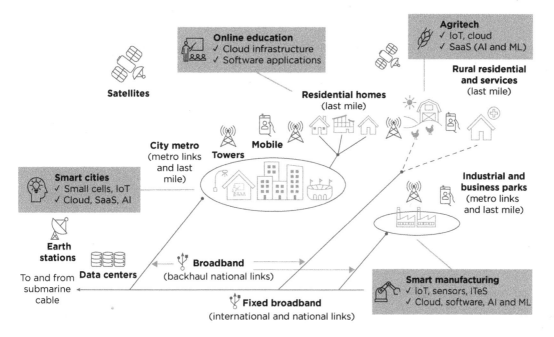

Source: IFC (2022).
Note: AI = artificial intelligence; IoT = Internet of Things; ITeS = information technology–enabled services; metro = metropolitan; ML = machine learning; SaaS = software-as-a-service.

capacity of submarine cables, grew by around 50 percent a year between 2010 and 2022, above the global annual growth of 45 percent over the same period (TeleGeography 2023). Data center capacity, measured in megawatts of information technology (IT) power, grew by 16 percent a year between 2010 and 2022, compared with 7 percent globally (TeleGeography 2023). Sub-Saharan Africa had around 163,000 telecom tower sites in 2022, a 9 percent increase from three years earlier (TowerXchange 2022).

The recent expansion of digital infrastructure in Africa has been insufficient to alleviate preexisting gaps. As of 2022, Africa accounted for 14 percent of global broadband internet subscriptions but had less than 2 percent of global digital infrastructure capacity (refer to figure 4.2, panel a). Mobile networks appear especially congested. As of 2022, the number of subscribers per tower in Sub-Saharan Africa was double that of the East Asia and Pacific and the Latin America and the Caribbean regions, and it was triple that of the Europe and Central Asia and the Middle East and North Africa regions (TowerXchange 2022).

Available digital infrastructure capacity in Africa is concentrated in a few countries. For submarine cables, the top five—in descending order, South Africa, the Arab Republic of Egypt, Nigeria, Algeria, and Kenya—accounted for two-thirds of the international internet bandwidth used in Africa in 2022. For data centers, the top five

FIGURE 4.2

Digital Infrastructure Gaps and Trends in Africa

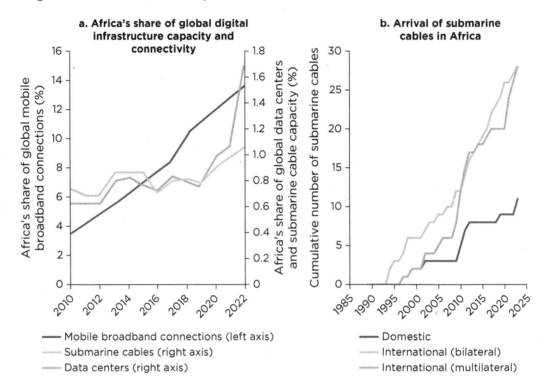

a. Africa's share of global digital infrastructure capacity and connectivity

b. Arrival of submarine cables in Africa

Mobile broadband connections (left axis)
Submarine cables (right axis)
Data centers (right axis)

Domestic
International (bilateral)
International (multilateral)

Sources: Panel a: International Finance Corporation (IFC) estimates based on data from TeleGeography and GSMA Intelligence; panel b: IFC estimates based on data from TeleGeography.

(also in descending order)—South Africa, Nigeria, Kenya, Egypt, and Ghana—hosted 96 percent of the available IT power in 2022.

Recent trends point to an acceleration of digital infrastructure expansion in Africa, especially for submarine cables and data centers since 2020 (refer to figure 4.2, panel a). Moreover, Africa's share of global digital infrastructure capacity remained broadly flat between 2010 and 2019, with an average of 0.8 percent for submarine cable capacity and 0.7 percent for data center capacity. Between 2019 and 2022, those shares increased by 34 percent for submarine cable capacity and by more than 100 percent for data center capacity.

With several major submarine cables expected to reach Africa's shores over 2022–27, the recent surge in the capacity of broadband and data infrastructure is likely to be sustained. The planned submarine cables, which include some major ones, such as 2Africa and Equiano, could boost capacity as much as sixfold between 2022 and 2027. Newer submarine cables typically connect multiple countries, compared with older cables, which were mostly domestic or connected just two countries (refer to figure 4.2, panel b). The construction of new cables aims to relieve growing congestion pressures on existing cables. As of 2022, submarine cables connecting Africa reached a utilization rate of 49 percent, compared with 37 percent globally. One-third of the submarine cables connecting Africa now have more than a 70 percent utilization rate, a threshold above which further utilization can result in network congestion and increased vulnerability of terrestrial networks to shocks.

Strengthening Digital Infrastructure Can Improve Service Affordability for End Users

Faster expansion of digital infrastructure may result in cheaper internet connectivity for end users. The cost of providing internet to individuals and businesses is largely driven by wholesale network access costs. These costs in turn stem from the transport, processing, and storage of digital data across end users' devices. This includes last-mile routes supported by mobile base stations or fiber optic cables, middle-mile routes consisting of transit infrastructure such as internet exchange points and high-capacity fiber optic cables, and first-mile routes that involve submarine cables and satellites. Each of these routes carries costs ultimately borne by end users. Digital infrastructure such as intercity fiber optic cables and city-level fiber loops are hard to duplicate and, as such, affect competition in downstream markets. As a result, the underlying business models of their deployment can affect competition in retail markets and ultimately internet access prices.

Submarine cables offer an opportunity to improve service affordability through cost savings. They often come with better technologies that allow network operators to carry greater internet traffic for a similar or lower cost than before their arrival, thereby generating economies of scale. They also generate savings on the costs of transporting data traffic between countries because they reduce the number of connection points between the origin and destination of data traffic. Such a reduction means less transit costs for local telecom operators. This mechanism is similar to the one at work in the airline industry: Opening a direct route between two countries eliminates any transit cost the airline operator would have incurred if it had relied on an indirect route.

Submarine cables can also generate savings on maintenance costs for telecom operators by limiting the cost of cable repair through redundancy. Submarine cable–related internet disruptions are a source of vulnerability and can increase operating costs for telecom networks because of the urgent need for repair. For instance, the Main One cable that stretches from Portugal to South Africa broke 3,000 kilometers south of Portugal in July 2017, disrupting internet service in several West African countries. That same month, the anchor of a container ship accidentally severed the only submarine cable linking Somalia to the global internet, cutting the country's internet access for weeks. Beyond the monetary and nonmonetary costs of submarine cable faults for the economy, they induce substantial repair and insurance costs for cable owners.

In the short term, the cost savings induced by submarine cables can be passed on to end users, including businesses, through a drop in price, depending on competition intensity, the ownership structure of the submarine cables (for example, whether they are owned by retail telecom operators or by an independent player), and the business model (that is, how submarine cable operators generate revenue). Cost savings are often passed through to end users as improvements on telecom packages at the same price. The degree of improvement depends on the intensity of competition not only in the retail market but also along the entire broadband value chain, including tower colocation markets,[1] wholesale internet protocol transit markets,[2] and international connectivity markets.[3] Moreover, submarine cables that are majority owned by a dominant telecom operator are associated with less generous packages than those owned by a neutral operator with no direct operations in downstream markets.

In the medium term, the drop in price may be accompanied by an improvement in the quality of connectivity. Indeed, increased demand induced by the price drop in the short term creates incentives for investment in middle- and last-mile broadband infrastructure (towers, fiber optic networks, data centers), which can ultimately improve the quality of connectivity for end users.

Internet service affordability involves price relative to income (or revenue) and, as discussed in chapter 3, is particularly limited in Africa compared with any other region.[4] However, the average revenue per user (ARPU), a measure of consumer expenditure per capita in the telecom sector, is among the lowest in the world (refer to figure 4.3, panel a). Mobile ARPUs in Africa are 35 percent below those in Asia, the second-least-expensive region. In general, low levels of ARPU are associated with low levels of capital expenditure (capex) (refer to figure 4.3, panel b). Low levels of capex are in turn associated with limited availability of quality digital connectivity. As such, without any change in the cost structure of the telecom industry, a further drop in prices could depress investment and the quality of connectivity. Submarine cables have the potential to address this trade-off by enabling cost savings that could improve affordability for a given level of quality of connectivity.

New quantitative analysis indicates that doubling the capacity of submarine cables could result in a drop of up to 14–21 percent in the price of broadband internet (refer to box 4.1). These effects dwindle over time, especially for mobile broadband. For instance, doubling the capacity of international connectivity is estimated to generate a contemporaneous drop in price of 6 percent for fixed broadband and 21 percent for mobile broadband. However, for fixed broadband internet, the cumulative price decline is 14 percent after three years and stabilizes at 7–8 percent thereafter. In contrast, for mobile broadband, the cumulative price decline reaches 11 percent after two years and continues dropping to become nil after five years. These effects vary by region. For instance, doubling the capacity of submarine cables in Sub-Saharan Africa is predicted to result in a 7–13 percent drop in broadband prices during the first year, compared with 23–28 percent in Latin America and 9–17 percent in Asia (Cariolle et al., 2024).

The analysis confirms that these price effects stem from cost savings in the short term, but in the medium term, these effects depend on competition intensity and quality improvements. Indeed, increased submarine cable capacity is associated with more concentrated telecom markets during the first three years, despite a sustained price drop. This means that in the first few years after the arrival of submarine cables, prices dropped mainly because of cost savings. Telecom markets get more concentrated because larger operators tend to have a larger ownership stake in submarine cables.

FIGURE 4.3

Average Revenue and Capital Expenditure per User in the Telecom Sector, 2022

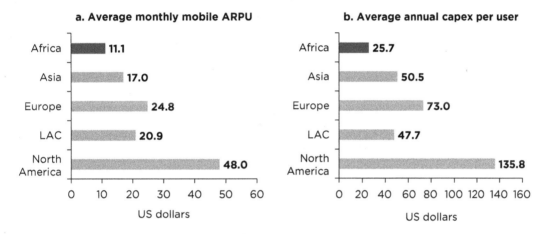

Source: GSMA Intelligence, https://www.gsmaintelligence.com/.
Note: ARPU = average revenue per user; capex = capital expenditure; LAC = Latin America and the Caribbean; telecom = telecommunications.

BOX 4.1

Methodology of the Study on the Impact of Submarine Cables on Internet Access Price

A background study to this book (Cariolle et al., 2024) examines the impact of submarine cable capacity on the cost of internet access. The analysis relies on data assembled from various proprietary sources such as TeleGeography and GSMA Intelligence, as well as public sources such as the International Telecommunication Union and the World Bank. The dataset consists of more than

continued

BOX 4.1 *(Continued)*

1,000 observations covering about 150 countries over 10 years, from 2011 to 2020, on:

- Submarine cable capacity, measured by international internet bandwidth used
- Internet access prices, measured by the price of the least expensive package in each country
- Competition intensity, measured by the degree of market concentration
- Regulation, measured by a composite index of 50 regulatory reforms pertaining to the status and functioning of the telecom regulator, its areas of intervention, the types of regulations, and the competition framework.

This information was complemented by measures of availability and quality of connectivity as well as proxies for market size, such as income, population, and access to electricity.

The analysis involved how changes in submarine cable capacity correlate with changes in internet prices, controlling for the availability and quality of internet, as well as country-specific shocks, regulations, and market size. A similar correlation was investigated between changes in submarine cable capacity and changes in market concentration. These correlations were assessed up to five years after the changes in submarine cable capacity and by region. They were also assessed across the 50 areas of regulatory reform to identify the most meaningful regulations. The estimation approach was further strengthened to get closer to the causal impact of submarine cables by focusing on international cables that typically connect multiple countries.

Investment Opportunities in Middle- and Last-Mile Digital Infrastructure

Recent arrivals of submarine cables in Africa offer some evidence about their potential to generate investment opportunities not only in first-mile digital infrastructure, but also in middle- and last-mile digital infrastructure (refer to box 4.2). The planned arrival of new submarine cables in Africa from 2022 to 2027 is expected to drive significant growth in international internet bandwidth and potentially generate investment opportunities.

BOX 4.2

Selected Success Stories of Digital Infrastructure Expansion in Africa

Several submarine cables in Africa can be associated with investment opportunities in middle- and last-mile digital infrastructure. For instance, the arrival of the Eastern Africa Submarine Cable System, a 10,000-kilometer submarine fiber optic cable in service since 2010 that runs along Africa's eastern coast, has enabled small telecom operators to gain access to as much international internet bandwidth as large operators.

Complementary terrestrial broadband infrastructure has followed suit. For instance, in 2017 Google initiated a pilot project, CSquared, that brought wholesale, carrier-neutral metro-area network fiber optic infrastructure to Accra, Ghana, and Kampala, Uganda. Since then the business model has been expanded in the Democratic Republic of Congo, Liberia, and Togo. Likewise, the sharing of telecom towers through independent operators has emerged in response to increasing demand for last-mile network capacity in a cost-effective manner. Helios Towers, for example, started operations in 2010 and has rolled out tower infrastructure across eight African countries at a fraction of what it would cost an operator to run its own tower, through the ability to colocate multiple operators on a single tower. After 10 years of operation, it became the first tower company from Africa to successfully list on the London Stock Exchange.

These business model innovations are often accompanied by increases in competition in the last-mile broadband value chain. For instance, the Comoros had maintained a state-owned telecom monopoly, with just 27 percent of the population using mobile telephony services in 2013 and fewer than 7 percent having mobile internet access. A second operating license was issued in 2015, resulting in the entry of a second operator. The subsequent increases in competition intensity were associated with a significant price drop—from $20 in 2014, before entry, to $10 in 2019, four years after entry. As of 2023, 38 percent of the population have mobile subscriptions, and 16 percent have access to mobile internet services, suggesting relevant progress, but still a large connectivity gap that needs to be addressed.

For Africa, the projected growth rate in international internet bandwidth by 2027 is 10 percentage points above the projected growth for Asia or Latin America. It will reach 402 terabits per second, surpassing the Middle East (refer to table 4.1) (TeleGeography 2023). The bulk of the projected capacity remains concentrated in Eastern and Southern Africa, followed by North Africa and then West and Central Africa. Coastal countries are significantly better covered than landlocked and island countries (refer to table 4.1).

The projected growth in international internet bandwidth in Africa could result in a price drop for both fixed and mobile internet access, beyond the historical downward trend on price.[5] The price of mobile broadband internet could drop by 10–11 percent during the first five years of the arrival of submarine cables. The expected price impact is lower for fixed broadband internet, at 3 percent during the first five years. The expected price drop would potentially bring in 5.2 million new mobile internet users and 151,000 new fixed broadband subscribers by 2027 (refer to table 4.2) (Cariolle et al., 2024).[6]

The potential benefits of submarine cables vary across countries, depending on the change in international internet bandwidth and the maturity of the market. In absolute terms, the largest increases in mobile broadband users would be expected in coastal countries in Eastern and Southern Africa, with potentially 2.6 million new users to be connected (refer to table 4.2), followed by West and Central Africa (1.7 million) and North Africa (1 million). Relative to the population size, the North Africa region is expected to have the biggest increase in broadband users in the region, owing to the maturity of its market, which carries larger network effects.

These expected effects fall short of universal broadband connectivity targets. One example is the projected number of new users—only about 1 million would be connected per year as a result of the price effects from the planned submarine cables. By comparison, universal broadband connectivity would require 100 million new users per year between 2020 and 2023 (refer to box 4.3). This gap suggests that submarine cables or affordability alone is not sufficient to achieve universal digital connectivity targets in Africa.

TABLE 4.1

International Internet Bandwidth Projections

Region	2022 (Tbps)	2027 (Tbps)	CAGR (%)
Africa	62.2	402.3	45
Eastern and Southern Africa	25.9	176.3	47
North Africa	24.9	138.0	41
West and Central Africa	11.4	88.1	51
Coastal countries	57.6	369.9	45
Landlocked countries	4.1	30.1	49
Island countries	0.5	2.3	37

Source: Internation Finance Corporation calculations based on country-level projections from TeleGeography (2023).
Note: CAGR = compound annual growth rate; Tbps = terabits per second.

TABLE 4.2

Geographical Disparities in Investment Opportunities

Outcome indicators	Africa	Eastern and Southern Africa	West and Central Africa	North Africa	Coastal countries	Landlocked countries	Island countries
Annual change in international internet bandwidth (%)	45	47	51	41	45	49	37
Mobile broadband penetration, 2022 (%)	27.0	22.5	24.1	49.0	30.8	17.0	18.8
Price of mobile broadband (% change)	-9.7	-9.0	-10.6	-8.6	-9.9	-10.3	-8.1
New mobile broadband users (millions)	5.20	2.55	1.69	0.96	4.50	0.63	0.07
New mobile broadband users, 2022 (% of population)	0.36	0.35	0.34	0.45	0.44	0.17	0.22
Fixed broadband penetration, 2022 (%)	10.6	5.2	3.0	43.0	13.4	2.3	5.2
Price of fixed broadband (% change)	-3.0	-3.1	-3.0	-2.5	-2.9	-3.3	-2.7
New fixed broadband users (thousands)	151	37	14	99	143	6	2
New fixed broadband users, 2022 (% of households)	0.05	0.02	0.01	0.20	0.06	0.01	0.02

Source: International Finance Corporation estimates.

BOX 4.3

Total Investment Needs—Why Do Estimates Vary?

Previous studies have estimated investment needs in digital infrastructure in Africa based on a target for new users to be connected. For instance, the United Nations Broadband Commission for Sustainable Development's (2019) report estimated that $2.7 billion of capital expenditures (capex) would be needed per year to reach universal broadband access between 2020 and 2030. A 2023 assessment by the International Monetary Fund suggests a total capex of around $45 billion would be required to reach universal 4G connectivity in Sub-Saharan Africa (Oughton, Amaglobeli, and Moszoro 2023). Costs can be a major driver of investment needs estimates because of country specificities and uncertainty around technological progress. However, most studies share similar average capex-per-user estimates, ranging from $30 to $60 depending on the target quantity for mobile connectivity and wholesale infrastructure cost assumptions. As such, variations in total investment needs estimates are mainly driven by the target number of users to be connected.

In this chapter, the focus is on the price effects of submarine cables as a driver of the number of new internet users for a given level of quality.[a] Other studies focus on the target of universal broadband access by 2030, which requires an estimated 100 million new users per year in Africa. Such a target is, however, nearly four times higher than the historical connectivity trends in the region, with 27 million new users per year on average from 2016 to 2021. These trends result not only from the effects of first-mile digital infrastructure such as submarine cables, but also from non-infrastructure-related factors such as network effects and changes in competition intensity, with the latter being driven by regulatory and policy reforms in the telecom sector. Moreover, the expansion of submarine cables has both price effects and nonprice effects, such as increased income and enhanced productivity growth for businesses resulting from the uptake in connectivity induced by the price effects of submarine cables.

a. Focusing on the price effects of submarine cables allows for a better understanding of how regulation can maximize the impact that strengthening digital infrastructure has on increasing digital connectivity and the associated investment opportunities. Regulation can be a powerful tool for enhancing the pass-through rate of the cost savings that are enabled by expansion of submarine cables.

When factors beyond the price effects of submarine cables are taken into consideration,[7] the expected expansion of submarine cable capacity could contribute to connecting nearly 100 million new mobile internet users and 10 million fixed broadband subscribers over 2022–27. Such an outcome reflects the high number of new mobile internet users associated with expansion of submarine cables. For instance, 133 million new mobile internet users and 14 million fixed broadband subscribers were connected over 2016–21 when submarine cable capacity expanded ninefold.

Estimated investment needs associated with the price effects range from $900 million to $1.3 billion of capex in middle- and last-mile digital infrastructure depending on the cost assumptions.[8] When nonprice effects are taken into consideration, the estimated investment needs range from $21 billion to $32 billion (refer to figure 4.4).[9] Around 39 percent of the cost is related to national and intercity fiber optic networks,[10] with the remainder related to data centers (15 percent), mobile towers and antennas (15 percent), and intracity fiber optic networks (31 percent). The estimated investment needs are equivalent to about $50 per user for the mobile segment, within the range of previous investment needs estimates but twice the historical trend for capex per user in Africa.[11] Beyond investment opportunities in middle- and last-mile digital infrastructure, the arrival of submarine cables can support the emergence of cloud computing in Africa, which is crucial for a continued drop in the cost of technology for businesses (refer to box 4.4).

FIGURE 4.4

Capex Needs Associated with Growth in International Internet Bandwidth

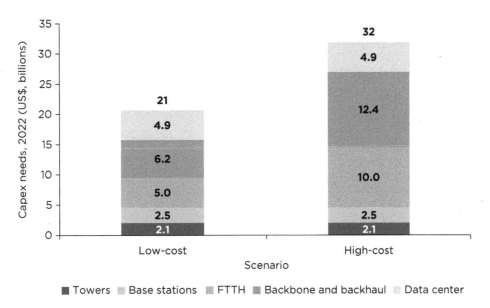

Source: International Finance Corporation estimates.
Note: Distribution reported on the basis of $15,000 per kilometer of fiber optic cable in the low-cost scenario and $30,000 per kilometer of fiber optic cable in the high-cost scenario. Capex = capital expenditure; FTTH = fiber to the home.

BOX 4.4

Cloud Computing and Enterprise Technology Solutions in Africa

Cloud computing, that is, on-demand computing resources based on data storage and processing centers outside a company's premises, serves as a digital infrastructure that helps make technology services more affordable for businesses. An expanding array of technology solutions used by businesses run on the cloud, including enterprise productivity solutions and enterprise resource planning software. Cloud computing eliminates the up-front cost of setting up in-house data and computing infrastructure and keeping up with rapid technological changes, thereby improving access to affordable digital technology solutions for businesses. Such improvement in affordability can be further enhanced by the availability of international connectivity through submarine cables and the presence of local data-hosting facilities.

In Africa, the latest boom in data center capacity has been associated with a faster drop in the price of data transfer, especially for low-capacity data transfer. However, capacity remains concentrated in a few large and populous countries, with 92 percent in the Arab Republic of Egypt, Kenya, Nigeria, and South Africa. This contrasts with other regions such as Asia and Latin America, where data center capacity is less concentrated. Moreover, the data center market remains nascent with two major neutral players—for example, Teraco and African Data Centers—as opposed to integrated telecom operators and a few small-scale cloud service providers such as Internet Solutions and Telkom/BCX.

Africa's data center capacity is expected to more than double over the next five years, driven by demand from cloud service providers. Cloud service providers typically develop availability zones to implement cloud platforms, with two or three locations in each zone. In developed markets, they tend to build one data center in the availability zone and partner with neutral data center operators for second and third facilities to ensure redundancy. In developing markets such as Africa, they often partner with data center operators instead of building their own facilities. Amazon Web Services (AWS)

continued

BOX 4.4 *(Continued)*

built a facility in South Africa in 2021, and Google is expected to follow suit. Beyond South Africa, the presence of cloud service providers is limited to a few small-scale facilities to store critical contents locally. Examples include the city of Lagos, Nigeria, which hosts all three major cloud service providers (Microsoft Azure, Google Cloud, and AWS), followed by Nairobi, Kenya, with Microsoft Azure and AWS, and Cairo, Egypt; Mombasa, Kenya; and Rabat, Morocco, with a single cloud service provider.

Regulatory Reforms Can Maximize the Impact of Digital Infrastructure Expansion

Telecom regulations have significantly evolved in Africa since the mid-2000s, but several countries still exhibit gaps in areas that are crucial to competition. Indeed, most countries (more than 40) have a national broadband plan and a separate telecom regulator with a wide range of mandates covering licensing, spectrum, quality of services, interconnection, universal service, and consumer protection.[12] These regulators have several instruments to support the functioning of telecom markets, including dispute-resolution mechanisms, appeals to decision, concept of market dominance, and ability to impose sanctions and penalties.

Key regulatory reforms remain absent in many countries. Regulatory reforms in the fixed broadband segment are among the least implemented by most countries in Africa (refer to figure 4.5). These reforms pertain to the status of the main fixed broadband operator, which is often a state-owned monopoly and provides services across the entire value chain—from internet access to end users to access to local and long-distance fixed lines, access to international connectivity, and domestic broadband infrastructure. Regulation of interconnection and access to infrastructure also remains nascent across the continent. Moreover, foreign operators are still not allowed to operate or own telecom infrastructure in several countries, and infrastructure sharing is not mandated in several countries.

With appropriate regulatory reforms, competition could be enhanced, and the arrival of submarine cables could further reduce prices for end users. Without an enabling regulatory environment that supports open and nondiscriminatory access to submarine cable landing stations and along the broadband value chain, the impact of new submarine cables on price would be limited. A statistical analysis of historical regulatory reforms shows how they can contribute to a larger price drop than under the status quo (refer to figure 4.6, panel a). For instance, the introduction of a national broadband

FIGURE 4.5

State of Telecom Regulation in Africa, 2020

Number of countries that have implemented reforms

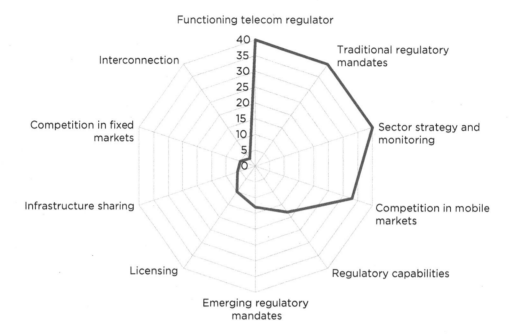

Source: International Finance Corporation estimates based on data from ITU (2020).
Note: ITU provides a set of 50 indicators that measure different areas of telecom regulations. These indicators have been grouped into 10 regulatory areas. *Functioning telecom regulator* includes the presence of a separate telecom regulator, with diversified funding sources, enforcement power, dispute-resolution mechanism, and the ability to sanction with the possibility of appeals; *regulatory capabilities* refers to the autonomy of the regulator in decision-making, accountability, public consultations, and the existence of a competition authority; *traditional regulatory mandates* refers to the regulator's mandate to measure quality of service, award licenses, regulate price, assign frequency spectrum, and manage universal service and consumer issues; *emerging regulatory mandates* include broadcasting, content, internet content and information technology services; and *licensing* refers to the types of licenses provided and the possibility of an exemption. ITU = International Telecommunication Union; telecom = telecommunications.

strategy was the biggest contributor to submarine cables' impact on mobile broadband price, followed by reduced barriers to using Voice-over-Internet Protocols (for example, WhatsApp), consumer protection, and foreign participation in facility-based operators. Such reforms are crucial for the cost savings associated with the arrival of submarine cables to be passed through to end users.

Moving forward, new regulatory reforms are needed to enhance private investments in digital infrastructure and maximize the potential impact of the planned submarine cables on price. Figure 4.6, panel b, shows the expected price effects of the arrival of submarine cables in Africa over 2022–27, depending on regulatory reforms. For both

FIGURE 4.6

Enhancing Effects of Regulatory Reforms on Mobile Broadband

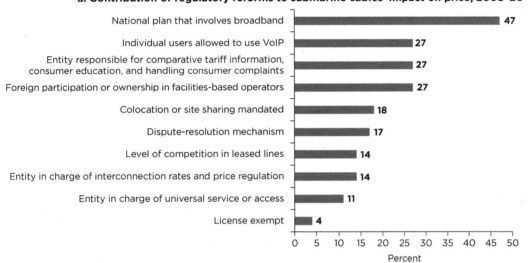

a. Contribution of regulatory reforms to submarine cables' impact on price, 2008–20

Category	Percent
National plan that involves broadband	47
Individual users allowed to use VoIP	27
Entity responsible for comparative tariff information, consumer education, and handling consumer complaints	27
Foreign participation or ownership in facilities-based operators	27
Colocation or site sharing mandated	18
Dispute-resolution mechanism	17
Level of competition in leased lines	14
Entity in charge of interconnection rates and price regulation	14
Entity in charge of universal service or access	11
License exempt	4

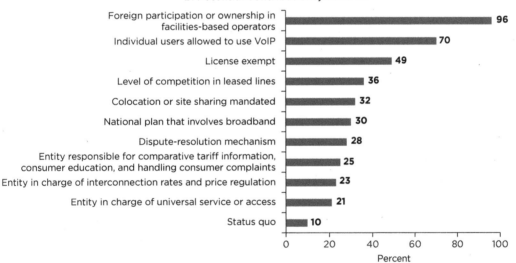

b. Potential contributions, 2022–27

Category	Percent
Foreign participation or ownership in facilities-based operators	96
Individual users allowed to use VoIP	70
License exempt	49
Level of competition in leased lines	36
Colocation or site sharing mandated	32
National plan that involves broadband	30
Dispute-resolution mechanism	28
Entity responsible for comparative tariff information, consumer education, and handling consumer complaints	25
Entity in charge of interconnection rates and price regulation	23
Entity in charge of universal service or access	21
Status quo	10

Source: International Finance Corporation estimates.
Note: The charts show the percentage change in price that is caused by each regulatory reform; as such, the percentages do not add up to 100 percent. The contributions were calculated as the average change in each regulatory indicator times the impact of the interaction between submarine cable capacity and regulation, divided by the marginal impact of submarine cables' capacity. As such, they reflect both the regulatory areas that experienced the biggest improvement over 2008–20 or 2022–27 and the magnitude of the impact of these regulations in boosting the price effects of submarine cables (panels a and b). The analysis assumes that each area of regulatory reform was brought to its best standard in 2022 on a scale ranging from 0 to 2. As such, the price effects reflect a combination of how far the average African country is from the best standard and the marginal impact of the regulatory reform. VoIP = Voice-over-Internet Protocol.

fixed and mobile broadband price, regulations aimed at improving competition intensity have the biggest impact on price reduction. These include foreign participation in fixed broadband markets and facility-based operators (tower companies and wholesale broadband operators); liberalization of the incumbent fixed-line operator market; reducing barriers to entry for global digital platforms (related to Voice-over-Internet Protocol); and competition in international gateways, leased lines, and mandated colocation and infrastructure sharing.

Summing Up

The prospects for the expansion of submarine cables in Africa can alleviate the digital divide and, therefore, create investment opportunities in middle- and last-mile infrastructure. The expansion of submarine cables by 2027 may generate up to $6 billion in annual investment needs for middle- and last-mile infrastructure. These investments would facilitate mobile and fixed broadband penetration, with an expected drop in prices that would potentially bring in 5.2 million new mobile internet users and 150,000 new fixed broadband subscribers by 2027. Beyond price effects, improvements in productivity and complementary infrastructure, such as electricity, could bring additional investment opportunities and up to 10 million fixed broadband new subscribers over the period.

Competition is key to maximize the impacts of investment in digital infrastructure. The increase of quality in connectivity would facilitate the use of cloud computing and other applications that may contribute to further utilization of digital technology for businesses. Effective regulations of fixed broadband networks, shared infrastructure, and openness to international players can enhance the investment opportunities in middle- and last-mile infrastructure while generating more benefits to customers.

Notes

1. In these markets, telecom operators purchase access to tower infrastructure to install and operate their active network equipment, such as antennas, base stations, and power stations.
2. In these markets, telecom operators purchase capacity to route their traffic along the domestic network.
3. In these markets, telecom operators purchase access to capacity to route their data traffic to foreign destinations.
4. In 2022, the price of a fixed broadband package with a five-gigabyte allowance represented 16 percent of the average income in Africa, compared with 5 percent in low- to middle-income countries. For a mobile data package, such a ratio amounted to 9.3 percent in Africa, compared with 3.6 percent in low- to middle-income countries (data from the ITU's ICT Price Baskets; income is measured by gross national income per capita).
5. These historical trends are taken as the average change in price during years with limited growth in international internet bandwidth: minus 3 percent for mobile broadband and zero percent for fixed broadband.

6. The analysis relies on a model of the diffusion of fixed and mobile broadband internet that allows deriving the number of first-time users as a function of change in price, controlling for the price of device, income, literacy, and access to electricity and considering network effects.

7. For instance, economywide effects associated with submarine cables, such as improvement in income for individuals and enhanced business productivity growth; see Hjort and Tian (forthcoming).

8. The estimate is sensitive to the cost per kilometer of fiber optic cable deployed, which depends on the deployment mode (aerial versus underground) and varies across countries depending on local wages. The estimated range is based on a cost per kilometer of fiber optic ranging from $15,000 to $30,000.

9. *Nonprice effects* refer to factors like quality of internet, income, literacy, and access to electricity that affect the uptake of the internet beyond price. The investment needs of $900 million to $1.3 billion derive from the change in internet penetration induced only by a price drop. However, the demand equation shows that the nonprice factors significantly affect internet penetration. These nonprice effects are taken into consideration by using the overall elasticity of internet penetration to submarine cable capacity, instead of just the portion of that elasticity coming from a change in price.

10. Part of the investment needs in middle-mile fiber optic could be met by activating underutilized fiber optic networks owned by state-owned enterprises and utilities. This underutilized infrastructure amounts to an estimated half a million kilometers, according to the International Finance Corporation (Rossotto 2021).

11. The United Nations Broadband Commission for Sustainable Development (2019) reports $27 of capex per new user, whereas the ITU (2020) reports $64 capex per user. These figures are based on average capex per user in Africa calculated using data from GSMA Intelligence over 2017–22.

12. References based on the number of African countries with de jure regulations in each area as of 2020. The data come from the ITU's ICT Regulatory Tracker, which tracks de jure regulations across 50 areas covering the institutional framework of the telecom regulator, its mandate and regime, and the competition framework of the telecom sector.

References

Cariolle, Joel, Georges V. Houngbonon, Tarna Silue, and Davide Strusani. 2024. "Submarine Cables, Internet Access Price and the Role of Competition and Regulation." Unpublished manuscript, International Finance Corporation, Washington, DC.

Hjort, Jonas, and Lin Tian. Forthcoming. "The Economic Impact of Internet Connectivity in Developing Countries." *Annual Review of Economics.*

IFC (International Finance Corporation). 2022. "Banking on SMEs: Driving Growth, Creating Jobs." Global SME Finance Facility Progress Report. IFC, Washington, DC. https://www.ifc.org/content/dam/ifc/doc/mgrt/2022-gsmef-progress-report.pdf.

ITU (International Telecommunication Union). 2020. *Connecting Humanity: Assessing Investment Needs of Connecting Humanity to the Internet by 2030.* Geneva: ITU. https://digitallibrary.un.org/record/3895170/files/Connecting%2520nHumanity.pdf?ln=en.

Oughton, Edward, David Amaglobeli, and Mariano Moszoro. 2023. "Estimating Digital Infrastructure Investment Needs to Achieve Universal Broadband." IMF Working Paper 23/27, International Monetary Fund, Washington, DC. https://www.imf.org/-/media/Files/Publications/WP/2023/English/wpiea2023027-print-pdf.ashx.

Rossotto, Carlo M. 2021. "One Million Kilometers of Fiber Optic Cables for Development." *Medium*, March 15, 2021. https://ifc-org.medium.com/one-million-kilometers-of-fiber-optic -cables-for-development-6e80f0f5dab9.

TeleGeography (database). "Transport Networks," "GlobalComms," and "Data Centers" modules, Washington, DC (accessed 2022–23), https://www2.telegeography.com/.

TowerXchange. (database), Delinian Ltd., London (accessed 2022).

United Nations Broadband Commission for Sustainable Development. 2019. "Working Group on Broadband for All: A Digital Infrastructure Moonshot for Africa." https://www.broadband commission.org/working-groups/digital-infrastructure-moonshot-for-africa/.

CHAPTER 5

Tech Start-Ups and Digital Platforms

Marcio Cruz, Beliyou Haile, and Mariana Pereira-López

Key Messages

- The success of mobile payments in Africa showcases how tech start-ups and digital platforms can disrupt markets by providing innovative and affordable services. They address financial exclusion by fostering technologies that are easy to adopt, cost-effective, and user friendly, resulting in reduced transaction costs for payments. Disruptive start-ups can potentially turn other growth constraints faced by businesses across various sectors into profitable opportunities, thereby enabling digitalization by providing technology solutions adapted to local contexts.

- Africa's digital start-up ecosystem is still nascent but stands out as one of the fastest-growing worldwide, underscored by a sevenfold increase in deals between 2015 and 2022. Start-up growth is currently concentrated in major cities in the Arab Republic of Egypt, Kenya, Nigeria, and South Africa, but other locations are seeing an acceleration. Digital tech firms in Africa are younger and smaller and grow more slowly than those in other regions. Sixty percent of tech firms in Africa are less than 10 years old, and 85 percent of them have fewer than 10 employees. Yet, as in other regions, younger tech firms are more disruptive than their older peers.

- The link between the incorporation of disruptive technologies and funding among tech start-ups in Africa is weak. Despite evidence suggesting that firms incorporating disruptive technologies are more likely to succeed, they struggle to obtain funding in Africa. Disruptive ventures in Latin America receive 99 percent more funding than nondisruptive ones, but in Africa they only get 40 percent more. As in other regions, teams with a higher share of women receive significantly less funding in the African tech sector.

Introduction

This chapter describes the role of tech start-ups and digital platforms in Africa in addressing some of the barriers to firms' digitalization. These ventures can provide innovative solutions to address high technology costs, enhance skills, compensate for the lack of digital literacy, expand access to markets, and close information gaps. The analysis in this chapter contributes to bridging the data gap regarding the entrepreneurial landscape in the region by harmonizing and combining data from various commercial platforms, including PitchBook, Crunchbase, Preqin, Refinitiv, Briter Bridges, Africa: The Big Deal, LinkedIn, and web-scraped data, along with new primary data collected by the International Finance Corporation (IFC).[1] The following questions are addressed:

- What are the key characteristics of tech entrepreneurship in the region?

- To what extent do digital tech firms incorporate disruptive technologies into their offerings?

- How can tech entrepreneurship enable digital adoption across African firms?

First, this chapter delves into the role of digital tech firms in the success of mobile payments in Africa in order to draw lessons about supply-driven technologies leading to leapfrogging (skipping a phase in technological development). Second, it describes the landscape and profile of tech entrepreneurship in the region and analyzes how start-ups have incorporated disruptive technologies (emerging technologies with the potential to change the way the market operates) into their offerings. Third, it assesses the barriers entrepreneurs face in the local ecosystem and discusses opportunities for investment in start-ups that could enhance the productive use of digital technologies by all businesses in Africa.

Role of Digital Tech Firms in the Success of Mobile Payments in Africa

The success of mobile payments in Africa is an example of how supply-driven disruptive technologies can target new markets with affordable and appropriate solutions. Chapter 1 shows how mobile payments served as an entry point for the digitalization of firms in Africa, but similar patterns of diffusion are not observed for other digital applications for businesses. The success of mobile payments in Africa involves several components; including the use of disruptive technologies and new business models to provide more efficient and affordable solutions for payment transactions, reducing the cost of adoption, which is an important barrier highlighted in chapter 3. Many people are aware of the success of M-Pesa in Kenya (Suri and Jack 2016).[2] Analyzing the drivers behind the rapid diffusion of mobile payments provides valuable insights for other disruptive technologies.

Mobile payments have spread quickly in Africa because of several factors. First, this technology is relatively easy to adopt and user friendly, and it reduces transaction costs for payments.[3] Mobile payments do not require a high level of financial literacy and can yield immediate and visible benefits (Begazo, Blimpo, and Dutz 2023; Suri et al., 2023). Second, mobile payments were an Africa-tailored solution deployed in a way that was accessible (through an extensive network of agents) and attractive for low-income, low-skill households and microbusinesses with basic access devices (basic mobile phones using SMS). Mobile payments addressed a local-specific problem, namely the failure of the traditional banking system to meet the financial needs of all households and enterprises, with strong network effects—the benefits of adoption increase with more people and firms using them (refer to Alvarez et al., 2023). Initial deployment of these solutions also benefited from regulations that did not impose significant burdens or additional costs.

An example of market disruption in the mobile payments sector is Wave, a digital payment start-up launched in 2017 in Côte d'Ivoire and Senegal. By 2022, it had grown to be francophone Africa's first unicorn (a privately held start-up with a market valuation of $1 billion). Wave targeted midsize to large markets such as Côte d'Ivoire and Senegal, where mobile money penetration remained low although incumbent firms had been operating for more than a decade. It has subsequently expanded to Burkina Faso, The Gambia, Mali, and Uganda. The company operated at a cost 50–70 percent below that of the incumbent and was thus able to offer more affordable, faster, and convenient usability that encouraged high-frequency small transactions, reaching 10 million registered accounts by 2022 (African Business 2023; Lévi 2021). Tech start-ups that address and build products around overcoming market frictions, such as high costs and low-quality services, can have greater impact and find a quick market fit through better service offerings. In the process, they inject more competition across markets.

The success of mobile payments in Africa has been uneven across the region. Countries in East Africa have led mobile money adoption, with 69 percent of the population in Kenya age 15 years and older having a mobile money account (the figure increases to almost 100 percent if households with at least one person using mobile payments are considered); in Uganda, 54 percent of that population has a mobile money account. The comparable figure for Morocco, however, is only 6 percent. Mobile money is not strongly related to penetration of financial institutions, mobile subscriptions (refer to figure 5.1), or per capita income.

Successful stories stem instead from an important entrepreneurial component, combining disruptive technologies and new business models. How can some of these features be replicated to diffuse digital technologies for other business functions, such as administration, planning, and sales or other sector-specific technologies? To further understand the role of tech start-ups and digital platforms as potential facilitators of technology diffusion across other business functions in Africa, the following sections analyze the entrepreneurial landscape, document how digital tech start-ups are incorporating disruptive technologies into their offerings, and assess the "premium to disruptiveness" received by those firms in terms of funding.

FIGURE 5.1

Mobile Money Accounts and Mobile Subscriptions

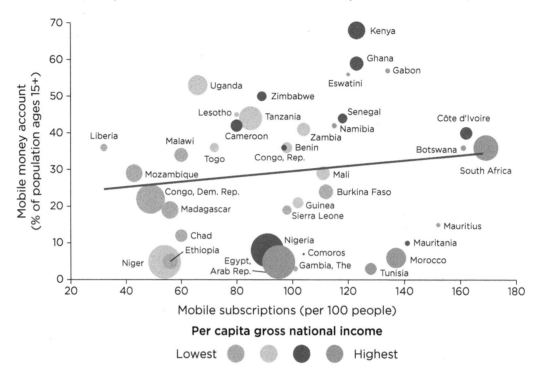

Sources: International Finance Corporation using data from the Global Findex Database 2021, World Bank (mobile money accounts), United Nations (adult population), and World Bank (mobile subscriptions).
Note: The solid line shows predicted values of mobile money accounts from a linear unconditional regression. Circle sizes represent the size of adult population ages 15–64 years. The value of mobile subscriptions can exceed 100 because people can have more than one mobile subscription.

Landscape of Digital Entrepreneurship in Africa

The African digital start-up ecosystem is among the fastest growing in the world. Over the past decade, Africa has consistently registered record investment figures, even amid the global downturn generated by the COVID-19 pandemic (Disrupt Africa 2022). In 2022, Africa attracted more than $3 billion in venture capital investment,[4] well above the $185 million observed in 2015. Furthermore, Africa has 11 so-called unicorns, most of which are focused on the financial technology (fintech) sector. Although the number of tech companies and deals in 2022 was half that in Latin America, the number of firms and deals in this space has nevertheless soared in Africa (refer to figure 5.2).

FIGURE 5.2

The Tech Start-Up Ecosystem in Africa Is Booming

a. Start-ups, deals, and value

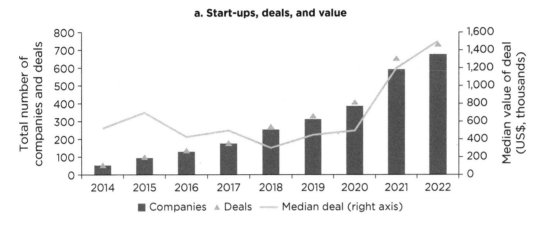

b. Africa's tech growth rate is highest in the world

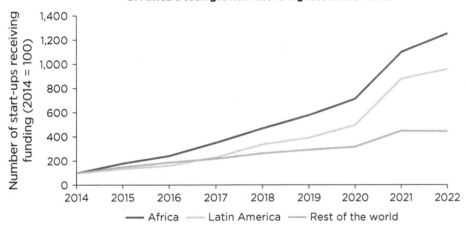

Source: Colonnelli et al. (2024), based on PitchBook data, 2023.

Profile of Digital Tech Firms

Digital firms in Africa are younger than those in other regions. More than half of them are less than 10 years old. Still, there is variation within the region. For example, South Africa has a larger proportion of older firms, and the mean age of companies is 25 years. In Nigeria, the average age of firms is eight years.

Tech firms in Africa are smaller and grow at a slower pace than in other regions. Data on employees from LinkedIn show that tech entrepreneurship is still concentrated in the segment of companies with fewer than 10 employees, which makes up 86 percent of the total (Colonnelli et al., 2024). Although this structure mimics that of other sectors in Africa, firm size is smaller than in comparator regions such as Latin America, where the proportion of businesses with fewer than 10 employees is 9 percentage points lower. Furthermore, African firms in general start out smaller than in other regions, including Latin America, Europe, and North America. African firms start to grow only after about 10 years, and even then, their median size remains below 10 employees.

Regional and Sectoral Concentration

Although most entrepreneurial activity is concentrated in the "big four" countries (Arab Republic of Egypt, Kenya, Nigeria, and South Africa), they are picking up elsewhere. The big four account for 56 percent of firms in the tech sector, even when a group of smaller and not necessarily investment-ready firms is included. Their dominance is observed for both established firms and start-ups (firms ages five years or less), pointing to persistence in firms' location. Yet, there is an increasing role for other countries such as Ghana, Morocco, and Tunisia, which account for 17 percent of all tech firms in Africa. The big four's share, at 70 percent, is even higher for "big deals"—or firms that reached $100,000 or more in funding. More than being concentrated in a few countries, tech start-ups are concentrated in a few cities in these countries (refer to map 5.1). Smaller and less sophisticated firms are less geographically agglomerated.

Market size is a critical factor leading to start-up concentration in the big four countries.[5] Yet, some other African countries, notably Ghana, Liberia, Senegal, Tunisia, Uganda, and Zimbabwe, are home to more digital tech firms than might be expected from their market size, proxied by gross domestic product (GDP). Similar qualitative results are observed when estimating the gap between digital business density (number of digital businesses operating in the country) and its potential level according to population and GDP. A group of countries, mainly located in eastern Africa, have more businesses than expected on the basis of their market size.

Information technology (IT) services and e-commerce are the specific areas of business that boast the highest number of digital tech firms in Africa, whereas fintech receives the largest concentration of funding. Almost half of the tech firms in the region are in IT, a subsector that includes software programming, digital services, IT machinery and equipment, infrastructure and services, and data storage and management.[6] Many of these firms are small and do not involve high-potential entrepreneurship.[7] Despite the expansion of mobile payments in the region, fintech accounts for fewer than 1 percent of the firms operating in the tech sector (refer to figure 5.3). However, looking at which start-ups receive the most investment, fintech is the leading subsector, suggesting a market concentration that can be driven by economies of network (for example, the winner takes most of the market), particularly for mobile payments, where the value of the platform increases with the number of users.

MAP 5.1

Geographical Concentration of Tech Firms

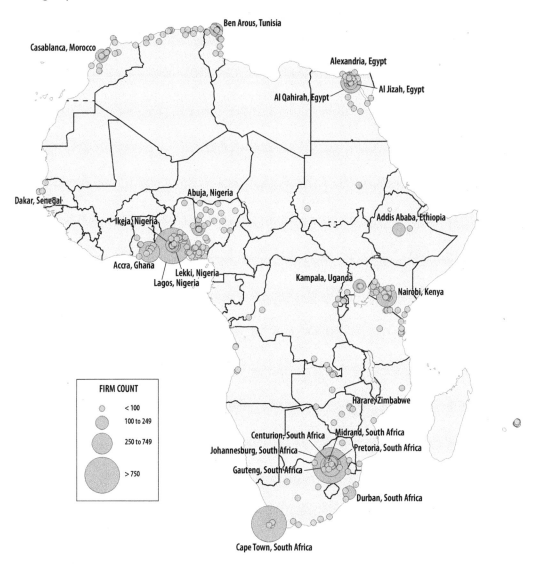

IBRD 47999 |
APRIL 2024

Source: Crunchbase data, 2023, https://www.crunchbase.com.

FIGURE 5.3

Almost Half of Africa's Tech Firms Focus on IT Services

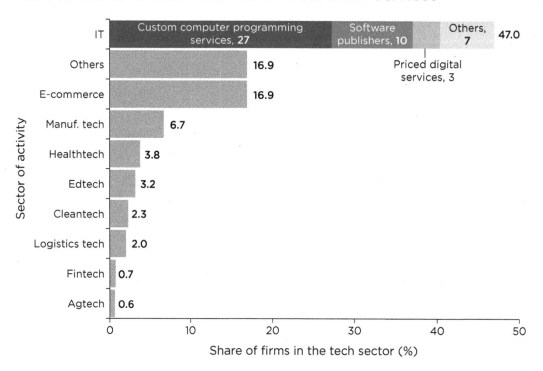

Sources: Colonnelli et al. (2024); International Finance Corporation calculations using data from LinkedIn, PitchBook, Preqin, and Refinitiv, including a sample of 130,122 tech firms.
Note: Agtech = agricultural technology; cleantech = clean technology; edtech = education technology; fintech = financial technology; healthtech = health technology; IT = information technology; manuf. tech = manufacturing technology.

Entrepreneurial Ecosystems and the Barriers to Digital Entrepreneurship

Successful businesses require a complementary entrepreneurial ecosystem. These factors are needed to foster access to knowledge, skilled labor, the right infrastructure, and business accelerators, incubators, and investors that channel resources and funding to high-potential firms (Audretsch, Cruz, and Torres 2022). An increasing number of organizations are aiming to support entrepreneurship in Africa and enhancing these factors.

The number of tech hubs (active organizations offering facilities and support for tech and digital entrepreneurs)—increased from 314 to 1,031 between 2016 and 2021 (Sarangé and Chuku 2021). Consistent with the geographical distribution of start-ups, these hubs are concentrated in the big four countries. However, 53 percent of these hubs focus on providing coworking spaces, which does not necessarily connect to funding. Moreover, 11 percent are accelerators (fixed- and short-term immersive cohort-based programs),[8] which offer mentoring and training programs, and 33 percent are incubators, which provide long-term support for start-ups through a broader set of ad hoc services. The remaining hubs serve as connections among researchers, entrepreneurs, and funding.

Findings from a novel survey of 264 small and medium-size accelerators, incubators, and investors in Africa highlight the nascent entrepreneurial ecosystem. These organizations are primarily young, small, and focusing on the accelerator and incubator phases (Colonnelli et al., 2024). Key points include that, first, most organizations are generalists rather than specialists in specific sectors. Second, most of the support tends to be nonfinancial, with more than 50 percent offering formal acceleration and incubation programs, and only 29 percent of these organizations providing equity funding. Third, although the selection of high-growth start-ups is critical to the success of these types of organizations (González-Uribe and Leatherbee 2018; Gonzalez-Uribe and Reyes 2021), 53 percent of them do not select start-ups on the basis of revenue criteria, 13 percent have a revenue threshold, and 10 percent base selection on growth; the remainder do not have clear criteria. African entrepreneurial organizations face critical constraints in identifying opportunities, with limited resources (56 percent) and information or data (46 percent) cited as major obstacles for both accelerators or incubators and investors. These challenges contribute to the higher perceived risk and more difficulties in securing funding for innovative start-ups.

Are Digital Tech Firms Enabling the Use of Disruptive Technologies?

The successful expansion of mobile phones and mobile payments shows that opportunities exist for private firms to disrupt markets and enable technology diffusion. As highlighted in box 5.1, not all business models that disrupt markets rely on disruptive technologies, but these types of technologies tend to be correlated with potential market disruption. The extent to which digital tech firms incorporate disruptive technology into their offerings can help to enable leapfrogging. The overall gap in disruptive technologies relative to top global entrepreneurial hubs (Palo Alto, Seattle, London, and Tokyo) is slightly lower compared with other emerging market regions, such as Latin America.[9] However, if mobile payments are excluded from the analysis, the distance to the frontier increases significantly. An analysis of the number of technologies incorporated (focusing only on those firms having at least one) shows that e-commerce is the sector in which Africa is closest to these top hubs (refer to Cruz, Pereira-López, and Salgado 2023).

Some key disruptive technologies that African digital tech start-ups have incorporated are related to mobile payments and cloud computing. However, the region still lags

BOX 5.1

What Are Disruptive Technologies?

Disruptive technologies have the potential to change the way a market operates, to create new markets, and to eventually overtake leading companies in mainstream markets. These types of technologies are increasingly embedded in other technologies or business offerings, leading to better performance. For example, on one hand, artificial intelligence started by creating a new and specialized market, but it has gradually been incorporated into other digital solutions. Financial technology companies, on the other hand, use digital technologies to improve their interaction with clients, reduce transaction costs, increase market outreach, and expand coverage.

Not all leading-edge technologies are disruptive. Some products or services with high technological content are too specialized to disrupt the markets. The concept of disruptive technology is, therefore, linked to the market. Take, for example, the case of Apple computers or the Ford Model T in the United States. Neither of these technologies was new, but they were disruptive in the way they were brought to millions of households and businesses (refer to Christensen 1997; Eli, Hausman, and Rhode 2023). The empirical analyses presented in this chapter follow the systematic approach to identifying these technologies used by Bloom et al. (2021), who implement a textual analysis of millions of patents (technology) and thousands of earning calls (market) from the United States.

in taking advantage of machine learning and artificial intelligence–powered solutions (refer to box 5.2). The share of African firms incorporating mobile payments into their offerings is 65 percent larger than in Latin America and twice the share observed in the frontier hubs (refer to figure 5.4). This is consistent with the fintech boom in the region and the widespread integration of mobile payments into digital tech firms, as well as the ubiquitous adoption of digital payments by firms across all sectors, discussed in chapter 1. However, Africa and especially Latin America have a higher share of firms offering cloud computing technologies compared with the frontier. Cloud computing provides a cost-effective substitute for in-house data storage infrastructure with the flexibility to quickly scale up or down as required (Daugherty and Wilson 2022). This can be pivotal for smaller firms grappling with limited resources and financial constraints.

BOX 5.2

How Can African Firms Best Leverage Artificial Intelligence for Their Success?

Artificial intelligence (AI), which is already being implemented by some of the disruptive firms in the African ecosystem, holds great potential to scale up and improve the quality of services by automating repetitive tasks and allowing employees to focus on the most complex and creative tasks. For example, through AI-powered chatbots, customers can obtain easy access to commonly requested information, allowing firms to provide these services to more consumers simultaneously. These technologies also allow service providers to augment their skills. Nurses and teachers, for example, can turn to these tools for knowledge, what Markoff (2016) and Agrawal, Gans, and Goldfarb (2023) regard as "intelligence augmentation." These uses could contribute to improving outcomes for patients, students, and consumers (Johnson and Acemoglu 2023).

Furthermore, AI is particularly valuable in Africa and other developing markets for two reasons. First, in low-information contexts, "machine learning can draw signals from new sources of data" (Björkegren 2023). Examples of this are credit scoring using machine learning (for example, Tala in India, Kenya, Mexico, and the Philippines; M-KOPA in Ghana, Kenya, Nigeria, South Africa, and Uganda), which helps people without financial access to obtain credit; identifying poor households for program targeting; and using satellite images to refine population estimates. These technologies can also be leveraged to build resilient food systems by analyzing large amounts of data, using models to predict food supply, and analyzing different scenarios related to potential supply chain disruptions and climate shocks.

Second, AI can compensate for the capability limitations of technology consumers, helping existing and new workers become more productive. Voice-powered AI gives access to digital technologies to people with limited literacy. Translation tools can break language barriers and expand access to information. Interactive conversations through chatbots or other solutions allow people with low levels of digital literacy to interact with more complex digital technologies.

continued

BOX 5.2 *(Continued)*

AI-driven image recognition can provide information in visual formats. Furthermore, learning experiences can be personalized by using these technologies. A recent empirical study examining the longer-term effects of a generative AI-based conversational assistant across thousands of workers finds that the AI tool increases productivity, as measured by issues resolved per hour, by 14 percent on average, with a 34 percent improvement for novice and low-skilled workers but minimal impact on experienced and highly skilled workers—helping less-experienced and lower-skilled workers move down the experience curve and generating durable learning.[a] Consistent with these findings, other related studies find that ChatGPT compresses the productivity distribution, with lower-skill workers benefiting the most.[b]

Despite the opportunities AI provides, Africa lags in these solutions because of various factors. First, there are still important infrastructure gaps. Second, scaling up AI solutions focused on the poor requires large investments, which may not necessarily be profitable for private investors and may benefit from support by governments and development finance institutions. Third, for these models to work, the machine learning algorithms must be trained with information. So far, the information is scarce to effectively train these systems in the many different languages and dialects spoken in Africa, which hampers the performance and accuracy of natural language-processing tasks (Björkegren 2023).

Finally, there are the widely known challenges, common to all countries, related to the misuse of data by businesses, including data privacy concerns, surveillance, and misinformation, as well as the potential manipulation of the associated algorithms by consumers (Björkegren, Blumenstock, and Knight 2023) and job displacement concerns.[c] All these risks pose regulatory challenges, especially in countries in which regulations are lagging. But private sector actions, such as developing more robust technologies, can address some of these problems.

a. On the basis of a US Fortune 500 company that specializes in business process software, with the majority of chat-based technical support agents in their sample working from offices based in the Philippines and answering technical support questions from US-based small and medium enterprises. See Brynjolfsson, Li, and Raymond (2023).
b. Refer to Noy and Zhang (2023).
c. To increase the likelihood that AI applications are translated into job opportunities, they need to be complementary to workers and enhance their capabilities (Johnson and Acemoglu 2023).

FIGURE 5.4

Use of Disruptive Technologies in Africa, Latin America, and Frontier Locations

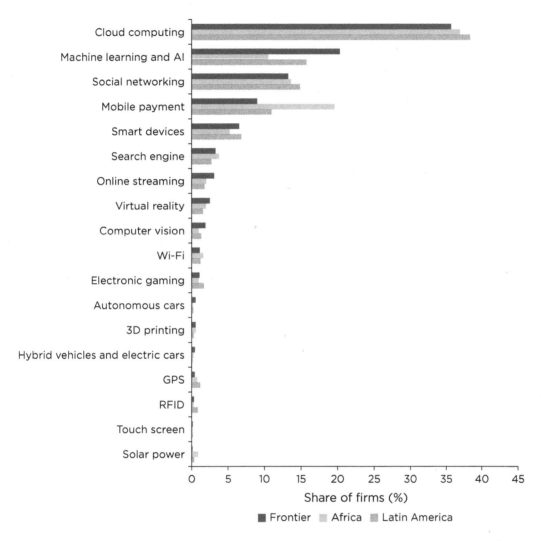

Share of firms (%)

■ Frontier   Africa   ■ Latin America

Source: Cruz, Pereira-López, and Salgado (2023) using data from Crunchbase, https://www.crunchbase.com.

Note: Each bar represents the share of firms in each region using each technology. Bars for each region do not add up to 100 percent because some firms might incorporate more than one disruptive technology into their offering. Frontier locations are defined as Palo Alto, Seattle, London, and Tokyo. Latin America is defined as South America plus Mexico. The technologies shown are based on the bigrams (two-word phrases associated with new technologies in patents) identified by Bloom et al. (2021). AI = artificial intelligence; GPS = Global Positioning System; RFID = radio-frequency identification. Other disruptive technologies such as OLED display, drug conjugates, wireless charging, software-defined radio, and lithium battery, are not shown in the graph as they have a share below 0.1% for Africa, Frontier, and Latin America locations.

African digital tech start-ups tend to integrate more disruptive technologies than their older counterparts. As expected, this pattern is similar to those of other regions and emphasizes the potential relevance of young firms in enabling technology diffusion (refer to figure 5.5). However, when examining variation across sectors and countries throughout the life cycle, it is notable that older firms in Africa, particularly in fintech and, to a lesser extent, in e-commerce, exhibit a relatively high level of disruptive technology activity. The fintech sector shows a different pattern because, on average, younger firms do not incorporate more disruptive technologies relative to older firms (Cruz, Pereira-López, and Salgado 2023). This result is mainly driven by Egypt, Kenya, and Nigeria (three of the big four), where older firms have incorporated more disruptive technologies. This is consistent with a sector characterized by higher entry costs, stricter regulations, and sectoral crossovers, meaning that before specializing in fintech, firms may need to consolidate in adjacent industries.

FIGURE 5.5

Age Profile of Disruptive Technologies

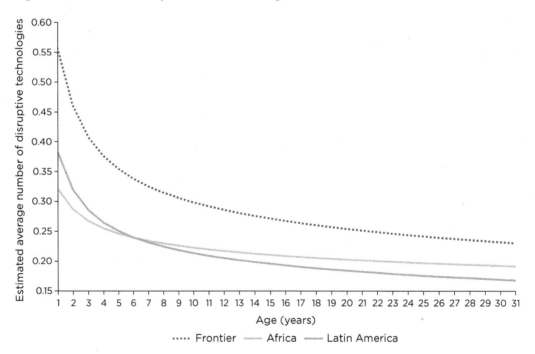

Source: Cruz, Pereira-López, and Salgado (2023) using data from Crunchbase, https://www.crunchbase.com.
Note: Frontier cities are defined as Palo Alto, Seattle, London, and Tokyo. Latin America is defined as South America plus Mexico. The figure shows the predicted value from a Poisson regression of the number of technologies over age by region. Given that many firms in the sample lack disruptive technologies, the average estimated value of the number of disruptive technologies (y axis) falls below 1.

Funding for Incorporating Disruptive Technologies Is Lower in Africa Than in Other Regions

African tech firms incorporating disruptive technologies attract more funds, but the additional funding associated with disruptiveness, the "premium to disruptiveness," is lower than in other regions. Disruptiveness, paired with a good-quality business proposal, entails risk but also has a large potential for future revenues. Therefore, firms including these technologies in their offerings would be expected to have a higher probability and a higher value of funding. Such firms in Africa have a 3-percentage-point higher probability of securing funding, compared with 7 percentage points in Latin America and 16 percentage points in the frontier locations. Firms incorporating disruptive technologies also obtain 40 percent more funding. Once again, the disruptiveness premium in Africa is lower than that in other regions: one-sixth of that observed for the frontier and less than half that in Latin America. This premium is particularly lower for start-ups, which could stem from a higher perception of risk compared with frontier locations, where better information tends to be available, allowing for risks to be more thoroughly evaluated and where local incumbents that impede the expansion of nonconnected start-ups by making access to essential business inputs more difficult may be less entrenched (refer to figure 5.6).

FIGURE 5.6

Being Disruptive Attracts 40 Percent More Funds for African Firms

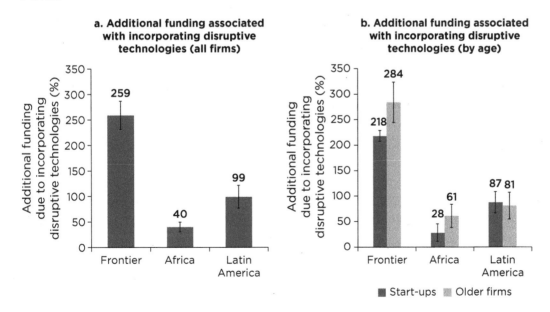

Source: Cruz, Pereira-López, and Salgado (2023) using data from Crunchbase, https://www.crunchbase.com.
Note: Frontier cities are defined as Palo Alto, Seattle, London, and Tokyo. Latin America is defined as South America plus Mexico. The lines represent 95 percent confidence intervals.

African tech firms that incorporate disruptive technologies receive earlier funding with lower initial amounts but perform better, with a higher probability of success in terms of exit or valuation growth.[10] Disruptive tech firms receive funding half a year earlier than nondisruptive firms, but the value of the first deal is 17 percent lower, as well as its first valuation. Even so, disruptive tech firms, on average, show a higher probability of success (almost 5 percentage points), a higher growth in valuation (44 percent), and, eventually, end up receiving more funding (5.3 percent growth in deals). Once again, these results corroborate the hypothesis that risk perception and information deficits in assessing risks prevent new ventures from getting more funding, even when they have great potential.

The characteristics of the tech firms' founders play a role in obtaining funding in the region. In Africa, tech sector founders with a postgraduate education have a probability 13 percentage points higher of securing funding and obtain an amount 48 percent higher than other entrepreneurs in the sector. If their education is from a foreign university, that probability rate increases by 1 additional percentage point, and the amount of funding increases by 5 percent. The allocation of funding toward highly educated individuals is not exclusive to Africa or the tech sector. It is likewise observed for nontech entrepreneurship in Africa (refer to figure 5.7).

Although having a team that includes women increases the probability of funding for African nontech firms by 4 percentage points, this is not the case in the tech sector. The value of funding for tech firms decreases significantly for teams with a higher share of women, a result not observed in Latin America. Furthermore, among big-deal firms (those that received funding exceeding $100,000), male-led teams can land, on average, 44 percent more funding than female-led teams. The contrast between tech and nontech in the region could indicate that even though more and more accelerators, incubators, and funds are targeting female-led projects, they have yet to reach the tech sector.

The factors that correlate most strongly with funding are whether the founder has experience participating in other firms (23-percentage-point increase in probability, 111 percent in funding) and—even more so—in other sectors (59-percentage-point increase in probability, 123 percent in funding). The latter points to the role played by spin-off companies in the region, especially in terms of big-deal companies. The infrastructure and trust established by their parent companies enable spin-offs to mitigate risks, secure more funding, and grow more rapidly. In general, in contexts in which there is a higher perception of risk or a dearth of information about projects, investors emphasize the characteristics and experience of founders in making their investment decisions.

FIGURE 5.7

Probability of Obtaining Funding on the Basis of Founder and
Firm-Level Characteristics in Africa

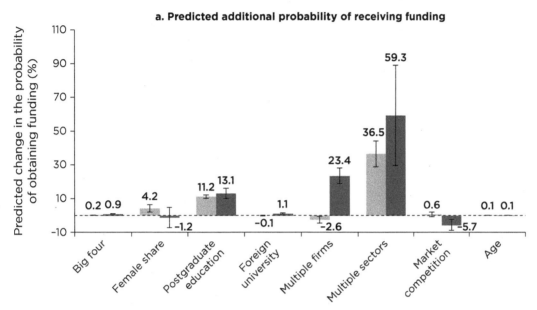

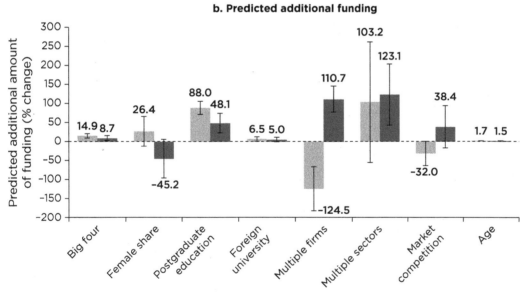

Source: Colonnelli et al. (2024) using data from LinkedIn, PitchBook, Preqin, and Refinitiv.
Note: The bars in panel a show the coefficients of a linear probability model in which the dependent
variable is whether the firm received funding. The lines represent 95 percent confidence intervals.
The sample includes 281,525 observations for nontech and 124,410 for tech. The bars in panel b
show the coefficients of a regression of the logarithm of the amount of funding over the different
characteristics of firms (expressed as a percent change). The lines represent 95 percent confidence
intervals. The panel includes 9,432 observations for nontech and 5,784 for tech.

Boosting the Pipeline of Meaningful Projects in Digital Tech

Even though investment has surged in Africa during the past decade, many further opportunities can be seized. Several sectors have potential given their market size, the type of market problems that firms can solve, and spillover effects on firms and workers. Fintech, e-payments, and e-commerce (refer to the first section of the chapter and box 5.3) are among the highest growth sectors in the region and can expand by taking advantage of the infrastructure that has been built over the past few years. Other sectors such as e-management, agricultural tech, education tech, and cleantech have large potential markets and start from a smaller share of investment in the region. These sectors are particularly relevant to boost productivity, build human capital to leverage the demographic dividend, and aid the clean energy transition.

BOX 5.3

Turning Market Gaps into Opportunities: E-commerce

E-commerce is, along with financial technology, the sector displaying the most investment and start-up growth in the past few years. Whereas some e-commerce companies have pursued the business-to-consumer market, the focus has recently been on the business-to-business segment. This segment shows untapped potential; on average, just 8 percent of formal firms in the region have online sales. Among these firms, 25 percent of their sales are conducted online. The share of sales using e-commerce is not significantly different for large firms, indicating that the use of digital channels for sales is not solely determined by company size, but rather by adoption and utilization.

Limited adoption of e-commerce, compared with mobile payments, can be attributed to several factors. First, adopters are not able to perceive the benefits. Second, the solutions usually require a higher level of digital literacy, especially when not accompanied by a network of agents. Third, many African countries have substantial gaps in logistics infrastructure, including lack of address, restricting the reach and growth of e-commerce firms. Building this infrastructure entails substantial investment and, consequently, requires securing more

continued

BOX 5.3 *(Continued)*

capital, makes the path to profitability longer, and poses survival risks for firms, particularly in a context of limited funding.[a] These constraints unveil opportunities for asset-light models relying on third-party logistics and logistical efficiencies. The feasibility of such models depends on the unique gaps in each country. In addition, the transportation of goods from a distribution center or hub to the end consumer's location (what is called last-mile delivery in the logistics industry) in Africa, and even among leading countries in e-commerce, suffers from the lack of an accurate and reliable street addressing system (Fredriksson 2021). This is most salient in business-to-consumer e-commerce.

The fast-moving consumer goods (FMCG) supply chain in Africa faces significant challenges. Informal vendors currently account for 90 percent of retail transactions, resulting in a fragmented supply chain that inefficiently connects suppliers and retailers. This fragmentation leads to high costs for distributors, retailers, and consumers. Additionally, the suboptimal delivery methods within this supply chain contribute to unnecessary emissions burdens.

Amid these challenges, several companies have recognized the immense potential in providing digital solutions to the informal sector and have transformed it into major market opportunities. Companies such as MaxAB in the Arab Republic of Egypt; Twiga Foods and Wasoko in Kenya; and TradeDepot, Sabi, and Omnibiz in Nigeria have emerged as key players in this space. Through their platforms, these firms have directly connected informal retailers with manufacturers, reducing markups caused by lengthy and fragmented distribution chains. They have also introduced logistical efficiencies through aggregation. The impact of this sector is significant, considering that 83 percent of jobs in Africa are in the informal economy, with a majority of retail businesses being run by women. Moreover, these companies have the potential to drive digital diffusion across businesses in Africa by integrating additional services such as credit, inventory monitoring, and data analytics into their platforms.

continued

BOX 5.3 *(Continued)*

TradeDepot: Digitalization of the FMCG Supply Chain

In Nigeria, local logistics start-up TradeDepot has developed a direct-to-retail distribution marketplace, cutting out wholesalers as mediators, focusing on digitalizing the FMCG supply chain, and more efficiently consolidating supply (combining shipments from different FMCG brands or manufacturers and distributors to generate efficiencies) and demand (informal retailers). Retailers can directly restock products via text, app, web, and call centers, and products are then directly delivered to their shops within a day or two. Distributors working through the digital marketplace receive these orders and deliver them via optimized routes, and FMCG brands receive market information on their products. In turn, the efficiency gains from organizing information flows and optimizing distribution channels translate into lower prices to retailers and, ultimately, consumers.

TradeDepot's organized digital FMCG supply chain landed the company a partnership with Unilever in 2019 to digitalize their distribution network in Nigeria. Rather than developing an in-house digital marketplace, Unilever leveraged TradeDepot's platform with established market fit, saving Unilever development costs. For TradeDepot, the success of a multinational FMCG brand partnership offered an unprecedented opportunity to increase scale.

a. For example, Omnibiz in Nigeria has an asset-light model without warehouses or a fleet and relies on third-party distributors, allowing it more flexibility.

E-management and Digital Solutions for Business Administration

Digital technologies have the potential to improve human capital, entrepreneurial, and firm capabilities in Africa. Evidence across countries has shown the large benefits of improving managerial practices (Bloom et al., 2013, 2020; Scur et al., 2021), for which training and methods could be shared and taught through digital platforms, reducing their costs. Furthermore, given the relationship between management practices and productivity and its complementarity with investment in innovation and research and development, using digital technologies can yield direct and indirect benefits. In addition, digital technologies can ameliorate information gaps related to management (firms are unaware of how good or bad their management practices are) by harnessing existing and new information (for example, online surveys) and using benchmarking tools.

A constraint for many digital businesses in Africa is limited market size, especially for "winner-takes-all markets" that characterize many digital business solutions. A recent analysis based on the Enlyft database of digital technologies used by firms in developing countries shows that, for all regions, the supply of some frontier digital technologies is relatively concentrated because of scale and network advantages. For example, the market share of software licenses applied to enterprise resource planning systems, a frontier technology for business administration, is concentrated in large global corporations, such as SAP, Microsoft, and Oracle (Cirera, Comin, and Cruz 2022).

Although the African markets might be relatively small for global conglomerates, there may be opportunities to tailor these solutions to local-specific conditions. Beyond affordability, a potential challenge for the diffusion of digital technology by businesses in Africa is the small market size, driven by a lack of productivity-enhancing technologies that match the existing skill levels. Digital solutions need to become cheaper, simpler, and available in local languages.

The potential for implementing simple (lower-cost) digital solutions that can lead to efficiencies in business functions is high. For example, Anderson et al. (2023) ran a pilot developing a simple app for marketing analytics (sales, products, and customers) and implemented it in Rwanda, resulting in higher sales (36 percent) and profits (29 percent). Chapter 2 estimates that more than 600,000 firms with five or more workers and up to 40 million own-account businesses in Africa are likely to benefit from further digitalization in business administration.

The wide adoption of mobile payments and e-commerce growth in the region can be a stepping stone for digital diffusion because new functionalities can be built on the mobile payments and e-commerce digital infrastructure. For example, as more small and midsize enterprises participate in business-to-business e-commerce, solutions aimed at more specific business and management functions, such as inventory management and monitoring of key performance indicators, can be introduced.

Sector-Specific Digital Solutions: Agtech

Agricultural technology, or agtech, currently accounts for less than 1 percent of digital tech firms, despite agriculture contributing a fifth of Africa's GDP and half of total employment (OECD and FAO 2016). Smallholder farms in Africa produce 70 percent of the region's food supply and support 60 percent of Sub-Saharan Africa's 1.2 billion people. Agricultural productivity in the region is among the lowest in the world, and technological progress and yields have mostly stagnated (Suri and Udry 2022).

The number of agtech services in low- and middle-income countries increased from about 50 in 2009 to more than 700 in 2019 (latest available), led by digital advisory and financial services (refer to figure 5.8). Among this group of countries,

FIGURE 5.8

Number of Agtech Services in Low- and Middle-Income Countries, by Use Case, 2009–19

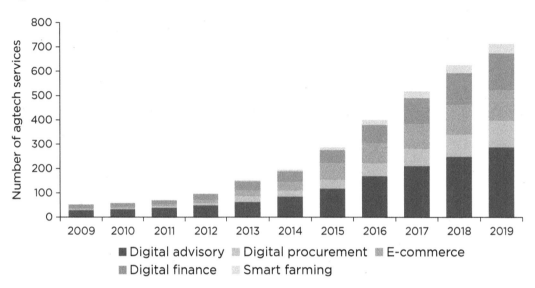

Source: Phatty-Jobe, Seth, and Norton (2020).
Note: Agtech = agricultural technology.

Sub-Saharan Africa witnessed the fastest growth and accounted for 62 percent of agtech services in 2020 (Phatty-Jobe, Seth, and Norton 2020). Climate advisory services for farmers and other actors who rely on rain-fed agriculture will help users adapt to weather variability and climate change. Investments in data collection tools such as unmanned aerial vehicles and Internet-of-Things (IoT) devices, analytical capabilities such as modelling and machine learning, and digital platforms will enable timely delivery of data-driven, customized (by commodity and location) agriculture and climate advisory services (Priebe 2022). Disseminating information through digital means is cheap once a platform and content have been developed, but those require fixed costs that reduce prospective profitability for private firms, potentially calling for partnerships with the public sector (Fabregas, Kremer, and Schilbach 2019; World Bank 2023).

Despite the growth in agtech services, Africa's agriculture remains the least mechanized and irrigated in the world, contributing to low productivity and resilience and high food loss and waste. Previous studies show that fewer than 1 percent of farming households owned a tractor, and 5 percent irrigated land (Christiaensen 2017). Through IoT-enabled digital platforms for fleet management, some start-ups (for example, Hello Tractor) are connecting tractor fleet owners with farmers and providing them with advanced tools for monitoring performance. Yet, further evidence is needed regarding the impact of these solutions on stimulation of technology upgrading by more user firms. Moreover, agtech start-ups also face similar barriers shared by other businesses, among them the shortage of working capital and low digital skills in the labor force (Abate et al., 2023).

The potential market for digital agriculture in Africa is estimated at more than $2 billion, more than 90 percent of which is still untapped (Tsan et al., 2019). Previous studies have identified potentially scalable agtech investment opportunities in addition to public investments and policies to enhance mobile penetration, the quality and affordability of internet connectivity, and digital skills in rural Africa (FAO and ITU 2022; Kim et al., 2020). These opportunities range from addressing asymmetric and incomplete information to alleviate credit constraints and amplify the options for insurance to sector-specific applications, such as product tracing and IoT, enabling cooling and storage to strengthen value chains and minimize food loss. Yet, these solutions need to overcome the challenges such as the dominance of small-scale agricultural operators and poor infrastructure in Africa.

Summing Up

Addressing market failures to facilitate financing of innovative early-stage disruptive businesses can strengthen the design and scaling of applications to boost firm digitalization in Africa. The success of mobile payments in the region shows that start-ups can disrupt markets by incorporating technologies that are relatively easy to adopt, user friendly, and cost-effective. The rapid diffusion of mobile payments across firms in Africa, as discussed in chapter 1, has an important entrepreneurial component, combining disruptive technologies and new business models and overcoming several barriers discussed in chapter 3, such as the high cost of adoption and lack of infrastructure and skills. Similar investment opportunities might be available for other business applications, but the incorporation of disruptive technologies has a weak relationship with prospects for financing among tech start-ups in Africa, relative to other regions.

Improving the pipeline of bankable projects by providing better access to information, markets, and finance can facilitate the spread of innovative digital applications. Businesses in Africa have a large market potential for digital solutions—from general functions, such as administration, planning, and sales, to sector-specific tasks and training of labor force. This market has specific needs for which rewarding disruptive solutions need to be combined with addressing lack of affordability, firm capabilities, and human capital that prevent a wider level of adoption across businesses in Africa while also being a barrier to tech start-ups themselves.

Notes

1. See Colonnelli et al. (2024) for further details about the dataset.
2. M-Pesa, a Kenyan mobile payment service that emerged from the mobile network operator Safaricom, Vodafone's Kenyan associate, started a mobile money revolution in the region in 2007,

using a model that entrepreneurs have tried to replicate, with mixed outcomes. Ten years after the launch of M-Pesa, mobile money has been used by at least one individual in 96 percent of households in Kenya and had lifted an estimated 2 percent of Kenyan households out of poverty (Suri and Jack 2016).

3. According to Suri (2017), using M-Pesa to send money had a cost equivalent of almost 30 percent of sending it via postal bank or bus delivery and 46 percent of sending it via Western Union, without accounting for other transportation or time costs.

4. This figure from Disrupt Africa (2022) encompasses only venture capital. Partech (2022) estimates around $6.5 billion in total for venture capital, equity, and debt in 2022.

5. See Zhu et al. (2022) for a broader discussion on the role of market size beyond the Africa region.

6. IT services include custom computer programming services, software publishers, priced digital services, all other miscellaneous electronic and computer equipment, computer facilities management services, semiconductor machinery manufacturing, computer and peripheral equipment manufacturing, and semiconductors and other electronic components.

7. *High-potential entrepreneurship* refers to those firms that are investment-ready or seeking investment and are, therefore, found in commercial datasets such as PitchBook, Crunchbase, and Preqin. Smaller firms only appear in noncommercial sources such as LinkedIn.

8. Cohen et al. (2019) provide further details on the role of accelerators.

9. Latin America is used as a region of comparison because, like Africa, it includes emerging markets that have experienced significant growth in technology adoption and entrepreneurship. These dynamics are more inward-related, which is different from other emerging regions like Asia, where the focus tends to be on trade and outward-related dynamics (Cruz, Pereira-López, and Salgado 2023).

10. An *exit* is the process by which an investor or investment firm realizes their investment and exits their ownership position in a company. It involves selling or divesting their stake in the company to generate returns on their investment (Investopedia 2021).

References

Abate, Gashaw T., Kibrom A. Abay, Jordan Chamberlin, Yumna Kassim, David J. Spielman, and Martin Paul Jr Tabe-Ojong. 2023. "Digital Tools and Agricultural Market Transformation in Africa: Why Are They Not at Scale Yet, and What Will It Take to Get There?" *Food Policy* 116: 102439. https://doi.org/10.1016/j.foodpol.2023.102439.

African Business. 2023. "Senegal Is Experiencing Mobile Money Revolution, Says Wave's West Africa Director." *African Business*, April 11, 2023. https://african.business/2023/04/technology-information/senegal-is-experiencing-mobile-money-revolution-says-waves-west-africa-director.

Agrawal, Ajay K., Joshua S. Gans, and Avi Goldfarb. 2023. "The Turing Transformation: Artificial Intelligence, Intelligence Augmentation, and Skill Premiums." Working Paper 31767, National Bureau of Economic Research, Cambridge, MA.

Alvarez, Fernando E., David Argente, Francesco Lippi, Esteban Méndez, and Diana Van Patten. 2023. "Strategic Complementarities in a Dynamic Model of Technology Adoption: P2P Digital Payments." Working Paper 31280, National Bureau of Economic Research, Cambridge, MA.

Anderson, Stephen J., Pradeep K. Chintagunta, Rupali Kaul, and Naufel Vilcassim. 2023. "Is (Smart) Technology Really Making Us Dumber? Marketing Analytics Improves the Mental, Managerial and Financial Performance of Entrepreneurs." Unpublished manuscript, November 30, 2023.

Audretsch, David, Marcio Cruz, and Jesica Torres. 2022. "Revisiting Entrepreneurial Ecosystems." Working Paper 10229, World Bank, Washington, DC.

Begazo, Tania, Moussa P. Blimpo, and Mark A. Dutz. 2023. *Digital Africa: Technological Transformation for Jobs.* Washington, DC: World Bank.

Björkegren, Daniel. 2023. "Artificial Intelligence for the Poor: How to Harness the Power of AI in the Developing World." *Foreign Affairs*, August 9, 2023. https://www.foreignaffairs.com/world/artificial-intelligence-poor.

Björkegren, Daniel, Joshua E. Blumenstock, and Samsun Knight. 2023. "Training Machine Learning to Anticipate Manipulation." Unpublished manuscript, July 18, 2023. PDF file. https://dan.bjorkegren.com/manipulation.pdf.

Bloom, Nicholas, Benn Eifert, Aprajit Mahajan, David McKenzie, and John Roberts. 2013. "Does Management Matter? Evidence From India." *Quarterly Journal of Economics* 128 (1): 1–51. https://doi.org/10.1093/qje/qjs044.

Bloom, Nicholas, Benn Eifert, Aprajit Mahajan, David McKenzie, and John Roberts. 2020. "Do Management Interventions Last? Evidence from India." *American Economic Journal: Applied Economics* 12 (2): 198–219. https://doi.org/10.1257/app.20180369.

Bloom, Nicholas, Tarek A. Hassan, Aakash Kalyani, Josh Lerner, and Ahmed Tahoun. 2021. "The Diffusion of Disruptive Technologies." Working Paper 28999, National Bureau of Economic Research, Cambridge, MA.

Brynjolfsson, Erik, Danielle Li, and Lindsey R. Raymond. 2023. "Generative AI at Work." Working Paper 31161, National Bureau of Economic Research, Cambridge, MA.

Christensen, Clayton M. 1997. *The Innovator's Dilemma: When New Technologies Cause Great Firms to Fail.* Boston: Harvard Business School Press.

Christiaensen, Luc. 2017. "Agriculture in Africa—Telling Myths from Facts: A Synthesis." *Food Policy* 67: 1–11. https://doi.org/10.1016/j.foodpol.2017.02.002.

Cirera, Xavier, Diego Comin, and Marcio Cruz. 2022. *Bridging the Technological Divide: Technology Adoption by Firms in Developing Countries.* Washington, DC: World Bank.

Cohen, S., D. C. Fehder, Y. V. Hochberg, and F. Murray. 2019. "The Design of Startup Accelerators." *Research Policy* 48 (7): 1781–97. https://doi.org/10.1016/j.respol.2019.04.003.

Colonnelli, Emanuele, Marcio Cruz, Mariana Pereira-López, Tommaso Porzio, and Chun Zhao. 2024. "Startups in Africa." Unpublished manuscript, International Finance Corporation, Washington, DC.

Cruz, Marcio, Mariana Pereira-López, and Edgar Salgado. 2023. "Disruptive Technologies and Finance: An Analysis of Digital Startups in Africa." Policy Research Working Paper 10633, World Bank, Washington, DC.

Daugherty, Paul, and H. James Wilson. 2022. *Radically Human: How New Technology Is Transforming Business and Shaping Our Future.* Boston: Harvard Business Press.

Disrupt Africa. 2022. *African Tech Startups Funding Report 2022.* Nairobi, Kenya: Disrupt Africa. https://disruptafrica.com/wp-content/uploads/2023/02/The-African-Tech-Startups-Funding-Report-2022.pdf.

Eli, Shari, Joshua K. Hausman, and Paul Rhode. 2023. "The Model T." Working Paper 31454, National Bureau of Economic Research, Cambridge, MA.

Fabregas, Raissa, Michael Kremer, and Frank Schilbach. 2019. "Realizing the Potential of Digital Development: The Case of Agricultural Advice." *Science* 366 (6471): aay3038. https://doi .org/10.1126/science.aay3038.

FAO (Food and Agriculture Organization of the United Nations) and ITU (International Telecommunication Union). 2022. *Status of Digital Agriculture in 47 Sub-Saharan African Countries*. Rome: FAO and ITU. https://www.fao.org/3/cb7943en/cb7943en.pdf.

Fredriksson, Torbjörn. 2021. "Cultivating New Capacities, the Case of E-commerce." In *Development Co-operation Report 2021: Shaping a Just Digital Transformation*. Paris: OECD Publishing. https://doi.org/10.1787/9d4714fc-en.

Gonzalez-Uribe, Juanita, and Michael Leatherbee. 2018. "The Effects of Business Accelerators on Venture Performance: Evidence from Start-Up Chile." *Review of Financial Studies* 31 (4): 1566–603. https://doi.org/10.1093/rfs/hhx103.

González-Uribe, Juanita, and Santiago Reyes. 2021. "Identifying and Boosting 'Gazelles': Evidence from Business Accelerators." *Journal of Financial Economics* 139 (1): 260–87. https://doi .org/10.1016/j.jfineco.2020.07.012.

Investopedia. 2021. "Exit." https://www.investopedia.com/terms/e/exit.asp.

Johnson, Simon, and Daron Acemoglu. 2023. *Power and Progress: Our Thousand-Year Struggle over Technology and Prosperity*. London: Hachette UK.

Kim, Jeehye, Parmesh Shah, Joanne Catherine Gaskell, Ashesh Prasann, and Akanksha Luthra. 2020. *Scaling Up Disruptive Agricultural Technologies in Africa*. International Development in Focus. Washington, DC: World Bank.

Lévi, Nicolas. 2021. "Mobile Money: Quel Avenir Pour Une Innovation Africaine Majeure?" Paper presented at Séminaire Transformations numériques, L'Ecole De Paris du Management, Paris, September 29, 2021. https://ecole.org/fr/seance/1472-mobile-money-quel-avenir-pour-une -innovation-africaine-majeure.

Markoff, John. 2016. *Machines of Loving Grace: The Quest for Common Ground between Humans and Robots*. New York: HarperCollins.

Noy, Shakked, and Whitney Zhang. 2023. "Experimental Evidence on the Productivity Effects of Generative Artificial Intelligence." *Science* 381 (6654): 187–92. https://doi.org/10.1126/science .adh2586.

OECD (Organisation for Economic Co-operation and Development) and FAO (Food and Agriculture Organization of the United Nations). 2016. *Agriculture in Sub-Saharan Africa: Prospects and Challenges for the Next Decade, Agricultural Outlook 2016–2025*. Paris: OECD.

Partech. 2022. *Africa Tech Venture Capital Report*. Berlin, Germany: Partech. https://partechpartners .com/africa-reports/2022-africa-tech-venture-capital-report.

Phatty-Jobe, A., A. Seth, and K. Norton. 2020. *Digital Agriculture Maps: 2020 State of the Sector in Low and Middle-Income Countries*. London: GSMA. https://www.gsma.com/r/wp-content /uploads/2020/09/GSMA-Agritech-Digital-Agriculture-Maps.pdf.

Priebe, Jan. 2022. *Data Driven Advisory Services for Climate Smart Smallholder Agriculture*. London: GSMA.

Sarangé, Clara, and Fortune Chuku. 2021. *Bolstering Innovators in Africa: Innovation Hubs' Catalytic Role as Ecosystem Support Organisations*. London: Briter Bridges. https://briterbridges.com/s /Afrilabs-Report-Final-FMO-EU-NLGv.pdf.

Scur, Daniela, Raffaella Sadun, John Van Reenan, Renata Lemos, and Nicholas Bloom. 2021. "World Management Survey at 18: Lessons and the Way Forward." IZA Discussion Paper No. 14146, Institute of Labor Economics, Bonn, Germany. https://docs.iza.org/dp14146.pdf.

Suri, Tavneet. 2017. "Mobile Money." *Annual Review of Economics* 9: 497–520. https://doi.org/10.1146 /annurev-economics-063016-103638.

Suri, Tavneet, Jenny Aker, Catia Batista, Michael Callen, Tarek Ghani, William Jack, Leora Klapper, Emma Riley, Simone Schaner, and Sandip Sukhtankar. 2023. "Mobile Money." *VoxDev Lit* 2 (2). https://voxdev.org/sites/default/files/2023-09/Mobile_Money_2.pdf.

Suri, Tavneet, and William Jack. 2016. "The Long-Run Poverty and Gender Impacts of Mobile Money." *Science* 354 (6317): 1288–92. https://doi.org/10.1126/science.aah5309.

Suri, Tavneet, and Christopher Udry. 2022. "Agricultural Technology in Africa." *Journal of Economic Perspectives* 36 (1): 33–56.

Tsan, Michael, Swetha Totapally, Michael Hailu, and Benjamin K. Addom. 2019. *The Digitization of African Agriculture Report 2018–2019.* Wageningen, the Netherlands: Technical Centre for Agricultural and Rural Cooperation/Dalberg Advisors. https://cgspace.cgiar.org/handle /10568/101498.

World Bank. 2023. *Digital Climate Information and Agriculture Advisory Delivery Mechanisms in West Africa.* Washington, DC: World Bank.

Zhu, Tingting Juni, Philip Grinsted, Hangyul Song, and Malathi Velamuri. 2022. *A Spiky Digital Business Landscape: What Can Developing Countries Do?* Washington, DC: World Bank.

CHAPTER 6

Financing Digitalization of Businesses in Africa

Marcio Cruz, Florian Mölders, and Mariana Pereira-López

Key Messages

- Digital infrastructure investments in Africa reached more than $32 billion between 2010 and 2021. For every dollar spent in the region by governments on public–private information and communication technology projects, private actors invested four. Yet, more private finance is needed to address infrastructure gaps and enable the productive use of digital technologies by firms.

- Funding for digital tech firms in African countries is small relative to their income levels. Only one-quarter of funded firms receive their first venture capital within the first five years. The African venture capital and private equity ecosystem relies predominantly on foreign capital. Start-ups in Africa are averse to debt, preferring equity, and do not want to give up control. Acceleration programs—which provide firms with guidance and funding—face high demand for grants, but firms are averse to government involvement and accelerators taking equity.

- African firms that apply for loans to carry out technology upgrades and for expanding production face higher application rejections than their peers in other regions. The financing gap for existing formal firms to digitalize their business administration is between $1.4 billion and $2.7 billion, based on different scenarios. The high cost of capital is an important barrier to the adoption of digital technologies in African economies. Emerging digital credit markets offer a potential increase in funding at lower cost. They can also facilitate access to traditional finance.

Introduction

This chapter analyzes the role of financing in facilitating opportunities in digital infrastructure, entrepreneurship, and adoption of digital solutions by firms. It underscores the need for further private financing to support the productive use of digital technologies across all sectors of the economy. It also discusses how policy reforms, especially regulations, must be put in place to stimulate private sector initiatives in this domain.

The chapter addresses the following questions:

- What is the status of investment in digital infrastructure?
- What are the key gaps in financing digital innovation through tech start-ups?
- How can capital be mobilized to support digital upgrades across all sectors?

The chapter outlines the characteristics of digital infrastructure investment in Africa. First, it discusses the role of development finance institutions (DFIs) and the public sector in de-risking projects and complementing and supporting private investment. Second, it examines funding and support for start-ups, including government-led efforts. Third, it analyzes the financial gaps, credit constraints (including the cost of capital), and potential benefits to be gained from increasing financing for firm digitalization.

Financing the Digital Transformation in Africa

The availability of financing with appropriate risk–return characteristics is key to addressing the different challenges posed by incomplete digitalization. The sources and types of financial instruments can be differentiated by three types of end user:

- Digital infrastructure providers;
- Technology start-ups supplying digital services and applications; and
- Traditional firms of all sizes that are digitalizing.

Addressing these diverse financing challenges requires tailored solutions involving public entities, private financiers, and DFIs. For large infrastructure investments such as submarine cables that have positive spillover effects, public and DFI financing can provide support, considering blended financing to lower the cost of capital and mitigate specific risks. Private investors have been already actively acting in this space. To leverage the benefits of these investments, complementary actions are needed to unlock financing to other end users. Tech start-ups usually rely on intangible assets, such as data and novel business models, making them least attractive for traditional banks. Grants can support initial growth when financing from venture capital (VC) and angel investors is limited. In sectors such as agricultural tech (agtech), health tech, and educational tech, where the social returns are high but private capital is limited, the public sector and DFIs can ensure viability and scalability. The local financial market to support these firms is limited, with large potential for expansion. For firm digitalization, obstacles such as high interest rates, limited information, and firms' lack of collateral might limit credit. Guarantees by the public sector or DFIs can help overcome these obstacles, along with support for artificial intelligence–based solutions that reduce the risks and lending costs for commercial banks.

Private capital's impact in this area can be maximized by enabling investment from productive actors in the value chain. Box 6.1 offers an example of complementary actions, based on public investments in infrastructure supported by the World Bank Group in Senegal, followed by reforms aiming to facilitate financing to tech start-ups to expand digital services and applications, along with complementary actions providing information and advice to support digital adoption by small and medium firms.

BOX 6.1

Mobilizing Finance for Digitalization

The World Bank helped enhance digital connectivity in West Africa through its support for the Africa Coast to Europe submarine cable, launched in 2012. This investment complemented previous cable connections, such as the Atlantis-2 in 2000 and South Atlantic-3/West Africa Submarine Cable in 2002. This infrastructure laid the foundation for improved access and reduced costs for broadband internet in Senegal and neighboring countries. In addition, the World Bank has helped increase access to energy in Senegal, something that indirectly facilitates adoption of digital technologies, through initiatives such as the Senegal Electricity Sector Support Project, which is making electricity more reliable and accessible in select rural areas, therefore enabling digital technologies to thrive.

Regulatory reforms resulting from these operations have facilitated entry and expansion of tech start-ups. Moreover, in 2018, the International Finance Corporation (IFC) invested in Partech Africa, a venture capital fund dedicated to financing tech start-ups across Africa, including Senegal. These collaborations and investments underscore the pivot toward attracting more private capital to sustain and grow Senegal's emerging tech ecosystem.

Lately, a World Bank loan to Senegal focused on promoting digital technology upgrades by firms. This program, in collaboration with the Agence de Développement et d'Encadrement des Petites et Moyennes Entreprises, the government agency that supports small and medium-size enterprises, has provided a diagnostic and funded technical assistance to support digitalization. IFC has also partnered with Orange Bank Africa, Orange Group's digital bank, to help businesses, including those in rural and underserved areas, to access loans online (IFC 2022, 2023). Understanding the impact and potential these actions have for mobilizing further private investment is critical to boost the productive use of digital technologies. Cruz, Dutz, and Rodríguez-Castelán (2022) show that despite remarkable improvements in digital infrastructure, there remain significant gaps in productive use of digital technologies by Senegalese firms.

HomeContent、

Investment in Digital Infrastructure

Digital infrastructure investments in Africa topped $32 billion between 2010 and 2021, with large participation from the private sector. Most of this investment went to the mobile subsector (refer to figure 6.1, panel a), which consists of cable and fiber optic, followed by internet (internet networks and operators) and terrestrial assets (communication towers, base stations). Most of these transactions were in Nigeria (66 percent), South Africa (14 percent), and the Arab Republic of Egypt (7 percent). Across Africa, private actors invested more than $4 for every dollar spent by governments on public–private information and communication technology (ICT) projects, a higher ratio than in other regions (refer to figure 6.1, panel b). Through these projects, which were mostly greenfield, private capital made an important contribution to closing digital infrastructure gaps in the region. Public investment constraints caused by high indebtedness and limited domestic revenues make financing from the private sector crucial to meeting Africa's digital infrastructure investment needs (Devine et al., 2021).

The average ICT infrastructure project in Africa is six times smaller than its equivalents in Latin America and the Caribbean and East Asia and Pacific (refer to figure 6.2). One in five ICT investment projects in Africa is backed by multilateral organizations. Of these projects, two-thirds are in the continent's poorest countries, and an additional one-fifth are in low-income countries with limited creditworthiness.

FIGURE 6.1

Private Investment in ICT Projects

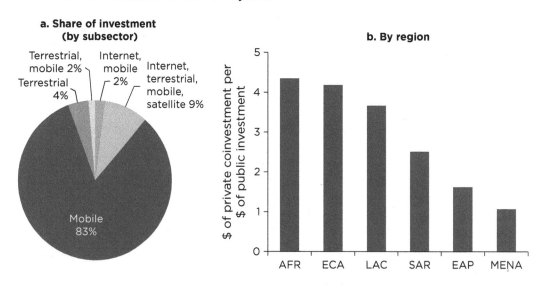

Sources: Panel a: IJGlobal; panel b: Private Participation in Infrastructure Project Database, World Bank. Note: Panel a shows the value of project and corporate finance transactions in telecommunications in Africa between 2010 and 2021. $ = US$; AFR = Africa; EAP = East Asia and Pacific; ECA = Europe and Central Asia; ICT = information and communication technology; LAC = Latin America and the Caribbean; MENA = Middle East and North Africa; SAR = South Asia.

FIGURE 6.2

Investment Levels in ICT Projects, by Region

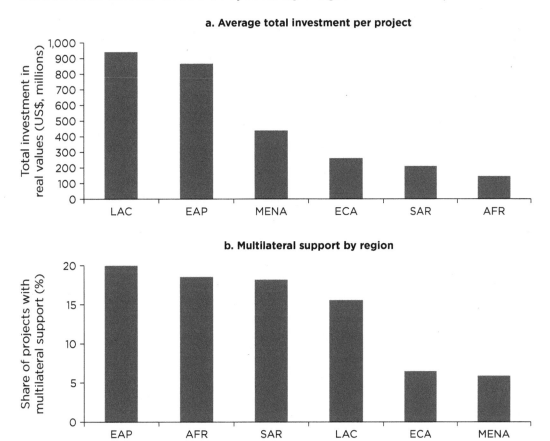

a. Average total investment per project

b. Multilateral support by region

Source: World Bank data on private participation in infrastructure.
Note: AFR = Africa; EAP = East Asia and Pacific; ECA = Europe and Central Asia; ICT = information and communication technology; LAC = Latin America and the Caribbean; MENA = Middle East and North Africa; SAR = South Asia.

DFIs can prioritize projects with longer maturities, particularly riskier projects that may be unattractive to commercial lenders, despite a potentially broad development impact. DFIs mobilize private capital for Africa primarily by investing in economic infrastructure and services. This accounted for 72 percent of total DFI capital mobilization in 2021 (OECD 2023).

Funding of Disruptive Tech Start-Ups

In comparison with other regions, the flow of financial support to digital technology start-ups in Africa is more restricted and limited. Start-ups draw on different combinations of financial sources at different points in their life cycle, reflecting their evolving risks. For example, firms are often initially funded through grants, friends or family, or personal savings. As the business develops, it usually transitions toward larger external funding sources such as VC or banks. However, a lower proportion of African firms in the VC and private equity (PE) ecosystem make it through all the different phases of such a funneling process—from early stage to initial public offering (IPO)—compared, for example, with their Latin American counterparts. Even with the increasing presence of accelerators, incubators, and VC firms focused on early-stage ventures, only a few firms manage to complete this funneling process. From the universe of VC-backed firms, only 12 percent raise later-stage funding, and only 3 percent go into IPO and post-IPO.

These characteristics of funding might be explained by the limitations of the entrepreneurial ecosystem in Africa. First, although funding is growing at high rates in Africa, it is still limited. Second, some of the tech solutions developed are not scalable enough because of market conditions and frictions such as fragmented supply chains, limiting their potential to attract investment. Third, exit options are limited,[1] with equity being the main type of funding (refer to figure 6.3).

Early-stage start-ups in Africa receive less funding than in other regions, with a value nearly 40 percent lower than their Latin American counterparts. These results are based on start-ups younger than five years old, comparing the median value of funding normalized by gross domestic product per capita across regions (refer to figure 6.4). This gap underscores the challenges faced by African start-ups in their initial growth

FIGURE 6.3

Funding of African Tech Firms, by Funding Type

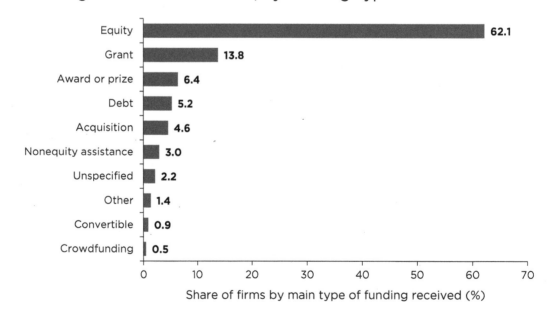

Source: Briter Bridges (2023).

FIGURE 6.4

Early-Stage African Tech Firms Are Less Well Funded Than Their
Peers in Other Regions

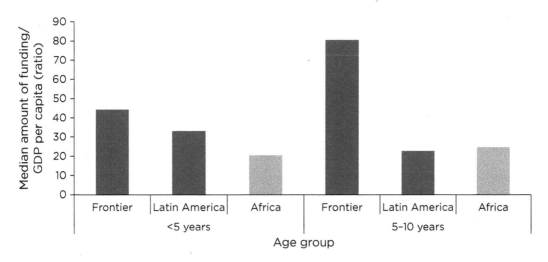

Sources: Crunchbase data, 2023; https://www.crunchbase.com, for amounts of funding and World
Bank for GDP per capita.
Note: Median funding is normalized by GDP per capita. *Frontier* is defined as London, Palo Alto,
Seattle, and Tokyo. GDP = gross domestic product.

and development phases. However, as firms mature (five to 10 years old), African start-
ups catch up, with a funding level 8 percent higher than that of those in Latin America,
although still 70 percent below frontier levels. Despite initial funding constraints, as
shown in chapter 5, younger African start-ups are more disruptive and innovative than
older firms.

Funding for tech entrepreneurs takes longer to be mobilized in Africa than in other
regions. In Sub-Saharan Africa, only one-third of funded firms secure their first VC deal
in their first five years, compared with more than half of firms in Latin America. By year
10 of operation, 60 percent of funded firms in Sub-Saharan Africa obtain their first deal,
compared with 75 percent in Latin America (Colonnelli et al., 2024). This means that
either the market appears to wait longer to finance investable ventures or that projects
take longer to become investable. This could be explained, as mentioned in chapter 5, by
a higher perception of risk, information gaps that do not allow the market to correctly
assess risks, or competition-related issues linked to access to a range of essential business inputs that take longer for new entrants to secure. In any case, investors prefer to
come in only after certain elements of risk have been resolved, which tends to be closer
to the usual exit time frame. In fact, for both the tech sector and other sectors in Africa,
the median value of funding ramps up after the seventh year of operation.

The African VC–PE ecosystem relies predominantly on foreign capital, primarily
from North America, Europe, and DFIs, to finance nearly all ventures (refer to figure 6.5).

FIGURE 6.5

Funding in Africa Is Fueled from Abroad

Investment flows between regions (share of total value)

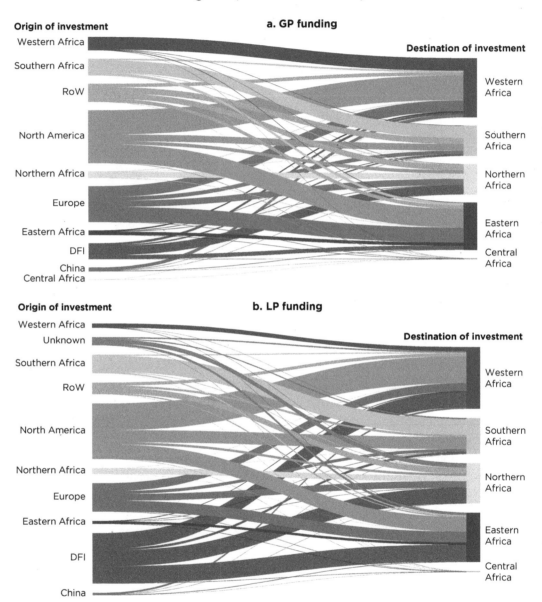

Source: Colonnelli et al. (2024).
Note: The figure shows the origin of investment partners participating in deals (left) and the within-Africa location (region) of the firm receiving the funding (right). DFI = development finance institutions; GP = general partner; LP = limited partner; RoW = rest of world.

These patterns broadly apply to both types of investments: general partners, which involves full operational control of a businesses with unlimited financial liability, and limited partners, which means that investors have little or no involvement in daily operations and limited liability. Among all other regions, only Latin America occasionally exhibits a comparable share of the deals funded by foreign capital. This fact also underscores the nascent stage of the African ecosystem. Other regions, such as Asia, have shifted from a foreign-financed ecosystem toward a smaller share of foreign capital in the past two decades.

There is increasing activity by accelerators, incubators (including syndicates, venture builders, and technology hubs), and seed funding investors to increase the pipeline of investable start-ups (refer to the discussion in box 6.2). Although there is no conclusive evidence so far about the impact of these activities or the most effective bundles of services (business education and training, mentorship, networking, and funding, among others), accelerators, incubators, and seed funding investors are expected to facilitate matching between potential investors and entrepreneurs. Likewise, they can help reveal the quality of start-ups and thus match investors to investable projects (Gonzalez-Uribe and Hmaddi 2022).

Creating an environment conducive both to attracting VC and to fostering long-term entrepreneurial success requires various complementary factors. It needs robust legal institutions, digital infrastructure, benefits from agglomeration of knowledge and human capital, a sizable market, and policies addressing exchange rate risks and capital controls. Indeed, investor protection, government effectiveness, internet bandwidth, and the share of the population with internet coverage were found to be positively associated with VC deals across 25 African countries between 2014 and 2019 (Jaoui, Amoussou, and Kemeze 2022). Likewise, contract enforcement and property rights protection are crucial for equity investments from largely international investors. Governments in the region are, therefore, increasingly promoting start-ups through comprehensive start-up legislation. Senegal and Tunisia have already embraced this approach, and 16 other countries are reportedly in the process of doing so (Investment Climate Reform Facility 2021). For these initiatives to succeed, collaboration among stakeholders is crucial to ensuring the right instruments and incentives are in place for all ecosystem members.

DFIs can improve the entrepreneurial ecosystem by funding VC firms, seed funds, incubators, and accelerators that support early-stage ventures in these markets. First, they can foster the ecosystem's selection of successful and potentially disruptive ventures. Second, by strategically channeling investments, they can catalyze additional private sector funding. Third, they can directly de-risk projects with high social returns but insufficient private sector appeal, thereby ensuring the realization of meaningful initiatives that might otherwise face undue challenges.

BOX 6.2

What Do Start-Ups in Africa Want and Need?

Funding and investment observed in the entrepreneurial ecosystem are equilibrium market outcomes. Disentangling the supply and demand factors driving these results can inform policies and investment opportunities. Supply factors relate to investors' perceptions of and preferences for risk. In these emerging markets, investors and funds might prefer to focus on companies with a good track record or on highly educated or experienced entrepreneurs. Demand factors or characteristics of entrepreneurs might limit this matching. Some of these factors or characteristics relate to the entrepreneurs' experience, incorporation of disruptive technologies in their offering, scalability, and investment readiness of the company. Even though a firm may be innovative, it might not be ready to receive investment because of some deficiencies in its capabilities or because the owners are not willing to cede some control (Cusolito, Dautovic, and McKenzie 2021). In this sense, the preferences of entrepreneurs matter in terms of how capital is deployed, especially for high-growth firms and in markets in which the variety and flexibility of instruments are still limited.

A background study for this book estimates preferences for capital of high-growth digital start-ups (Colonnelli et al., 2024). The analysis builds on a light-touch experiment in which firms are asked to rate a set of investors' and accelerators' profiles (depending on the stage of the firm). The study, aimed at eliciting the preferences of individuals in an experimental setting, follows the literature on résumé audit studies (Bertrand and Mullainathan 2004; Kessler, Low, and Sullivan 2019) and previous applications to venture capital markets (Colonnelli, Li, and Liu 2024). The design allows for an unbiased estimation of the preferences of start-ups for different sources of investors, terms, and partners by providing strong incentives in the form of helping firms match up with potential partners (investors, accelerators, or incubators), which helps ensure that the responses are truthful. The analysis provides rigorous information on high-growth start-ups in Africa, which is rarely available and can inform how to allocate capital in a cost-effective manner, in terms of what kind of services, such as accelerators and investment readiness programs, are in high demand.

Preliminary results indicate that the characteristics of a deal matter more than the characteristics of investors. These results are based on

continued

BOX 6.2 *(Continued)*

primary data collected from 3,128 firms in Africa (refer to figure B6.2.1). There appears to be a preference for nonfinancial support and local experience. In terms of the instruments, start-ups are averse to debt. Although they prefer equity, they do not want to give up control. Analyzing the preferences of earlier-stage entrepreneurs regarding acceleration programs, the preliminary results indicate that they want grants and that there is a reputation premium for internationally sponsored accelerators, whereas there is an aversion to government involvement or accelerators taking equity.

FIGURE B6.2.1

Funding Preferences of Start-Ups

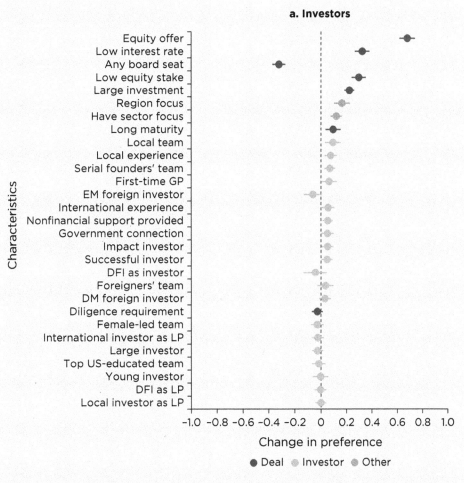

continued

BOX 6.2 *(Continued)*

FIGURE B6.2.1 *(Continued)*

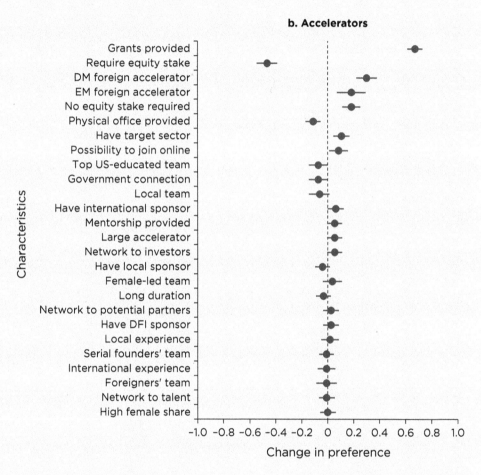

b. Accelerators

Source: Colonnelli et al. (2024).

Note: Results are obtained from a regression analysis. $Interest_{ij} = \beta_0 + \sum_{m=1}^{M} \beta_m$ $characteristics_{jm} + \alpha_i + e_{ij}$, where i is the entrepreneur who answers the survey; $Interest_{ij}$ is the level of interest of start-up i for investor or accelerator profile j; M is the total number of characteristics analyzed, m refers to each of the M characteristics, e is the error term; β_m is the coefficient associated with each characteristic of the accelerator, incubator, investor, or deal; and α_i is individual firm effects. Responses for $N = 3,128$ firms. DFI = development finance institution; DM = developed market; EM = emerging market; GP = general partner; LP = limited partner.

Financing Firms' Digital Upgrade

The development of financial markets fosters the adoption of advanced technologies, especially in industries with higher financing needs. There is a direct association between access to commercial loans and the use of digital technologies (Cirera, Comin, and Cruz 2022). Microbusinesses that obtain a loan are 18 percent more likely to use smartphones, nearly 15 percent less likely to use a 2G phone, and more than 9 percent more likely to use a computer (Atiyas and Dutz 2023). Additionally, for the case of agriculture, Abate et al. (2016) find that better access to credit enhances uptake of technologies.

African firms applying for loans for technology upgrades and production expansion have more of their applications rejected than firms in other regions. Figure 6.6 shows that, on average, small firms in (select) African countries had about one loan rejection in the past three years. Medium-size African enterprises had a lower average rejection number (0.89), followed by large firms (0.66). The higher average number of rejections for African firms is especially striking for small businesses, an estimated 0.58 higher than that of firms in other regions.

FIGURE 6.6

African Firms Find It Harder to Get Loans for Tech Upgrades

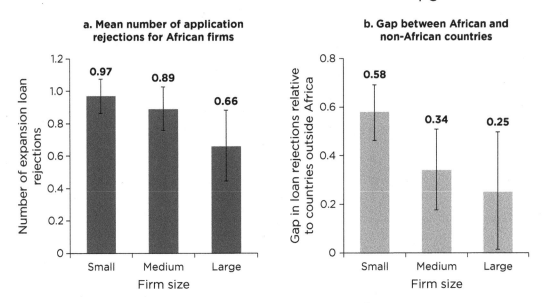

Sources: World Bank, Firm-level Adoption of Technology survey (select African countries); Cirera et al. (2024).
Note: Estimated margins after a linear regression of the number of loan rejections for expansion loans controlling for size, sector, and region fixed effects. Panel b plots the interaction term of the size groups with a dummy variable for Africa. The lines represent 95 percent confidence intervals.

Between 130,000 and 260,000 firms could potentially digitalize their internal processes if access to credit were improved. These estimates, based on methods and findings described in chapter 2, take into consideration some basic characteristics of the firms (for example, size, sector, region), where companies stand in their current digitalization process, their likelihood of adopting these technologies, and their financial constraints. Eleven percent of formal firms that have not digitalized their internal processes have the characteristics to potentially do so. If the sample is restricted to those firms with sales high enough to cover credit repayments, only 10 percent would be potential credit receivers. Furthermore, just 6 percent seem to be capital constrained.[2]

The estimated financing gap for the digitalization of business administration of formal firms in Africa is between $1.4 billion and $2.7 billion. These estimates are based on different scenarios (refer to figure 6.7). Although this is a small share of the overall funding gap in Africa, it represents the digitalization of only one business function, which is strongly associated with firm productivity, employment, and firm growth. Firms with the potential to digitalize have sales growth rates similar to those of digitalized firms,

FIGURE 6.7

Financing Gap for Formal Firms' Digitalization

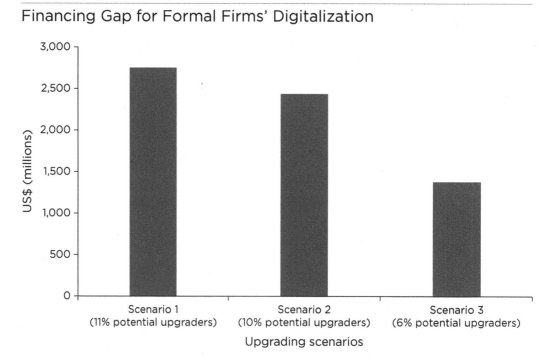

Source: International Finance Corporation calculations based on World Bank Firm-level Adoption of Technology surveys.
Note: Scenario 1 takes into account all firms with an estimated probability of using sophisticated digital technologies for business administration or operations planning, regardless of their financial situation. Scenario 2 restricts to those firms with gross profits large enough to cover the investment value in at least two years. Scenario 3 is the most restrictive, as it also excludes those firms with assets valued at lower than the median of the digitalized firms in their sector or size group, as a proxy of facing financial constraints.

but their productivity is 0.25 standard deviation lower. Furthermore, 46 percent of firms with the potential to digitalize are small, 35 percent are medium size, and 19 percent are large. Closing this financing gap will make an important contribution to completing digitalization, specifically by facilitating the adoption of digital technologies.

The interplay between available finance and the adoption of technology is nuanced, especially for micro-, small, and medium-size enterprises (MSMEs). Among firms with the potential to digitalize, 30 percent do not have the required asset levels to obtain traditional loans. Limited access to financial markets, insufficient liquidity, inadequate collateral, lack of financial literacy, and poor infrastructure complicate this relationship, further limiting the potential of these firms to digitalize.

Reducing the Cost of Financial Capital

The cost of capital, a significant barrier to technology adoption and digitalization in African economies, is the anticipated return investors expect to compensate for associated risks. The cost of capital consists of three elements: first, the risk-free rate of return that applies to all investments and serves as a baseline; second, country-level risk premiums that reflect the extra required yield for elevated risk in a specific country for potential defaults or exchange rate depreciations (a country's premium is computed by comparing the interest on its bonds with the interest on bonds for a country considered low risk that acts as a benchmark); and third, returns address project or sector-level risks. The average country risk premium is higher in Africa than in other regions, which contributes to higher cost of capital. In addition, markets assign a higher risk to sectors associated with new technologies or digitalization (refer to figure 6.8), which makes investments in those sectors likely more costly.

Traditional financial institutions generally rely on standardized financial records and credit histories to make credit decisions. However, many African companies, especially those in the informal economy, lack this track record, making it difficult for small and medium-size firms to access finance for technology investments. Moreover, the speed with which technology can become obsolete further complicates matters, making it difficult to assess the software's durability and the return on investment. Furthermore, the lack of technical skills to test, deploy, and maintain software adds uncertainty for financial institutions, further limiting their willingness to fund such projects.

Emerging digital credit markets provide more streamlined loan approval processes, which considerably lower transaction costs. An analysis of M-Shwari, a digital banking solution in Kenya, by Suri, Bharadwaj, and Jack (2021) revealed that digital loans complement rather than substitute for existing credit sources. Recent mobile money–based solutions relying on machine learning methods predict repayment of credit from mobile phone metadata and have shown a good prediction performance that could allow access for unbanked individuals, potentially helping microbusinesses (Björkegren and Grissen 2020). In addition to the potential of digital credit markets, digitalization (for example, mobile money) can facilitate access to traditional finance (refer to box 6.3).

FIGURE 6.8

Average Sector-Specific Risk across Emerging Markets and Developing Economies Using Industry Betas

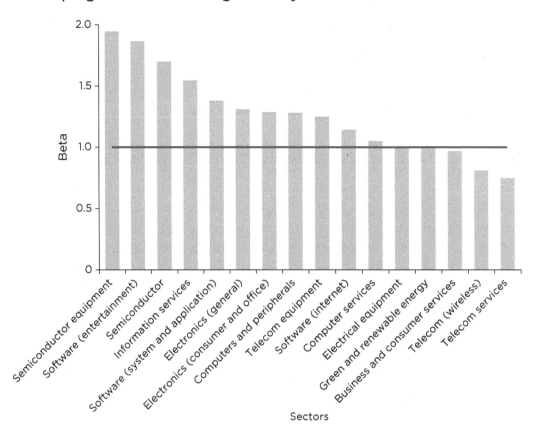

Source: Damodaran (2023).
Note: The beta quantifies the volatility of a stock or portfolio relative to the overall market, within the Capital Asset Pricing Model (CAPM). The CAPM is a financial model that describes the relationship between the expected return of an investment and its risk. Beta equals 1, indicated by the horizontal line, implies that a stock's price is expected to move with the market. Equities with a beta greater than 1 are considered more volatile than the market, meaning they might offer higher returns but come with higher risk. Telecom = telecommunications.

Recent research (for example, Meli, Djoumessi, and Djiogap 2022) also underscores the value of financial education for enhancing mobile banking uptake, highlighting the need for a comprehensive approach to improving both access to finance and adoption of technology among MSMEs.

One of the most pressing issues is the perceived high risk associated with investing in MSMEs and tech-focused firms, which is exacerbated by rapid technological changes and businesses' lack of tangible assets to use as collateral. Traditional financial institutions often see these factors as barriers, leading to high interest rates and stringent collateral requirements. This is particularly evident in the African context, where the funding gap for MSMEs was estimated at $417 billion in 2018/19.[3]

BOX 6.3

Combining Mobile Money with Traditional Financial Services Boosts Productivity

A recent study investigates the effects on labor productivity in Africa of combining mobile money use with access to traditional financial services (Konte and Tetteh 2023). Specifically, the paper builds on previous work that shows that mobile money can reduce financial transaction costs (Jack and Suri 2014) and facilitate access to trade credit and loans (Beck et al., 2018; Gosavi 2018). The paper shows that firm labor productivity is enhanced by synergistic effects of mobile money when used along with traditional financial services such as bank credit and account ownership.

Drawing on firm-level data from the World Bank Enterprise Survey across 14 Sub-Saharan African countries, the analysis reveals that although traditional financial services had a significant positive effect on labor productivity, mobile money alone did not show a robust impact. However, the combined use of both financial avenues leads to increased productivity. Specifically, combining access to bank capital with mobile money use increases productivity by 22 percent compared with firms that do not use any of these services (refer to figure B6.3.1). The findings are stronger for small and medium-size enterprises in which high-value and low-value transactions coexist. Mobile money is cost-effective in low-value transactions, whereas traditional financial services are relatively cheaper for high-value transactions. Furthermore, because small and medium-size firms are more financially constrained, receiving resources from banks and, at the same time, benefiting from transaction cost reduction offered by mobile money leads to higher productivity.

The untapped potential for private sector investment in mobile money platforms is striking. For instance, partnerships between commercial banks and mobile network operators could yield value-added products, facilitating digital credits to small and medium-size enterprises by leveraging transaction records as a new form of credit scoring. Through such collaborations, mobile money can directly elevate firm performance, particularly for firms with limited access to traditional financial avenues. Strategic enhancements, such as enabling bank-to-mobile money interoperability and increasing daily transaction limits, could further amplify this complementarity.

continued

BOX 6.3 *(Continued)*

FIGURE B6.3.1

Effects of Finance and Mobile Money on Productivity

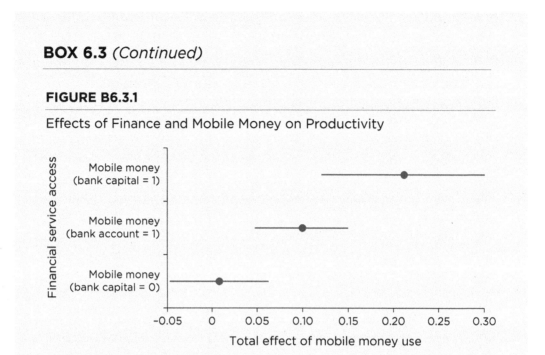

Source: Konte and Tetteh (2023).
Note: Dots indicate the estimated effect, and the extended lines surrounding them indicate the 90 percent confidence interval surrounding the estimate. Bank capital = 1 for firms that have a part or all of their working capital financed by traditional banks and 0 otherwise. The bank account dummy takes a value of 1 for firms that have a checking or savings account in a bank.

Another crucial issue is the role of the informal economy, which widens the gap between information about a given firm available to its owners and managers and their potential financiers. A considerable part of economic activity in African countries occurs outside formal financial systems. As a result, financing is lower, particularly for microbusinesses and young businesses that lack collateral accessible to larger, more established firms (Atiyas and Dutz 2023).

The financial constraints that firms face to acquiring technology, along with the many associated market failures, require policy responses. First, there is a need for financial sector regulatory reforms, such as the establishment of better credit infrastructure to ease access to capital for technology adoption and innovation. Furthermore, research has shown that credit enhancement tools such as partial credit guarantees can boost lenders' risk tolerance (Begazo, Blimpo, and Dutz 2023). It is also necessary to support and generate incentives for banks to improve their risk management as well as the quality of information, including credit bureau coverage, use of nontraditional sources, and the reform of secured transaction regimes, which can support the productivity and growth of enterprises (Ghassibe, Appendino, and Mahmoudi 2019).

To ameliorate such constraints, financial institutions are increasingly accepting innovative types of collateral, such as movable assets and intangibles (future sales, inventories, and cash flows). This increases the number of firms with access to finance by 10 percent on average, reduces interest rates, and extends terms, in particular for smaller and younger firms (Love, Martínez Pería, and Singh 2016). Digital collateral, an emerging form of securing lending that uses lockout technology to disable the flow of services remotely, can also reduce this credit market friction. Using a field experiment evaluation, Gertler, Green, and Wolfram (2021) found that digital collateral led to higher loan repayment and profitability for lenders.

Moreover, clear frameworks for data protection and cybersecurity can give firms the confidence to adopt digital solutions. For example, whereas cloud technologies provide computing and storage capacity at a lower cost, data privacy concerns and market concentration have deterred their broader adoption by businesses (Bayuo et al., 2022; McKinsey 2018). It is also important to ensure that tax policies targeted to digital services, especially mobile money, do not end up generating obstacles for digital adoption or disproportionally affecting lower-income households and small businesses.[4]

DFIs also have a role in supporting the flow of credit to small and medium-size enterprises intending to adopt digital technologies. For example, blended finance can offer guarantees, especially in underserved markets and for sectors such as agriculture and climate, which are critical for food security and sustainability, respectively. DFIs can also support capacity-building initiatives for financial institutions to develop expertise and knowledge for effectively assessing and financing tech adoption projects. This includes advisory services to enhance the capability of financial institutions to evaluate the viability and impact of tech adoption initiatives by small and medium-size firms (Begazo, Blimpo, and Dutz 2023).

Notes

1. "The process of selling off an investment in a company, typically through a merger, acquisition, or initial public offering (IPO), to generate a profit or return on investment" (Investopedia 2021).
2. We define *capital constrained firms* as those nondigitalized firms that have lower capital levels than the median digitalized firm in their size–sector–country group.
3. This figure is based on 2018/19 MSME financing gap data (IFC 2017).
4. See, for example, the case of Uganda, where a 0.5 percent tax on mobile money withdrawals generated an immediate 24 percent drop in transactions (Clifford 2020) and disproportionally affected the poor (ICTD 2021; IMF 2019; UNCDF 2021).

References

Abate, Gashaw Tadesse, Shahidur Rashid, Carlo Borzaga, and Kindie Getnet. 2016. "Rural Finance and Agricultural Technology Adoption in Ethiopia: Does the Institutional Design of Lending Organizations Matter?" *World Development* 84: 235–53. https://doi.org/10.1016/j.worlddev.2016.03.003.

Atiyas, Izak, and Mark A. Dutz. 2023. "Digital Technology Uses among Microbusinesses: Why Is Productive Use So Low across Sub-Saharan Africa?" Policy Research Working Paper 10280, World Bank, Washington, DC.

Bayuo, Blaise, Roxanne Bamford, Belinda Baah, Judith Mwaya, Chizi Gakuo, and Sophie Tholstrup. 2022. *Supercharging Africa's Startups: The Continent's Path to Tech Excellence.* London: Tony Blair Institute for Global Change. https://institute.global/policy/supercharging -africasstartups-continents-path-tech-excellence.

Beck, T., H. Pamuk, R. Ramrattan, and B. R. Uras. 2018. "Payment Instruments, Finance and Development." *Journal of Development Economics* 133: 162–86. https://doi.org/10.1016/j .jdeveco.2018.01.005.

Begazo, Tania, Moussa Blimpo, and Mark Dutz. 2023. *Digital Africa: Technological Transformation for Jobs.* Washington, DC: World Bank. https://doi.org/10.1596/978-1-4648-1737-3.

Bertrand, Marianne, and Sendhil Mullainathan. 2004. "Are Emily and Greg More Employable than Lakisha and Jamal? A Field Experiment on Labor Market Discrimination." *American Economic Review* 94 (4): 991–1013.

Björkegren, Daniel, and Darrell Grissen. 2020. "Behavior Revealed in Mobile Phone Usage Predicts Credit Repayment." *World Bank Economic Review* 34 (3): 618–34. https://doi.org/10.1093/wber /lhz006.

Briter Bridges. 2023. "Africa's Regional Innovation Ecosystem Mappings." https://briterbridges.com /regional-mappings.

Cirera, Xavier, Diego Comin, and Marcio Cruz. 2022. *Bridging the Technological Divide: Technology Adoption by Firms in Developing Countries.* Washington, DC: World Bank. https://doi.org /10.1596/978-1-4648-1826-4.

Cirera, Xavier, Diego Comin, Marcio Cruz, and Santiago Reyes. 2024. "The 'Incomplete' Digitalization of Firms in Africa." Background paper, World Bank Group, Washington, DC.

Clifford, Killian. 2020. "The Causes and Consequences of Mobile Money Taxation: An Examination of Mobile Money Transaction Taxes in Sub-Saharan Africa." GSMA, London. https://www .gsma.com/mobilefordevelopment/wp-content/uploads/2020/06/GSMA_The-causes-and -consequences-of-mobile-money-taxation.pdf.

Colonnelli, Emanuele, Marcio Cruz, Mariana Pereira-López, Tommaso Porzio, and Chun Zhao. 2024. "Startups in Africa." Unpublished manuscript, International Finance Corporation, Washington, DC.

Colonnelli, Emanuele, Bo Li, and Ernest Liu. 2024. "Investing with the Government: A Field Experiment in China." *Journal of Political Economy* 132 (1): 248–94.

Cruz, Marcio, Mark A. Dutz, and Carlos Rodríguez-Castelán. 2022. *Digital Senegal for Inclusive Growth: Technological Transformation for Better and More Jobs.* Washington, DC: World Bank. https://doi.org/10.1596/978-1-4648-1687-1.

Cusolito, Ana Paula, Ernest Dautovic, and David McKenzie. 2021. "Can Government Intervention Make Firms More Investment Ready? A Randomized Experiment in the Western Balkans." *Review of Economics and Statistics* 103 (3): 428–42.

Damodaran, Aswath. 2023. "Damodaran Online." https://pages.stern.nyu.edu/~adamodar/.

Devine, Hilary, Adrian Peralta Alva, Hoda Selim, Preya Sharma, Ludger Wocken, and Luc Eyraud. 2021. "Private Finance for Development: Wishful Thinking or Thinking Out of the Box?" Departmental Paper 2021/011, International Monetary Fund, Washington, DC.

Gertler, Paul, Brett Green, and Catherine Wolfram. 2021. "Digital Collateral." Working Paper 28724, National Bureau of Economic Research, Cambridge, MA.

Ghassibe, Mishel, Maximiliano Appendino, and Samir Elsadek Mahmoudi. 2019. "SME Financial Inclusion for Sustained Growth in the Middle East and Central Asia." IMF Working Paper 209, International Monetary Fund, Washington, DC.

Gonzalez-Uribe, Juanita, and Ouafaa Hmaddi. 2022. "The Multi-Dimensional Impacts of Business Accelerators: What Does the Research Tell Us?" Working Paper 115461, London School of Economics and Political Science, LSE Library, London.

Gosavi, Aparna. 2018. "Can Mobile Money Help Firms Mitigate the Problem of Access to Finance in Eastern Sub-Saharan Africa?" *Journal of African Business* 19 (3): 343–60. https://doi.org/10.1080 /15228916.2017.1396791.

ICTD (International Centre for Tax and Development). 2021. "There and Back Again: The Making of Uganda's Mobile Money Tax: Summary of ICTD Working Paper 123 by Adrienne Lees and Doris Akol." Research in Brief 72. ICTD, Brighton, UK. https://opendocs.ids.ac.uk/opendocs/bitstream /handle/20.500.12413/16873/ICTD_RiB_%2072_Uganda_2.0A.pdf?sequence=1&isAllowed=y.

IFC (International Finance Corporation). 2017. "MSME Finance Gap: Assessment of the Shortfalls and Opportunities in Financing Micro, Small and Medium Enterprises in Emerging Markets." IFC, Washington, DC. https://www.ifc.org/content/dam/ifc/doc/mgrt/121264-wp -public-msmereportfinal.pdf.

IFC (International Finance Corporation). 2022. "IFC Invests in AXIAN Telecom Bond to Support Digital Connectivity in Africa." Press release, February 9, 2022. https://pressroom.ifc.org/all /pages/PressDetail.aspx?ID=26816.

IFC (International Finance Corporation). 2023. "IFC Partners with Orange Bank Africa to Increase Digital Lending for Small Businesses in West Africa." Press release, July 3, 2023. https://pressroom .ifc.org/all/pages/PressDetail.aspx?ID=27645.

IMF (International Monetary Fund). 2019. *Uganda: 2019 Article IV Consultation—Press Release; Staff Report; and Statement by the Executive Director for Uganda.* IMF Country Report 19/125. Washington, DC: IMF.

Investment Climate Reform Facility. 2021. "Startup Acts: An Emerging Instrument to Foster the Development of Innovative High-Growth Firms." https://www.icr-facility.eu/event/startup-acts -an-emerging-instrument-to-foster-the-development-of-innovative-high-growth-firms/.

Investopedia. 2021. "Exit." https://www.investopedia.com/terms/e/exit.asp.

Jack, William, and Tavneet Suri. 2014. "Risk Sharing and Transactions Costs: Evidence from Kenya's Mobile Money Revolution." *American Economic Review* 104 (1): 183–223. https://doi.org/10.1257 /aer.104.1.183.

Jaoui, Fadel, Omolola Amoussou, and Francis H. Kemeze. 2022. "'Catch Me If You Can' on Drivers of Venture Capital Investment in Africa." *African Development Review* 34 (S1): S117–40. https://doi.org/10.1111/1467-8268.12655.

Kessler, Judd B., Corinne Low, and Colin D. Sullivan. 2019. "Incentivized Resume Rating: Eliciting Employer Preferences without Deception." *American Economic Review* 109 (11): 3713–44.

Konte, Maty, and Godsway Korku Tetteh. 2023. "Mobile Money, Traditional Financial Services and Firm Productivity in Africa." *Small Business Economics* 60 (2): 745–69. https://doi.org/10.1007 /s11187-022-00613-w.

Love, Inessa, María Soledad Martínez Pería, and Sandeep Singh. 2016. "Collateral Registries for Movable Assets: Does Their Introduction Spur Firms' Access to Bank Financing?" *Journal of Financial Services Research* 49: 1–37.

McKinsey. 2018. "Creating Value with the Cloud." *Digital McKinsey: Insights.* December. https://www.mckinsey.com/~/media/McKinsey/Business%20Functions/McKinsey%20Digital/Our%20Insights/Creating%20value%20with%20the%20cloud%20compendium/Creating-value-with-the-cloud.ashx.

Meli, Steve Douanla, Yannick Fosso Djoumessi, and Constant Fouropi Djiogap. 2022. "Analysis of the Socio-Economic Determinants of Mobile Money Adoption and Use in Cameroon." *Telecommunications Policy* 46 (9): 102412. https://doi.org/10.1016/j.telpol.2022.102412.

OECD (Organisation for Economic Co-operation and Development). 2023. "Mobilisation." OECD. Stat (accessed March 13, 2024). https://stats.oecd.org/Index.aspx?DataSetCode=DV_DCD_MOBILISATION.

Suri, Tavneet, Prashant Bharadwaj, and William Jack. 2021. "Fintech and Household Resilience to Shocks: Evidence from Digital Loans in Kenya." *Journal of Development Economics* 153: 102697. https://doi.org/10.1016/j.jdeveco.2021.102697.

UNCDF (United Nations Capital Development Fund). 2021. *The Impact of Mobile Money Taxation in Uganda.* New York: UNCDF. https://www.uncdf.org/Download/AdminFileWithFilename?id=16141&cultureId=127&filename=the-impact-of-mobile-money-taxation-in-ugandapdf.

CHAPTER 7

Policies to Unlock Digital Private Investment

Zineb Benkirane, Marcio Cruz, and Mariana Pereira-López

Key Messages

- Policies are needed to support tech entrepreneurs in developing and adapting digital technologies for the local operating context. Likewise, policies need to facilitate firm adoption and use of digital technologies for productive purposes. This requires implementing complementary actions, from regulatory reforms to firm-level interventions, that affect firm inputs, outputs, and capabilities, as well as incentives to attract high-talent entrepreneurs to innovative and disruptive businesses.

- Reducing the cost of trading digital goods and facilitating the integration of digital services would make technology more affordable in Africa. Despite Africa's heavy reliance on imports from outside the continent, it still has one of the highest applied tariffs on digital goods globally. The African Continental Free Trade Area is expected to reduce prices and increase the imports of digital goods. Yet, the current and proposed coverage of tariff reductions on digital goods is limited, given that tariff reductions target intra-region trade, and most of these goods are sourced outside Africa.

- Broader regulatory reforms are needed to boost competition, reduce risk, and encourage further private investment in digital infrastructure, innovative start-ups, and digital adoption by businesses. Operationally speaking, these reforms should start at a small scale to incentivize and pilot private sector–led innovations. Infrastructure sharing can facilitate competition and reduce deployment costs to improve connectivity. In low-income countries, priority reforms should focus on increasing access to digital enablers, such as internet and devices, complemented by actions to facilitate the productive use of digital technologies by businesses and making digital adoption more affordable. Middle-income countries more advanced in digitalization should prioritize reforms enabling fuller use of digital technologies for productive purposes.

Introduction

This chapter analyzes the role of policies in facilitating fuller use of digitalization, including reforms to foster private sector investment in this domain. The chapter first posits that stimulating private investment in digitalization requires action in various complementary areas. Second, it analyzes how trade policy can foster digital adoption through further market integration, with in-depth estimates of the potential impact of the African Continental Free Trade Area (AfCFTA). Third, it provides further examples of regulatory reforms, sectoral investments, and firm-level interventions, including a discussion on how country priorities may vary according to country income level. Finally, the chapter considers how various stakeholders can support actions to unlock private investment opportunities in the digital space.

The Role of Policies

The scope of the policies required to unlock private investments that could enhance firm digitalization is broad. They encompass various complementary elements, such as access to electricity, human capital, regulations, competition, and access to finance for enabling the productive use of technologies. Recent academic publications and various reports from the World Bank Group have emphasized several policies to support technology upgrading.[1] The design of these policies must be tailored to each country's local context. Box 7.1 provides a checklist for the design of these policies and more specific recommendations for the African context.

New evidence presented in this book can inform actions that policy makers, development finance institutions (DFIs), trade organizations, and investors in various domains, such as trade and market integration, need to undertake. Other areas, discussed in previous chapters, refer to regulatory reforms to enhance the impact of investments in digital infrastructure (refer to chapter 4), the potential market failures and opportunities for private investments in digital solutions (refer to chapter 5), and the benefits from broader access to finance, linking the needs of different end users of finance with digitalization (refer to chapter 6).

BOX 7.1

Policy Priorities: Diagnostic Checklist to Facilitate Technology Adoption

Previous work undertaken as part of the World Bank Productivity Project series has pointed to several policy recommendations for boosting technology adoption by firms. The following steps would need to be embedded in a country's firm technology adoption framework to design effective policies:

- Identify the types and sizes of the market failures.
- Assess the quality of infrastructure.
- Identify regulatory bottlenecks.
- Facilitate access to finance for technology upgrading.
- Institutionalize an open trade regime that supports access to external knowledge and technology.
- Build institutions to address coordination failures in the provision of information and training of the workforce in the availability and use of digital technologies.
- Improve the provision of and the markets for business advisory and technology extension services.
- Enhance awareness, improve targeting mechanisms for government support, and strengthen government capabilities.

Beyond suggestions for policy makers and public agencies, the private sector can benefit from diagnostic tools and instruments for technology upgrading at the firm level (for example, business advisory services, technology extension services, technology centers, and finance instruments, including grants and vouchers). Cirera, Comin, and Cruz (2022) provide further detail, combined with evidence from the World Bank's Firm-level Adoption of Technology survey. They also emphasize the importance of the supply side of technology in driving adoption.

The World Bank's 2023 report *Digital Africa: Technological Transformation for Jobs* (Begazo, Blimpo, and Dutz 2023) emphasizes the impact of digital and complementary technologies on jobs and poverty reduction. The analysis focuses on improving internet affordability and infrastructure, innovation and education policies, and digital inclusion. Policies to promote affordability and access

continued

BOX 7.1 *(Continued)*

to infrastructure highlighted in the study include pro-competition regulation in areas such as licensing. Innovation policies aim at enabling enterprises and households to use digital technologies more productively and provide inclusive applications to consumers. To facilitate the widespread use of digital technologies, increased access to business advisory services, technology information, skills training, along with long-term investments in high-quality secondary and tertiary education, are among the available instruments.

Amin and Gallegos (2023) discuss the importance of affordable devices for all, focusing on internet-enabled mobile devices for individuals in developing countries. Hence, their policy recommendations center on boosting the affordability of internet-enabled devices in low- and middle-income countries, focusing on areas such as reducing import duties and other taxes on these devices and offering subsidies or financial incentives to both manufacturers and consumers. Moreover, financing initiatives, such as microloans or pay-as-you-go models, make devices more accessible. Fostering local digital content and services drives demand, and developing digital literacy programs enhances user capabilities.

Trade and Market Integration Policies

Effective trade policies can make digital technologies more affordable and foster their adoption. Simplified import and export regulations, along with the reduction of tariffs on technology products, can streamline the firm-level acquisition processes of equipment and digital tools. In this context, the AfCFTA trade agreement (officially started in 2021, encompassing 54 African Union member states) seeks to foster economic integration by progressively eliminating tariffs between members on 90 percent of traded goods, promoting trade in services, and implementing rules of origin to ensure preferential treatment of products. Beyond goods and services, the AfCFTA covers investment, intellectual property rights, and competition policy. By 2030, the AfCFTA has the potential to create a single market of more than 1.3 billion people with a combined gross domestic product exceeding $3 trillion. The agreement sets varying timelines for cutting tariffs based on countries' respective development levels.

The AfCFTA is expected to lower tariffs on digital goods, but the overall regionwide impact on imports for these goods might be minimal. Simulations from a background study for this book (Bastos, Castro, and Cruz 2024) indicate that, for the region as a whole, imports of digital goods are expected to grow by only 0.3 percent and exports by 1.0 percent on average. This result stems from the fact that AfCFTA members are not currently targeting significant reductions in tariffs for countries that are not signatories of the agreement (refer to box 7.2). Country-specific estimates suggest, however, that a few countries could see higher digital imports, while exports could rise by as much as 6.0 percent compared with the baseline.

AfCFTA would lead to much higher trade in a counterfactual scenario with elimination of external tariffs of digital goods. A counterfactual scenario with full liberalization of digital goods suggests that imports of these products would increase by 8.0 percent, compared with 0.3 percent in the current AfCFTA setup, and exports would increase by 3.0 percent, compared with 1.0 percent in the baseline scenario. For several countries, the increase in imports of digital goods would be closer to or larger than 20.0 percent (Bastos, Castro, and Cruz 2024).

Regional initiatives such as the African Union's Digital Transformation Strategy for Africa (2020–30) aim to secure a digital single market by 2030. This strategy dovetails with existing programs, such as the Policy and Regulation Initiative for Digital Africa, focusing on a range of goals, including economic growth, job creation, and poverty eradication. The Digital Economy Initiative for Africa supports these ambitions by targeting comprehensive digital enablement by 2030.

Besides offering a broader set of alternatives for those adopting technology, conducive trade policy can also expand markets of tech start-ups supplying digital applications. Regional integration and regulatory convergence (capital requirements, taxes, standards, intellectual property, and so forth) can facilitate the expansion of markets for digital solutions. Start-ups can access larger markets and, therefore, benefit from better potential for scaling up in other countries on the continent, further enhancing their appeal to investors. Furthermore, the harmonization of standards and regulations reduces regulatory compliance costs, allowing start-ups to allocate resources more efficiently and focus on creating innovative solutions. It also reduces uncertainty for investors. An example of this market expansion is the case of interoperability in payment systems, which would enable mobile payment providers to have a larger potential market.

Trade integration and the reduction of uncertainty resulting from trade agreements can also contribute to attracting foreign direct investment (FDI). According to the United Nations Conference on Trade and Development (UNCTAD 2023), Africa captured only 3.5 percent of global FDI inflows in 2022. In the framework of the AfCFTA, a Protocol on Investment was adopted in 2023 to create a coherent and unified continental investment framework. It also establishes a Pan-African Trade and Investment Agency for investment promotion, technical support, and investment facilitation. These actions can support further integration into the global value chain.

BOX 7.2

Will the African Continental Free Trade Area Reduce Prices and Increase Trade of Digital Goods in Africa?

Africa has low import penetration for digital goods compared with the global average, and intra-African trade in digital goods remains minimal. In 2019, Africa imported $59.4 billion worth of digital goods, with 35.0 percent sourced from China and 27.0 percent from the European Union. Digital goods constitute a smaller share of African manufacturing imports (about 20.0 percent) compared with the rest of the world (around 30.0 percent). The Arab Republic of Egypt, Nigeria, South Africa, and Tunisia collectively account for 56.0 percent of Africa's digital goods imports.

Despite its heavy reliance on imports from outside the region, Africa imposes one of the highest applied tariffs on digital goods globally. These tariffs have remained relatively constant in Africa, in contrast to significant declines observed in non-African countries over the past decade. Tariff protection on digital goods varies across countries and correlates negatively with income per capita, with tariffs ranging between 0 and 15 percent. Tariffs on digital goods are near 10 percent in large economies (measured by population size), such as Ethiopia, Ghana, and Nigeria.

Despite the comprehensive liberalization expected from AfCFTA, our analysis indicates that the agreement is unlikely to have a significant impact on reducing tariff protection on digital goods in Africa. Hence, the import-weighted tariff on these products is expected to decrease by only 0.3 percentage point, from 6.3 to 6.0 percent, on average, across countries, because of the agreement (refer to figure B7.2.1, panel a). Despite tariff reductions of 4.4 percentage points, from 4.9 to 0.5, on average, within AfCFTA members (refer to figure B7.2.1, panel b), there is an absence of tariff reductions on imports of digital goods from outside of the trade area, which constitute most digital goods imports. To cut costs, AfCFTA negotiations should consider including tariff concessions on digital goods imports from nonmember countries. Cost reduction would be more pronounced for the poorest countries with the highest tariffs on digital goods.

continued

BOX 7.2 *(Continued)*

FIGURE B7.2.1

Expected Change in Tariffs after Implementation of the AfCFTA by 2030

Source: Bastos, Castro, and Cruz (2024).
Note: Country-level estimates are based on Import-weighted tariffs. AfCFTA = African Continental Free Trade Area.

Finally, further market integration can also enhance technology upgrade by expanding the opportunities related to the market size of firms in general. Extensive literature focused on export promotion activities has shown that more information and exposure to external markets tends to increase the likelihood of exporting (Olarreaga, Sperlich, and Trachsel 2020), which is also associated with improved performance and digital adoption. Furthermore, evidence suggests that further exposure to export markets increases the likelihood of adopting more advanced technologies (Atkin, Khandelwal, and Osman 2017; Cirera, Comin, and Cruz 2022; Lileeva and Trefler 2010). New evidence for Tunisia, based on an ongoing experiment on export promotion, suggests that some of these initiatives can have significant effects on export performance for treated firms (Ali et al., 2024).

Broader Regulatory Reforms and Public Programs

This section discusses broader regulatory reforms that would increase investment opportunities in digital businesses in Africa. They include infrastructure sharing and data protection, start-up acts, financial regulations, sectoral and competition policies, and firm-level interventions.

Infrastructure Sharing and Data Protection

Infrastructure sharing and access to essential infrastructure can improve competition and reduce deployment costs of telecommunications services.[2] Challenges such as regulatory capacity, dispute-resolution mechanisms, incentives for first-mover advantage, lack of trust, and technological issues hinder successful implementation of regulatory reforms. Evidence from chapter 4 also suggests that a national broadband strategy can enhance the benefits of investments in digital infrastructure through price reductions. Lack of regulation regarding access to the fiber optic backbone is also a limitation, with a significant portion controlled by state-owned enterprises or operators with state shareholdings. Tower companies play a crucial role in network deployment and passive infrastructure sharing, leading to substantial cost savings. Estimates across six African countries suggest potential price reductions from sharing infrastructure in rural areas of up to 52 percent per user for monthly broadband internet connection costs (Oughton 2023). Yet, mandatory infrastructure sharing can sometimes create barriers to expansion, as seen in cases in which authorization is required to deploy fiber infrastructure, potentially duplicating or competing with existing incumbents.

Universal Service Funds (USFs), when well structured and governed, can help extend telecommunications and broadband services to underserved or unconnected areas. USFs can be financed through levies on telecom operators. Most countries in Africa have introduced or are in the process of introducing USFs (Okeleke, Bahia, and Borole

2023). The implementation of USFs often includes the creation of infrastructure in rural or remote regions where it would otherwise be commercially unviable for private operators to establish networks. By offering subsidies or financial incentives, these funds encourage telecom providers to extend their services into these less profitable areas. Additionally, they might support initiatives to provide affordable devices and connections, as well as digital literacy programs to enable effective use of these technologies.

Several emerging countries that have had successful experiences with building public infrastructure can serve as examples for Africa. India has been in the forefront of building digital public infrastructure, based on a triad of identity, payments, and data management. This process has been established through public–private partnerships. India is building public infrastructure to facilitate innovation through digital platforms and further use of digital technologies by individuals and firms. For example, by generating records of digital transactions in a framework that facilitates standardized data sharing while protecting data privacy, this system can reduce asymmetric information in the credit market. In doing so, it enables the use of data as a collateral to micro- and small businesses (Alonso et al., 2023; Dixit 2023). This framework can also enable further applications of artificial intelligence (AI), including ongoing activities with chatbots, to support farmers and innovations by local tech start-ups (Nilekani and Bhojwani 2023). Other experiences, such as Brazil's instant payment system (Pix), can provide additional options for the public sector to strengthen competition and stimulate innovation in the financial sector (Saiyid 2023).

Moreover, clear frameworks for data protection and cybersecurity can give firms the confidence to adopt digital solutions, because they provide certainty regarding compliance. Technology clusters and innovation hubs, supported or established by governments, can act as incubators where start-ups, academic institutions, and established firms collaborate on technology solutions. On the financing side, governments can enhance access to capital for techcentric small and medium enterprises (SMEs) through low-interest loans or grants or by bolstering the venture capital ecosystem.

Start-Up Acts

Governments in Africa are increasingly promoting start-ups through comprehensive legislation and regulatory frameworks. These reforms usually aim at fostering entrepreneurship and enabling the development of new high-growth firms (start-up acts). For example, Senegal and Tunisia have already embraced this approach, and 16 other countries are reportedly in the process of doing so (ICR 2021). The Tunisian Startup Act includes a legal framework that simplifies the start-up launching process. It also incorporates targeted incentives such as grants, tax benefits, and subsidies for patent registration, as well as employment programs to develop skills. Moreover, it includes financial system measures, entitling new firms to issue convertible bonds, a Startup Guarantee fund, foreign exchange accounts to promote internationalization, and special conditions for customs.

For these initiatives to succeed, a participatory approach involving various ecosystem stakeholders, including the recipients of these policies, combined with rigorous impact evaluation are critical. Broader participation is needed to better understand the needs and ensure the right instruments and incentives are in place for all ecosystem members and not designed to disproportionately benefit entrepreneurs with stronger political connections. For instance, in Senegal, the design of the Startup Act consisted of a wide consultative and participatory process of the entrepreneurial community. However, despite the importance of experimenting with new regulatory solutions to incentivize new business models, evidence of their impact is still lacking. Therefore, policy makers need to embed monitoring and evaluation frameworks to make the necessary adjustments toward implementation.

The development of challenge funds and business plan competitions that solicit motivated and bright entrepreneurs constitute an additional pathway to foster entrepreneurship. Evidence from business plan competitions in Nigeria suggests that these competitions can spur high-growth entrepreneurship (McKenzie 2017). However, they should be accompanied with extensive capacity building for interested entrepreneurs to create quality business plans and put forward realistic and feasible ideas. Targeted communication campaigns are also needed to ensure that business competitions reach the right people and attract innovative and scalable digital projects, including actions that improve the network of local entrepreneurs with foreign investors. The incentives could also target country- or subregional-specific bottlenecks that could enhance the productivity of other businesses.

Financial Regulations

Several financial sector regulators have established frameworks that allow small-scale, live testing of innovations by private firms in a controlled environment. Such flexibility, defined as "regulatory sandbox," could expedite the approval process for new types of financing or risk-assessment methods aimed at technology adoption. This would encourage more financial institutions to offer innovative financing options at lower rates, ultimately reducing the cost of capital for firms. An example of such a framework is the Sierra Leone Sandbox, created by the Bank of Sierra Leone in collaboration with development partners (World Bank 2020). The primary objective of this initiative is to stimulate demand for financial services by allowing businesses to pilot innovative solutions before they are fully introduced to the market. In doing so, the sandbox reduces the regulatory uncertainty and financial risks associated with deploying new technologies or services.

Regulatory support for further integration of mobile money platforms can enhance technology adoption rates. The surge of mobile money in Africa has required some innovations in terms of regulations and institutions (Suri et al., 2023). Many regulatory challenges are associated with mobile money, given the need to foster the adoption of advanced solutions while safeguarding competition and protecting customers. Thus, regulations might need to be designed at the component level, including customer registration, exchange and storage of e-money, foreign transfers, and interoperability (Aron 2017; Suri et al., 2023).

Sectoral and Competition Policies

Regulatory reforms that boost competition incentivize firms to develop, adopt, and use technology more effectively. Pro-competition regulation is critical across many dimensions, starting with a regulatory environment stimulating price reduction among internet service providers, new entry and expansion of tech start-ups, and firms adopting better technologies to be more competitive. Evidence has shown that for firms to adopt and use technologies more effectively, they need the appropriate incentives, which depend on the competition environment (Iacovone, Pereira-López, and Schiffbauer 2023).

There are significant synergies between the digital and climate transition agendas in Africa. Investments in electricity often require public investments in distribution and transmission networks as well as subsidies for private investments in renewables to compensate for carbon externalities.[3] Synergies between the digital and education agendas also exist. Reducing gaps in skills and capabilities requires public as well as private investment in education. Finally, the need for skills-appropriate digital apps and new technologies requires specific subsidies and other enabling mechanisms for digital entrepreneurs.

Given the prominence of agriculture in the region, conducive agricultural tech (agtech) policies and strategies can have broad-based benefits. Nonetheless, only a few African countries have so far developed national digital agriculture policies. Countries should prioritize the development of agtech policies and institutional frameworks to create an enabling environment for agtech research and innovation; incentivize investors and agtech start-ups to support local and affordable solutions for productive use, especially for low-income, low-skilled farmers; promote widespread adoption; and ensure safe and responsible use of technologies and data.

Digitalization of Government Services

While technology can be key in streamlining tax identification, detection, and collection, its use can also yield positive spillovers on digital technology's supply and demand (Okunogbe and Tourek 2024). Digitalizing tax administration stimulates firms' demand for innovative solutions to engage with the government, fostering entrepreneurial activity. Additionally, it catalyzes technology adoption across sectors, as evidenced by higher rates of voluntary e-invoicing among firms with partners mandated to adopt e-invoicing (Bellon et al., 2023). Many African countries can benefit from further from digital instruments for tax collection. Nonetheless, further research is necessary to explore these spillovers comprehensively, as well as to identify potential limitations, including incentives, costs, and data privacy and security risks, as well as understanding its political economy implications (Okunogbe and Santoro 2023).

The adoption of electronic procurement processes may also enhance competition and facilitates entry from higher quality contractors. Evidence from India and Indonesia suggests that electronic procurement has improved quality and reduced delays on infrastructure projects (Lewis-Faupel et al., 2016). E-government can also promote digital adoption by firms by simplifying their access to information and interaction with government agencies. Moreover, government procurement can also generate demand for innovative tech solutions. Health tech, for example, still appears to investors as high risk because of divergent regulations and lack of successful exits. In this context, further engagement between governments and start-ups can lead to the development of disruptive solutions with high social returns.

Firm-Level Interventions

Supportive policy mechanisms can pave the way for companies to more easily embrace new technologies. Tax incentives and subsidies, including concessional finance, when governments can afford them, can act as catalysts for firms to invest in specialized technologies or research and development initiatives and can help overcome financial hurdles encountered during technology adoption by user firms and during technology development and scaling by tech start-ups.

Training and business advisory services that improve firm capabilities can also facilitate firm-level uptake of technology. Given the critical role of firm capabilities, including digital skills and management practices, as complementary factors for firm-level digital adoption and the associated information failures (for example, "managers don't know what they don't know"), a mix of information (benchmarking) and targeted support for firms might be suitable.[4] Furthermore, training programs, accompanied by strong monitoring and evaluation, could generate complementary skills and best practices that might lead to more intensive and advanced use of technologies.

Other potential support mechanisms could be vouchers for insourcing professional managers as well as financial support for small and high-growth firms to develop these capabilities. Cirera, Comin, and Cruz (2022) emphasize the role of business advisory services, technology extension services, and technology centers. Many of these interventions have mixed results in terms of impact, but they could potentially be enhanced by closer connection with the private sector. Moreover, policies could benefit further from wide access to digital enablers as a channel that can reduce the cost of delivering information and advisory services to businesses. Recent experiments with the use of digital information provision in East Africa offer causal evidence of positive effect input purchase choices made by farmers (Fabregas et al., 2024). Other evidence from Guatemala and Mexico suggests that training sessions over videocalls through digital platforms are feasible for businesses, but the impact does not last beyond six months (Davies et al., 2024).

Priority Actions for Countries and DFIs

What are the policy implications for countries amid a wide variation in levels of digitalization of businesses? The challenge facing policy makers seeking to assess the implications at the country level is that digitalization varies within countries.[5] For example, in Kenya, the share of micro-, small, and medium (formal and informal) businesses with internet access and with a website in the county of Nairobi is above 30 percent and 20 percent, respectively, compared with below 5 percent of businesses in other areas of the country (Cruz and Hernandez Uriz 2022). These regional disparities are common across most countries in Africa.

Improving access to digital enablers, such as internet and devices, should be a priority action to support low-income countries. Access to digital enablers is disproportionately more expensive in lower-income countries (and subnational regions further from the capital city or major metropolitan areas), particularly those that are landlocked or affected by fragility and conflict. These economies need to prioritize reforms that facilitate further investment in digital infrastructure, lowering the cost of connectivity and entry-level devices. They also need to expand and upgrade their broadband infrastructure to handle the explosive growth in data, enabling broader digitalization (World Bank 2024).

When making efforts to improve infrastructure, targeted policies that facilitate the productive use of digital technologies by businesses are needed. As documented in chapter 5, tech start-ups and fully digitalized businesses tend to be concentrated in a few cities with wider access to human capital and infrastructure, a trend observed worldwide. Thus, prioritizing the diffusion of existent digital solutions and the development of simpler and more context-appropriate technologies across the continent, addressing specific local needs, can significantly benefit these regions, as well as improve trade integration to reduce the cost of digital goods as inputs for production.

The wide variation in the productive use of digital technologies across and within firms suggests that policies need to account for the specific challenges facing firms. Incomplete digitalization and the lack of productive use of digital technologies already adopted by firms are not an exclusive challenge of low-income economies. Yet, among digitally enabled businesses (those with access to devices and internet connectivity), there are levels of incomplete digitalization, suggesting that these businesses are not adopting these digital technologies to perform business functions, and if they do so, they are not using these technologies intensively as the most frequently used method to perform these tasks.

DFIs should focus their support on the implementation of pro-competitive digital infrastructure, complementing this with support for the increased uptake of firm-level productive use of digital technologies. DFI-led operations geared to governments should prioritize reforms that unlock private investment by facilitating a reduction in the cost of adoption, including those highlighted in the previous section. Regulatory reforms are needed to enhance the effects of investments in digital infrastructure on reducing the prices of internet connectivity (chapter 4), including facilitating access to dark fiber. DFI support should also focus on facilitating the entry of digital tech firms, which provide innovative digital solutions such as applications that reduce the barriers of cost, knowledge, and skills to the productive use of digital technologies (chapter 5). DFI support should also hone in on regulatory reforms coupled with concessional finance to improve access to information, reduce risk, and facilitate access to credit for tech start-ups and SMEs adopting digital technologies (chapter 6). Complementary trade reforms that reduce tariffs on digital products from outside the AfCFTA and enable further digital trade in services are needed to facilitate the adoption of higher-quality inputs by more firms, along with other policies to boost trade in digital services within African countries. Regulatory reforms that boost competition incentivize firms to adopt and use technology more effectively (Iacovone, Pereira-López, and Schiffbauer 2023).

Shifting from digital access to productive use by businesses requires further complementary actions and coordination among DFIs, government, and the private sector. A key message from the analytical findings of this book is that improving digital access through broader connectivity is not necessarily translated into wider digital use for productive purposes. This message has been emphasized by other recent studies (for example, Cirera, Comin, and Cruz 2022) and is reinforced by the more nuanced findings of this book showing that the challenge for adopting digital technologies for productive purpose goes well beyond access, as shown by the findings on incomplete digitalization. The multifaceted challenges and barriers to digital transformation in Africa require specific solutions involving commercial, public, and multilateral development bank funding.

Concluding Remarks

This book estimates a large potential market for digital upgrade among businesses in Africa. This includes more than 600,000 formal firms and up to 40 million microbusinesses that possess a high probability of digital upgrade, with characteristics similar to those of firms that already benefit from these technologies across the continent. Most of these firms already have access to digital enablers, such as mobile phones or computers with access to internet. Many of them already use mobile payments. Yet, there is significant potential to benefit from fuller use of digitalization. In many cases, particularly for small and microbusinesses, digital upgrade means that those firms can enhance their capacity to deliver and perform their tasks more efficiently.

Despite notable progress in digital infrastructure, the cost of data and connectivity in Africa remains relatively high. Additionally, machinery, equipment, and software are disproportionately expensive in the region. These barriers, coupled with a lack of other complementary factors, such as human capital, finance, demand, and firm capabilities, make the overall process of technology upgrade unattractive for many businesses.

This incomplete state of digitalization, where many businesses are already digitally enabled but face obstacles to further digitalization, presents investment opportunities for the private sector. Investments in new digital technologies have the potential to further disrupt the way in which many products across agriculture, manufacturing and services are produced and distributed, making it easier to obtain and interpret information, and in the process helping workers upgrade their skills as they work. This book emphasizes three key areas for investment:

- Investing in digital infrastructure, particularly in the middle- and last-mile segments, to leverage the potential expansion of submarine cables by 2027

- Developing digital services and applications that address the challenges of affordability and low skills, capitalizing on the increased availability and adaptability of disruptive technologies such as AI to provide tailored solutions for local businesses, and enhancing the workers' capabilities with complementary tools; and

- Increasing access to finance by improving information accessibility to reduce risks associated with digital and other productive investments.

Policy makers can facilitate these investments by implementing reforms that create a conducive business environment for digitalization.

Notes

1. See Alfaro-Serrano et al. (2021), Verhoogen (2023), World Bank (2024), and box 7.1.
2. See Begazo, Blimpo, and Dutz (2023) for further details on the potential benefits of infrastructure sharing.
3. See IEA and IFC (2023).
4. Alfaro-Serrano et al. (2021) provide a systematic review of evaluation of interventions supporting technology adoption on firms.
5. As described in chapters 1 and 2, most firms in the region (with five or more workers) already have access to digital devices, especially mobile phones, and at least half of them have access to computers and internet. There is still a large gap among lower-income countries, and within these countries there are still large disparities across regions (for example, digital update is significantly lower outside the capital cities) and firm size, with small and particularly microbusinesses being significantly deprived of digital devices and connectivity.

References

Alfaro-Serrano, David, Tanay Balantrapu, Ritam Chaurey, Ana Goicoechea, and Eric Verhoogen. 2021. "Interventions to Promote Technology Adoption in Firms: A Systematic Review." *Campbell Systematic Reviews* 17 (4): e1181. https://doi.org/10.1002/cl2.1181.

Ali, Nadia, Giacomo De Giorgi, Aminur Rahman, and Eric Verhoogen. 2024. "What Do Market-Access Subsidies Do? Experimental Evidence from Tunisia." Unpublished manuscript, Columbia University, New York, January 2024.

Alonso, C., T. Bhojwani, E. Hanedar, D. Prihardini, G. Uña, and K. Zhabska. 2023. "Stacking Up the Benefits: Lessons from India's Digital Journey." Working Paper 23/78, International Monetary Fund, Washington, DC.

Amin, Rami, and Doyle Gallegos. 2023. *Affordable Devices for All: Innovative Financing Solutions and Policy Options to Bridge Global Digital Divides.* Washington, DC: World Bank.

Aron, Janine. 2017. "'Leapfrogging': A Survey of the Nature and Economic Implications of Mobile Money." Working Paper 2017-02, Centre for the Study of African Economies, University of Oxford, Oxford, UK.

Atkin, David, Amit K. Khandelwal, and Adam Osman. 2017. "Exporting and Firm Performance: Evidence from a Randomized Experiment." *Quarterly Journal of Economics* 132 (2): 551–615. https://doi.org/10.1093/qje/qjx002.

Bastos, Paulo, Lucio Castro, and Marcio Cruz. 2024. "The Quality and Price of Africa's Imports of Digital Goods." Policy Research Working Paper 10718, World Bank, Washington, DC. http://hdl.handle.net/10986/41163.

Begazo, Tania, Moussa P. Blimpo, and Mark A. Dutz. 2023. *Digital Africa: Technological Transformation for Jobs.* Washington, DC: World Bank.

Bellon, Mattiew, Era Dabla-Norris, and Salma Khalid. 2023. "Technology and tax compliance spillovers: Evidence from a VAT e-invoicing reform in Peru." *Journal of Economic Behavior & Organization* 212 (C): 756–77. https://doi.org/10.1016/j.jebo.2023.06.004.

Cirera, Xavier, Diego Comin, and Marcio Cruz. 2022. *Bridging the Technological Divide: Technology Adoption by Firms in Developing Countries.* Washington, DC: World Bank.

Cruz, Marcio, and Zenaida Hernandez Uriz. 2022. *Entrepreneurship Ecosystems and MSMEs in Kenya: Strengthening Businesses in the Aftermath of the Pandemic.* Washington, DC: World Bank Group. https://hdl.handle.net/10986/38230.

Davies, Elwyn, Peter Deffebach, Leonardo Iacovone, and David McKenzie. 2024. "Training Microentrepreneurs over Zoom: Experimental Evidence from Mexico." *Journal of Development Economics* 167: 103244. https://doi.org/10.1016/j.jdeveco.2023.103244.

Dixit, Siddharth. 2023. "India's Digital Transformation Could Be a Game-Changer for Economic Development." *Let's Talk Development* (blog). World Bank, Washington, DC. https://blogs.worldbank.org/en/developmenttalk/indias-digital-transformation-could-be-game-changer-economic-development.

Fabregas, Raissa, Michael Kremer, Matthew Lowes, Robert On, and Giulia Zane. 2024. "Digital Information Provision and Behavior Change: Lessons from Six Experiments in East Africa." Working Paper 32048, National Bureau of Economic Research, Cambridge, MA.

Iacovone, Leonardo, Mariana Pereira-López, and Marc Schiffbauer. 2023. "Competition Makes It Better: Evidence on When Firms Use It More Effectively." *Research Policy* 52 (8): 104786. https://doi.org/10.1016/j.respol.2023.104786.

ICR (Investment Climate Reform Facility). 2021. "Startup Acts: An Emerging Instrument to Foster the Development of Innovative High-Growth Firms." ICR, Bonn. https://www.icr-facility.eu/event/startup-acts-an-emerging-instrument-to-foster-the-development-of-innovative-high-growth-firms/.

IEA (International Energy Agency) and IFC (International Finance Corporation). 2023. *Scaling Up Private Finance for Clean Energy in Emerging and Developing Economies.* Paris: IEA. https://www.ifc.org/en/insights-reports/2023/scaling-up-private-finance-for-clean-energy-in-edmes.

Lileeva, Alla, and Daniel Trefler. 2010. "Improved Access to Foreign Markets Raises Plant-Level Productivity ... for Some Plants." *Quarterly Journal of Economics* 125 (3): 1051–99. https://doi.org/10.1162/qjec.2010.125.3.1051.

McKenzie, David. 2017. "Identifying and Spurring High-Growth Entrepreneurship: Experimental Evidence from a Business Plan Competition." *American Economic Review* 107 (8): 2278–307. https://doi.org/10.1257/aer.20151404.

Nilekani, Nandan, and Tanuj Bhojwani. 2023. "Unlocking India's Potential with AI." *Finance and Development* 60 (4): 15–16.

Okeleke, Kenechi, Kalvin Bahia, and Sayali Borole. 2023. "Universal Service Funds in Africa." GSMA Intelligence, London. https://data.gsmaintelligence.com/research/research/research-2023/universal-service-funds-in-africa.

Okunogbe, Oyebola, and Fabrizio Santoro. 2022. "Increasing Tax Collection in African Countries: The Role of Information Technology." *Journal of African Economies* 32 (suppl. 1): i57–i83. https://doi.org/10.1093/jae/ejac036.

Okunogbe, Oyebola, and Gabriel Tourek. 2024. "How Can Lower-Income Countries Collect More Taxes? The Role of Technology, Tax Agents, and Politics." *Journal of Economic Perspectives* 38 (1): 81–106. https://doi.org/10.1257/jep.38.1.81.

Olarreaga, Marcelo, Stefan Sperlich, and Virginie Trachsel. 2020. "Exploring the Heterogeneous Effects of Export Promotion." *World Bank Economic Review* 34 (2): 332–50. https://doi.org/10.1093/wber/lhy034.

Oughton, Edward J. 2023. "Policy Options for Broadband Infrastructure Strategies: A Simulation Model for Affordable Universal Broadband in Africa." *Telematics and Informatics* 76: 101908. https://doi.org/10.1016/j.tele.2022.101908.

Saiyid, Mustafa. 2023. "Pix: Brazil's Successful Instant Payment System." *IMF Country Reports* 23 (289). International Monetary Fund, Washington, DC. https://doi.org/10.5089/9798400249266.002.

Suri, Tavneet, Jenny Aker, Catia Batista, Michael Callen, Tarek Ghani, William Jack, Leora Klapper, Emma Riley, Simone Schaner, and Sandip Sukhtankar. 2023. "Mobile Money." *VoxDev Lit* 2 (2). https://voxdev.org/sites/default/files/2023-09/Mobile_Money_2.pdf.

UNCTAD (United Nations Conference on Trade and Development). 2023. *World Investment Report 2023: Investing in Sustainable Energy for All.* Geneva: UNCTAD.

Verhoogen, Eric. 2023. "Firm-Level Upgrading in Developing Countries." *Journal of Economic Literature* 61 (4): 1410–64. https://doi.org/10.1257/jel.20221633.

World Bank. 2020. "Global Experiences from Regulatory Sandboxes." Fintech Note No. 8, World Bank, Washington, DC. http://hdl.handle.net/10986/34789.

World Bank. 2024. *Digital Progress and Trends Report 2023.* Washington, DC: World Bank. https://www.worldbank.org/en/publication/digital-progress-and-trends-report.

APPENDIX A

Firm-level Adoption of Technology and Research ICT Africa Surveys

The World Bank's Firm-level Adoption of Technology (FAT) survey provides granular information on technology adoption by firms. It is a nationally representative survey that collects detailed information about the technologies adopted and used to perform general and sector-specific business functions. Along with firms' digital technology use, it also collects information on various firm characteristics. More details about the FAT survey are provided by Cirera, Comin, and Cruz (2022).

In Africa, the data are available for six countries: Burkina Faso, for 2021; Ethiopia, 2022; Ghana, 2021; Kenya, 2020; Malawi, 2019–20; and Senegal, 2019. In each country, the survey consists of five modules. Module A collects information about the general characteristics of the firms. Module B collects information on technologies used to perform general business functions that are common across all firms, such as business administration and sales. Module C covers sector-specific technologies. Module D consists of questions about the barriers to and drivers of technology adoption. Module E collects information on the firm's balance sheet and employment.

The survey is stratified by firm size, sectors, and regions within countries. In Africa, the FAT survey covers 6,830 firms across agriculture, manufacturing, and services. The sector-specific modules cover 12 subsectors with different levels of stratification across countries. The survey focuses on formal firms with more than five workers, except for Senegal, for which data are collected for both formal and informal firms. Table A.1 provides a summary of the number of firms by country.

The Research ICT Africa (RIA) survey covers micro- (fewer than five workers) and informal businesses. It includes 3,906 firms from Ethiopia, Ghana, Kenya, Nigeria, South Africa, Tanzania, and Uganda, collected in 2022. Table A.2 shows the distribution of firms by country. A few questions from the RIA questionnaire were harmonized with the FAT survey in the 2022 round.

TABLE A.1

FAT Survey: Number of Observations per Country, by Firm Size and Sector

Country	Size			Sector			
	Small	Medium	Large	Agriculture	Manufacturing	Services	Total
Burkina Faso	335	187	78	80	140	380	600
Ethiopia	999	330	147	149	573	754	1,476
Ghana	773	382	106	85	275	901	1,261
Kenya	408	419	385	150	318	744	1,212
Malawi	284	122	76	0	137	345	482
Senegal	1,219	395	172	204	679	903	1,786

Source: Firm-level Adoption of Technology survey, World Bank.
Note: Additional data for the following countries were used as a benchmark in the analysis of chapter 1: Bangladesh, Brazil, Cambodia, Chile, Croatia, Georgia, India, Republic of Korea, Poland, and Viet Nam. Further details on the analysis are provided by Cirera et al. (2024). FAT = Firm-level Adoption of Technology.

TABLE A.2

RIA Survey: Number of Observations per Country

Country	Number of observations
Ethiopia	499
Ghana	544
Kenya	547
Nigeria	718
South Africa	568
Tanzania	510
Uganda	520

Source: Research ICT Africa survey.
Note: Further details are available in Atiyas et al. (2024). RIA = Research ICT Africa.

References

Atiyas, Izak, Marcio Cruz, Mark A. Dutz, Justice Mensah, and Andrew Partridge. 2024. "Digital Technology Choices among Microenterprises in Africa." Background paper, International Finance Corporation, Washington, DC.

Cirera, Xavier, Diego Comin, and Marcio Cruz. 2022. *Bridging the Technological Divide: Technology Adoption by Firms in Developing Countries.* Washington, DC: World Bank.

Cirera, Xavier, Diego Comin, Marcio Cruz, and Santiago Reyes. 2024. "The 'Incomplete' Digitalization of Firms in Africa." Background paper, World Bank Group, Washington, DC.